DAMAGE INCORPORATED

METALLICA
and the Production of Musical Identity

Glenn T. Pillsbury

Routledge
Taylor & Francis Group
New York   London

Routledge is an imprint of the
Taylor & Francis Group, an informa business

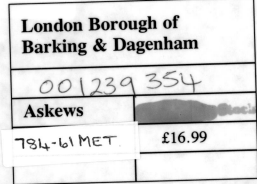

Published in 2006 by
Routledge
Taylor & Francis Group
270 Madison Avenue
New York, NY 10016

Published in Great Britain by
Routledge
Taylor & Francis Group
2 Park Square
Milton Park, Abingdon
Oxon OX14 4RN

© 2006 by Taylor & Francis Group, LLC
Routledge is an imprint of Taylor & Francis Group

Printed in the United States of America on acid-free paper
10 9 8 7 6 5 4 3 2 1

International Standard Book Number-10: 0-415-97373-2 (Hardcover) 0-415-97374-0 (Softcover)
International Standard Book Number-13: 978-0-415-97373-1 (Hardcover) 978-0-415-97374-8 (Softcover)
Library of Congress Card Number 2005030680

Library of Congress Cataloging-in-Publication Data

Pillsbury, Glenn T., 1970-
Damage incorporated : Metallica and the production of musical identity/ Glenn T. Pillsbury.
p. cm.
Includes bibliographical references (p.   ), discography (p.   ), and index.
ISBN 0-415-97373-2 (hb) -- ISBN 0-415-97374-0 (pb)
1. Metallica (Musical group) 2. Rock musicians--United States--Biography. 3. Heavy metal--Social aspects--United States. 4. Heavy metal—United States--History and criticism. I. Title.

ML421.M48P55 2006
782.42166092'2--dc22   2005030680

Taylor & Francis Group
is the Academic Division of Informa plc.

Visit the Taylor & Francis Web site at
http://www.taylorandfrancis.com

and the Routledge Web site at
http://www.routledge-ny.com

Contents

Acknowledgments

Writing a first book is never a solitary process. It is a massive undertaking that marks a significant portion of one's life. No matter that the completion of the project falls ultimately to an individual, the presence of others is always there and subtly (or not so subtly) shapes the final outcome. I was extraordinarily lucky to have arrived at the University of California, Los Angeles (UCLA) into an environment overflowing with enthusiasm and collegiality, as well as really good scholarship. Robert Walser and Susan McClary fostered an exceptional intellectual climate of faculty and students that has developed into one of the most important programs in musicology in the United States. I came to UCLA specifically to study with Rob and his interest in my work remained steadfast, and I want to acknowledge his mentorship as both a musicologist and a humanist.

I am also very excited for the opportunity to acknowledge the group of graduate student colleagues who have had such an important impact on the project in front of you: David Ake, Steven Baur, Andrew Berish, Durrell Bowman, Dale Chapman, Maria Cizmic, Stuart De Ocampo, Francesca Draughon, Charles Garrett, Daniel Goldmark, Gordon Haramaki, Olivia Mather, Cecilia Sun, Grace Tam, and Jacqueline Warwick. Their intellectual camaraderie is imprinted in everything that follows.

Finally, thank you to Rhonelle, my chief editor and partner for many years; this could not have been completed without your help and support.

vii

Introduction

What is this crap? The guitars sound like rusty chainsaws and the singer barks like he wants to be let outside to chase a cat. This band has a big underground buzz, but they're not going anywhere. I'll stake my entire reputation on that.

Jeff Gilbert, early reviewer of Metallica's *Kill 'Em All,* **1984**

Los Angeles, 1996—It starts small, toward the end of the two-hour concert, as stage technicians grab fire extinguishers to put out what appears to be a sudden electrical fire. Moments later a loud explosion and sparks spew from one of the six massive lighting towers encircling the floor-filling stage. As the tower slowly begins collapsing in on itself, almost bowing in death, another blast in a different tower blows the lighting tech stationed there out over the arena, his arms and legs flailing 50 feet in the air as he desperately reaches for the safety line attached to his belt. The initial fire has grown worse, though. With the musicians ducking and scrambling for cover amidst the chaos of collapsing rigging and falling glass, a burning technician careens wildly onto the stage as others race after him to smother the flames. At virtually the same time, lights on several other lighting towers explode; as they collapse, the stage area is filled with smoke, stretchers, and EMTs working to treat the wounded. Suddenly, the entire concert arena is thrown into total darkness. The crowd goes wild. When a light does appear a few moments later, it is a solitary incandescent light bulb hanging from a wire, its glow casting illumination over a small set-up of drums, amps, and mike stands. The only remaining lighting tower comes back online, but faintly. The four members of Metallica, at the center of so much destruction only minutes before, emerge unscathed into the new setup, turning on three more light bulbs and fiddling with the new amps in the atmosphere of stripped-down looseness. Looking out into the crowd, singer James Hetfield grins and asks, "What the hell was that?" before the band launches into a short closing set of its early 1980s material.

The elaborate stage(d) pandemonium of the *Load* tour in 1996 and 1997, designed as a tongue-in-cheek send-up of Metallica's immense worldwide success, occurred during the final moments of the performance of the song "Enter Sandman," the most recognizable symbol of the group's status. As the first single from the multiplatinum selling album *Metallica* (1991), "Enter Sandman" marked a radically different musical and commercial approach from the band's earlier albums: the goal was to write shorter, more direct material and bring it to a wider audience via the capabilities of mainstream promotional tactics such as music video and radio. The strategy worked exceptionally well, so well in fact that sales of *Metallica* nearly eclipsed the combined sales of every other Metallica record. While that success did not explicitly portend the wild events of the 1996–1997 tour, the concert aesthetic of that tour certainly attempted to address the significance of the *Metallica* era.

Of course, 15,000 fans paid at least $30 to be a part of Metallica's negotiation between high-paid superstars and a tight-knit rock band, and that transaction forces us to consider how the mediation of the concert spectacle acts as but one frame for the performance of identity. In *Damage Incorporated* I am interested in the many ways identity can be created and represented, and what performance through music offers to the topic of identity as a whole. In a project about Metallica, the issue of commerce stands as an obvious point of inquiry in the situation described above, but identity in popular music is a complex web of issues reaching out to other points, such as gender and race. As a web, none of the individual components operates alone, but all are influenced by strands of interconnectedness and continue to be in flux and in process across time. Musically, this mutability is perhaps best represented in the concept of genre, a wholesale attempt at categorization that distills elements of identity into a recognizable pattern of action and language. At times cynically reduced to mere marketing tools in the service of commerce, musical genres actually represent specific rhetorical devices that deeply inform how we interact with and make sense of particular aesthetic expressions.

Damage Incorporated offers an interdisciplinary study investigating a range of topics that intersect in the music and cultural influence of Metallica. As part of a collection of heavy metal bands—among them Slayer, Anthrax, and Megadeth—grouped together under the rubric "thrash metal," Metallica's music presents a number of avenues for investigation that can contribute to some of the major concerns of popular music studies. By focusing on a single artist throughout, I aim to use Metallica as a lens through which those larger issues can be examined. Specifically, I focus on identity in popular music as the engagement with sets of performing conventions, and with Metallica's performance of certain conventions of genre, race, and gender serving as a constant impetus. Distinctions within those topics are never fixed, and investigating that essential fluidity means we must investigate how larger processes of history and culture shape contemporary manifestations of them. The five chapters engage broadly with larger questions of the politics of culture, race, American history, musical analysis, and the character of musical discourses in the context of commerce, while the subject of Metallica serves as the conduit for those investigations.

Within the field of academic popular music studies, *Damage Incorporated* is a response to two books: Susan Fast's critical study of Led Zeppelin, *In the Houses of the Holy*, and Robert Walser's *Running with the Devil*. The existence of Fast's book, in particular, says much about the state of popular music studies as a discipline. Since the early 1990s the field of popular music musicology has undergone a powerful process of growth and maturation in tandem with the development in mainstream musicology known as critical musicology. Importantly, the best products of that process have eagerly adapted the ideas and methodologies of other humanistic areas, such as literary theory, feminism, ethnic studies, film, and art history into their repertoire of approaches and directed the powerful tools of cultural studies toward the criticism and contextualization of musical detail. In her book *In the Houses of the Holy*, Fast expertly wields a broad range of theoretical methodologies and an encyclopedic knowledge of Led Zeppelin's music to address important critical issues about the band. She has availed herself of the important progressive work in popular music studies from the last ten years and her individual chapters are quite useful. As a book on a single artist, however, it largely neglects to situate its existence in a postcanonic era. In other words, Fast at times overlooks how her credentials as a musicologist are allowed to stamp her work with the authority of the academy and to cover up the complicated issues of writing about a single artist.

The broad theoretical reach of Robert Walser's *Running with the Devil: Power, Gender, and Madness in Heavy Metal Music*, with its prescient application of ideas of history, philosophy, and sociology to the music of heavy metal, is another important initiator for many of the issues discussed in my own project. At the same time, my project on Metallica seeks to expand the terrain covered in *Running with the Devil* to explore in greater depth certain issues as well as reexamine some of its topics from a different angle. For instance, Walser was primarily concerned with a version of metal that was much more commercially visible than that generally played by Metallica. While his ideas on virtuosity and gender, for example, provide a significant contribution to the study of those topics, I want to explore how those issues are performed differently in music like Metallica's. Virtuosity in metal bands such as Metallica is, as Walser notes, much more about *ensemble* virtuosity than the *soloistic* virtuosity of Eddie Van Halen or Randy Rhoads, and the two kinds draw on very different resources for their presentation. How is it different and why is it that way? How do the two kinds interact? Also, I approach Walser's notion of the performance of masculinity (exemplified most typically in the glam metal bands of the late 1980s) via the performance of heterosexual "normalcy," a version of masculinity that consciously tries to avoid the very existence of gender (much less feature it as a form of play). Indeed, if Walser's views on gender androgyny are in any way defending its appearance in glam metal bands from disparagement by narrow-minded fans of "real" men who play "real" metal, I am interested here in going behind the claims by detractors to find out just how real men express themselves and what it means for musical identity.

Although the materials in this project proceed in a basically chronological fashion, I do not intend for them to serve as a strictly biographical study of Metallica. To nonacademics in particular, the notion of writing a book on a band with the cultural stature of Metallica brings with it images of the authoritative discussion of canonical figures in music (as in the case of *In the Houses of the Holy*). This is, after all, the way music history is presented in the average college music appreciation course and in treatments on public television and VH1. Biography has long been a hallmark of musicology, a tradition achingly visible in the *Kleinmeister* paradigm, an adjunct to musicology's previously central businesses of canon building and edition making. The archetypal "Man and His Music" model (it is actually a real series of books), a chronologically-based argument for individual greatness, provides a ready-made form into which individuals can be poured so as to claim a spot in the pantheon of eternal prestige. That unfortunate concept has certainly guided projects on popular music artists, and biography remains a tricky endeavor. Not the least of its problems lies in the way the entire notion of prestige (as it has traditionally operated) has been so thoroughly questioned as historically contingent and ideologically suspect. The significance of so much progressive musicology from the 1980s and 1990s has been to tease out narrow assumptions about how music supposedly works and to contest the way those assumptions have both shaped the discussion of musical meaning and excluded marginalized voices. Biography typically works to position its subjects as exceptions to cultural and social norms, and the traditional pursuit of prestige also requires a certain level of completeness through a rigorous pursuit of detail. However, to my mind the value of completeness necessarily competes with the value of usefulness, in that some details of biography serve only as details of biography. This is not to argue against completeness or attention to detail, but to observe that usefulness is always a better choice. Footnotes, after all, are designed to accommodate completeness.

Still, a project on a single artist is inherently biographical at some level and this project on Metallica is no exception: the chronological layout of my chapters ensures some sort of survey-like approach to the band's career. In particular, I begin in 1983 and end in 2000. In my attempts to explore the musical and cultural influence of Metallica I have not tried to produce a grand narrative of the band's history, or sought to put forth a discussion of one all-encompassing topic, and I have not conceived of the chapters as signposts or milestones in the life of Metallica. Instead, I ground each chapter on a single song or a group of songs that illuminate issues of musical identity within American musical culture. As such, I use the music of Metallica as a hermeneutic window to get at broader issues of reception history and meaning in popular music. My discussions proceed, therefore, according to an inside-out process, where critical musical analyses of specific songs gesture outward to important cultural elements that shape the meaning of the analysis. Details of biography are of course crucial, but such matters already form the core of most of the popular literature on Metallica. Indeed, several books and booklets have been published in the past decade containing exhaustive biographical accounts. Moreover, avoiding a full-fledged biography allows me to introduce details of the band's career as they become relevant to my discussions of music without the need to exhaustively retell the same stories, stamping the authoritative voice of scholarly popular music studies on the proceedings. Thus, existing biographical material proves useful in its turn, but I regard it more for its important historiographical value than for its archival value. Ultimately, I am interested not only in what the band members, fans, and critics say about Metallica, but also in how they actually say it.

This project begins with 1983 because that was the year of Metallica's first commercial release, *Kill 'Em All*. While that year seems like an obvious point at which to begin, where should it stop? That is to say, how should a project on Metallica deal with the fact that the band continues to write, record, and perform new material? While musicological projects outside of popular music studies can sometimes be faced with this issue, it is nevertheless particularly acute in this discipline. How one acknowledges the continued existence and viability of the subject reflects importantly on the overall style of presentation in the project. Focusing on a single artist, therefore, also engages with questions of biography when the subject remains an active participant in the industry. Because Metallica remains very active, previously untold details of the band's past will continue to surface, casting a new light on this present undertaking. Of course no historical project can avoid that situation. I use the year 2000 as an end date for this project because I see the 1990s—the decade of *Metallica*, *Load*, and *Reload*, and the vast increase in Metallica's cultural position—as a distinct period of musical and stylistic change for the group. This is not to ignore the way that that decade must not necessarily reflect a time of explicit coherence, musically or otherwise, nor do I ignore important differences between the *Metallica* years and *Load/Reload* years of the second half of the decade. However, the crisis brought about by the "selling out" controversy offers a potentially unified series of events that *does* impinge on the decade as a whole. While that controversy, in its most visible form, has stalked Metallica since 1991 (and will no doubt be raised continually in the future) the musical hiatus experienced by the band in 2001 (the first year ever in which Metallica did not play a single concert) and 2002 made it possible to consider the development of the selling out controversy across a fairly neat segment of time.

Finally, the issues of biography, completeness, and usefulness all arise in the question of writing from the dual perspectives of fan and scholar. Indeed, I come to this project with a long history as a Metallica fan and a metal guitarist, and I continue to interact with the band's music as a fan and musician. That experience and perspective enables me to draw on a great deal of material and ensures a deep familiarity with the music at hand, allowing me to present the material in ways largely unavailable to outsiders; in a sense, I have been researching this project, in some form, for much of my life. Writing as a fan also allows me to inject those personal experiences with Metallica into the project, and I do not hesitate to bring that history directly to bear on the exploration of the topics and issues outlined here. At the same time, fandom can become a deleterious blind spot, particularly as one treads the fine epistemological lines of biography. There is a difference between writing about music one has a great deal of enthusiasm for, and writing about that music in ignorance of the complex ways it interacts with larger social issues or reaffirms problematic representations of those issues.

As in many popular music projects, I spend a good deal of time discussing the texts here from the standpoint of production rather than concentrating on their reception. Such an approach is not to claim for production a certain definitiveness that is necessarily lacking in a study of reception though. When we think of production and reception as two distinct poles, we can easily lose the sense of their interconnectedness and overlap in the production of meaning. The selling out controversy mentioned above exemplifies this kind of important crossover. The dense cultural tangle of reception issues that arises through the accusation of and the defenses against selling out have fundamental roots in the musical details of the band's 1990s music. Still, the analytical tools of musicology—the ability to elaborate the effects of the production of musical details—form a significant contribution to popular music studies. In addition to its traditional emphasis on history, musicology brings to the scholarly arena the willingness to engage with musical texts on a detailed level in support of larger arguments. The insistence that musical sounds result from specific, yet culturally mediated, choices on the part of musicians, together with an ability to deal with those concrete musical events, constitute one of musicology's important contributions to popular music studies.

Indeed, what to *do* with the music in popular music remains one of the most contested aspects of popular music studies. As I elaborate in several places, musicology generally aligns itself somewhere in between the approaches of (mainly British) neo-Marxist sociology and (mainly American) ethnomusicology. Yet, from that perspective, lyrics and subculture analysis form the important core material, while musical details are often consigned to the status of "just is." The more recent claims by music theorists that explication of musical details might best be handled by trained experts in Schenkerian-dominated music theory characterize another part of the analytical spectrum. Thus, on one side sociologists and cultural critics view musical details as technical obfuscations of more important cultural issues within popular music. But, in the hands of music theorists, details are parsed to a degree that significantly downplays or excludes any linkage with larger contexts. I take musical detail seriously because many of Metallica's aesthetic negotiations throughout its career, particularly across the fulcrum of 1991, are evinced in discrete, musically detailed ways. However, those obvious musical changes only have meaning when considered alongside other nonmusical aspects of the band's aesthetic, and, I believe, as part of the context provided by the generic tensions within heavy metal. Throughout this project I reiterate the ways such distinctions function as sites for larger meanings. I aim, therefore, to exploit musicology's position as a "best of both worlds" solution to the problem of "the music" by insisting on the importance of discrete musical choices as well as the role cultural mediation plays in giving those choices meaning.

The use of notated transcription to represent musical events also occupies an important part of the debate about the discussion of musical details in popular music. In particular, standard musical notation is a highly specialized tool, requiring a certain level of proficiency on the part of the reader. To the uninitiated, notation can seem not much more than a lot of obfuscating squiggles that stand in the way of some direct connection to the music. Additionally, because of its specialized nature, the use of notation brings with it a certain amount of ontological baggage: it can be claimed to represent the music *as it really is.* This is an important political claim because when the music under consideration circulates aurally (as is the case with most popular musics), the use of notation to represent those musical styles introduces the very real possibility of *mis*representation. For instance, the fact that standard notation has no significant capacity for incorporating musical elements such as timbre into the analytical fold means ignoring one of the central ways musical details produce meaning (and genres are musically distinguished) in popular music. Moreover, if the use of notation is at best an attempt at fixed translation or distillation of events unfolding in time, at worst it operates in the service of prestige. By notating a piece of music one can claim to argue for it really being Music (with a capital M), and for many analyses the notated score or example must be present before the analysis can begin. In such cases, notation subtly transforms the object of analysis into the notation itself, and transforms practices into texts.

Guitar-driven styles of music such as heavy metal introduce another element in the notation question: tablature. Designed centuries ago as an instrument-specific system of notation, tablature's great significance for rock and metal coincided roughly with the appearance of guitar-based magazines in the late 1970s and early 1980s. The pedagogical purpose of those magazines necessitated a simple method for presenting musical scores without requiring exhaustive priming in standard notation. Guitar tablature fills that requirement quite well by representing notated pitches according to a corresponding location on the fretboard of the guitar as well as eliminating rhythmic indications completely, and magazines usually get around that missing component by printing musical examples in *both* tablature and standard notation. Since the purpose of most tablature in guitar magazines has been to notate riffs, solos, and entire songs assumed to be already familiar to the reader, rhythms are notationally deemphasized. At the same time, these magazines have occasionally encountered resistance to tablature from readers who feel its particular directness represents a kind of dumbing down of "real" musical details. Traditional notation and the effort to learn to read it, then, operate for those readers as a defense against mindless hacks while also serving as a means of elevating the music according to the prestige of specialization afforded other notated musics.

Nevertheless, it is possible to use notation as a diagram, a visual method of representing sound rather than a verbalized language. In this way, notation functions as a supplementary component that draws on the powerful discursive possibilities enabled by transcription without producing the overtly complex reduction favored by many theorists. Thus, I envision my use of transcription throughout *Damage Incorporated* as brief graphical illustrations designed to augment individual analytical references. I also incorporate guitar tablature for some examples because through them I explore a method of analysis that relies on the fundamental physical layout of the guitar. In particular, I investigate how the half-step basis of the instrument provides a way of understanding the peculiar kinds of chromaticism that appear in thrash metal bands like Metallica. Indeed, recognizing that elemental layout as the interface for expression also provides a way of theorizing the significance of specific intervallic relationships in metal (such as the minor second and the tritone) that moves beyond the categorizations of modal theory which serve as a foundation for analysis of rock harmony. In those examples I concentrate less exclusively on pitch and instead explore how the relationship between pitches and the physical shapes and guitaristic gestures of their performance contribute to the creation of musical meaning.

In a project on a popular music artist as important as Metallica it would seem there could be no better source of information than from the members themselves. After all, they wrote the stuff, didn't they? If anyone could speak about its meaning it would be those who actually wrote it, right? However, I did not build this project around personal interviews, and I had two concerns with the idea that interviewing Metallica would have been an indispensable component to my study of the band (even beyond the basic issue of access). The first is the amount of influence bestowed upon the author/artist as the final interpretive source. That authors or composers are thought to hold the real answers to interpretive questions effectively robs their work of its inherently rich polyvocal possibilities. Moreover, that line of thinking operates very clearly according to assumptions that understand (and value) artistic expression as the direct manifestation of a stable and complete self. Selves, however, are never stable and complete since various historical and cultural forces always help to shape and redefine selfhood. Artistic expression may indeed seem to come from an individual, but that expression is always also larger than that individual, contingent as it is on many other factors for its meaning.

My second concern with the necessity of personal access to Metallica is that the band's position as a performer in a commercial industry always mediates their speech in some way. Indeed, major performers such as Metallica have given thousands of interviews, covering a broadly homogenous set of questions, as part of the complex system of role-playing that drives the interaction between music industry talent, mass media, and audience. Particularly when the group is still very active, like Metallica is, we must be quite cautious about assuming any interview with a card-carrying musicologist wouldn't simply replicate the rhetorical strategies characteristic of the interview genre itself. In other words, some sort of transcendent honesty cannot be assured (even if such a thing were possible). While it is never my intention to accuse anyone of lying or misrepresenting themselves, at the same time we must not also forget the ways interviews always function at some level as rhetorical performances that share with visual appearance and musical choices in the presentation of the band's identity to the public. My response, then, was not to struggle to find questions never before asked or to hope for an opportunity to procure little-known historical details, but (like my interest in the journalistic and fan accounts of Metallica) to turn the answers Metallica has already given into useful historiographical data.

Along those lines, writing about a band as successful as Metallica brings with it a distinct set of questions related to issues of subjectivity. Critical interpretation stems largely from understandings of who is speaking and what they are trying to say, as well as who is listening. Yet, the recognition that in popular music there might be a subject made up of a group of people needs to be addressed. In particular, who or what are we referring to when we say that Metallica speaks? Film studies have been engaged with this issue for some time and in most criticism, a film's author is assumed to be its director. Literary critics also appear to have it easier than musicologists. And even musicologists studying music from the classical canon work seamlessly with an understanding that the composer who signs the piece represents their subject. Yet, in all of those cases subjectivity only seems uncomplicated because many of the factors that would make them more complicated have remained less studied, or at least have been downplayed. When we examine subjectivity in the context of popular music, however, a well-established set of intellectual passageways always exists in the complicating commercial factors inherent in the creation and presentation of identity. The commercial nature of most popular music always stands as a given, as a backdrop, and as a potential caveat in most work in the field. While similar structures of commerce have been investigated for classical music, those studies typically reside on the margins of musicological scholarship. The standard use of record sales (for any number of purposes) as the primary commercial interface in popular music studies does not as yet have an equivalent for traditional musicological subjects, but not because such an equivalent cannot be found or does not exist. Rather, popularity has simply never been a recognized component of critical inquiry in those areas.

Even beyond the complicating factors of commerce, with a rock *band* we necessarily have a set of competing interpretive speakers as well. First, there is a subjectivity of the thing called Metallica which delineates one method of interaction. On the other hand, there are the identities and subjectivities of the individual band members, which offer (in this case) four other kinds of interpretive entry points. Sometimes the distinction between the two is really important, and other times less so. Writing about a band therefore balances the assumption that the individual band members can be represented as a unified collective, with the recognition that important critical insight can be gained from the fact that the band members can be understood as individuals. Indeed, the later chapters of *Damage Incorporated* depend a great deal on the possibilities raised by this tension in subjectivity. Metallica's involvement in the Napster case in 2000, for example, functions not only as an episode in the selling out controversy that affected the thing called Metallica, but it also marks a clear example when one member of Metallica, drummer Lars Ulrich, articulated most of the band's defense. Ulrich, of course, claimed to speak on behalf of the band and, in reading his statements and watching him on television, we are meant to imagine the other three members standing right behind him, speechless and ghost-like, nodding in agreement. But such imaginings only draw our attention away from the fact that the words are still Ulrich's, and his rhetoric the product of one person's immersion in a larger game of subjectivity. Similarly, James Hetfield's position as the primary musical innovator in Metallica and the only member to write lyrics (until the collective lyrics on *St. Anger* [2003]) means something altogether different in the *Load/Reload* era of the 1990s than it might have in the 1980s. The fact that Hetfield's lyrics in the 1990s consciously take up topics related to his own psychology matters significantly for discussions of the songs from that time. Of course, biographically-based readings and interpretations must not be the sole outcome of those discussions, but Hetfield's stylistic change nevertheless introduces an important component to the long-range study of the band. In that sense, the focus of subjectivity develops into a more detailed examination of one member as the crucial driving force behind the collective.

The sound and musical techniques of 1980s thrash metal have been little studied by scholars, and while the style has received a small amount of attention as part of heavy metal generally, a detailed investigation of how its characteristics are finely deployed provides an important contribution to the understanding of many issues in popular music studies. The term *thrash metal* usually evokes images of scruffy and violent young men pulverizing their audience's ears with Phrygian-mode transgression and lyrics hailing Satan, but thrash metal refers, at its most basic level, to rhythm. Chapter 1 therefore takes both of those components together—scruffy young men and their rhythms—to explore the idea of genre from the standpoint of thrash metal itself. I discuss how its musical techniques become codified into a recognizable set of cultural meanings that function within and against larger understandings of how heavy metal operates and informs musical identity. Beginning with its combination of American hardcore and turn-of-the-decade British metal, I ground my study of thrash metal in Mikhail Bahktin's idea that genres are never fully invented but are moments in a conversation, in this case conversations about musical style. As conversations, they resist solid and impeccable formulations, deviations from which might constitute an entirely separate genre. In particular, I am interested in the way Metallica's earliest recordings contribute to the very sense of a thrash metal genre, and moreover, how the members of the group situated their music within the context of a genre. Indeed the rhythmic basis of thrash metal informs other discussions about form, structure, and the complex cultural terrain involving the value of musical complexity.

I theorize the musical aesthetic of thrash metal as movement through *cycles of energy* working on many different levels to focus power and intensity into bodily experience. These range from the meta experience of the mosh pit and the insistent speed of the beat that assaults and affects the bodies of the performers and audience, to the particular physicality of playing riffs using a heavy amount of palm muting (a guitaristic technique that offers a great amount of timbral shading and control based on slight alterations of the guitarist's picking hand during performance). Moreover, Chapter 1 explores how the various combinations of rhythmic intensities in the guitars and drums underlie most of the formal characteristics of thrash metal songs in ways much more pronounced than in other styles of rock. The effect of the changes from section to section is also phenomenological, and our understanding and experience of them depends greatly on the temporal thickness of subjectivity. Ultimately, rhythmic intensities do not signify nearly as strongly by themselves. Rather, the *changes* in intensity provide the crucial context for their signification, and the various contexts then create the cycles of energy that make thrash metal songs so effective. In this way, thrash metal's modular style of composition exemplifies musicologist Richard Middleton's notion of thinking about form as process (rather than treating form as a precast mold), as well as operating as something of a middle ground between Charles Keil's conception of open and closed processes. Finally, from the beginning Metallica attached important cultural significance to their approach to form, viewing their efforts as compositional in ways that specifically enabled them to claim a higher form of cultural prestige than would otherwise be available to thrash metal musicians.

Consciously aligning themselves with some vague construct of "European-ness," Metallica pointed to the very presence of slower, less intense songs like "Fade to Black" (1984) as evidence of their stylistic diversity. Chapter 2 explores a group of songs (including "Sanitarium" [1986] and "One" [1988]) representing what I call the "Fade to Black Paradigm," and which deliberately eschew the constant aggression and force of most of Metallica's other songs. Moreover, this kind of song finds no significant place in the work of any other thrash metal group in the 1980s. From the perspective of the thrash metal genre, "Fade to Black" represents an important divergence offered by an otherwise recognizable thrash metal band. Quietly arpeggiated chords, a straight, nondistorted vocal timbre, and a clear sense of minor-mode tonality designed to be heard as expressive accompany the sense of despair found in the lyrics. Indeed, the importance of the lyrical subject in "Fade to Black" lies at the core of my discussion. The lyrics deal with the topic of suicide, here presented as interior images experienced by one who has decided to commit suicide. However, Metallica's song does not try to pull back from the edge of suicidal depression, turning around to fight through the emotional pain and live another day. Rather, I argue that "Fade to Black" (particularly the final guitar solo) actually forces the listener to witness the narrator's suicidal moment. "Fade to Black," like the other songs of the Paradigm, is ultimately a bleak song, but in confronting the topic of suicide so directly it continues thrash metal's willingness to explore and deal with difficult issues in a direct manner.

Metallica's exploration of emotional states far removed from transgressive occultism, violence, or straightforward celebrations of genre identity has been a contentious aspect in their reception. It has been praised by critics as right-thinking artistic development as well as being used by some fans as evidence of a fundamental softness, weakness, and of having "sold out" (discussed at length in later chapters). On a deeper level, however, the incorporation of musical and affective traits from other genres of popular music into the Fade to Black Paradigm recontextualizes those same traits in order to express emotions that the aggressive sounds of thrash metal cannot. Yet because musical elements do not exist in a social vacuum, but are crucially dependent on the constant construction of personal identities for their meaning, the process of appropriation is inextricably linked to notions of identity.

Chapter 3 examines the rhetoric surrounding structural complexity and ensemble virtuosity from the perspective of race and gender. I am particularly interested in how an aesthetic of intelligent detachment, together with an explicit concern over the mechanisms of control, contributed to Metallica's success during the 1980s. Drawing on the work of film scholar Richard Dyer and cultural theorists such as George Lipsitz, I argue that the construction of detachment and the insistence by the band that its political commentaries on personal independence and control represented merely explorations of certain issues like drug abuse and corporate corruption cannot be seen as completely value-neutral. The particular ideologies set forth in songs such as "Master of Puppets" (1986) and "Eye of the Beholder" (1988) not only reveal a quasi-Libertarian philosophy, but they also work by invoking the powerfully normative mechanisms involved in the cultural construction of "whiteness." So far, music has had very little visibility in the body of critical study on whiteness, and I see my discussion of Metallica's performance of whiteness (typically opposite some conception of "blackness") as an important contribution to those investigations. In both songs, I argue that Metallica avoids explicit sloganeering, preferring instead to wrap their views in complex musical structures and precise performance that appear to conceal any sense of responsibility for direct action behind a veneer of color-blind musicianship. The band's declarations of unmarked heterosexuality further enhanced their image as one unaffected by fame and excess. Along these lines, contemporary critical discussion frequently hailed Metallica's apparent normalcy, lyrical intelligence, and its ensemble virtuosity as having finally separated hard rock from the blues and, in so doing, progressing away from blackness. Especially by the late 1980s, rock critics celebrated the erasure of a more traditional, sexuality-based rock masculinity, and, in the specific case of the blues, the apparent erasure of the sticky issues entangling race and popular music. Indeed, by casting Metallica as the ultimate nonblues rock band—in fact by separating them from the blues-rock tradition altogether—critics could also preserve the blues' status as an exotic and "authentic" African-American musical tradition.

If structural complexity can represent one method of engaging with the power of whiteness, Chapter 4 extends my inquiries into race to engage with the topic of musical exoticism. "Wherever I May Roam," from the album *Metallica* (1991), opens with a Phrygian-mode melody wrapped in the sound of a sitar. The surrounding musical texture instantly informs us that we're not anywhere close to a Western locale but are instead somewhere in the "East." At the same time, Hetfield's lyrics are very much about the freedom and independence of the Road, an experience we have come to understand as part of the specific cultural significance of American history and the allure of the West. These two topics, and their combination into one riff, have much to say about the dialectic between Self and Other in what Scott Lash and John Urry have theorized as the age of posttourism. Chapter 4 examines how the presence of the Phrygian mode, typically the most direct musical symbol of the non-West but also fundamental to the musical grammar of heavy metal, mediates the expression of Self and Other. Metallica's decision to employ the specific timbre of a sitar in a song written by an American heavy metal band about the Road is only eclipsed by the sense of it being an utterly unremarkable decision. I explore how that very unremarkableness belies the broad reach and power of post-Orientalist musical tourism in Western society.

To that end, Chapter 4 also assesses the very label "Phrygian" in the context of metal. While it is clear that such a label makes sense as a description of the central riff in "Wherever I May Roam" (as I will argue), the uncritical application of mode-based theoretical terminology can just as easily conceal much about the way metal riffs (particularly those by Metallica) are produced. An understanding of the physical apparatus of the guitar is equally important for the analysis of riffs, particularly as it pertains to the theoretical concept of pitch class wherein the same pitch letters (A through G and their chromatic alterations) hold equal significance, regardless of octave, in the analysis of a single line of music. I focus instead on what I term the "expressive registers" of the guitar in order to emphasize the distinction between, for example, the Phrygian E–F pair in different octaves or across octaves. In other words, I argue that the E–F pair played in the lowest octave of the guitar operates in fundamentally different ways than the E–F pair residing an octave higher. Moreover, applying the term "Phrygian" to E–F pairs usually obscures the much more important half-step relationship between those two pitches in metal riffs. It also often downplays the more important rhythmic characteristic of the riff, a characteristic totally foreign to modal terms like Phrygian.

In the final chapter, I lay out a wide-ranging series of issues all contributing to a large-scale theorization of the phenomenon of selling out in popular music. The maelstrom of Metallica's selling out controversy throughout the 1990s not only represents the latest significant instance of the topic in popular music, but the complexity of their case also brings together a number of issues regarding the role and status of art in the postmodern era. It is within that eruption that I find a rich tapestry of interlocking topics that touch on all of my main concerns across this project. Studying the notion of selling out requires we examine the construction of identity through musical genre, race, and gender as they are expressed via the mechanisms of commerce. Often dismissed as the ravings of duped and misguided fans too caught up in the mythology of rock authenticity, the accusation of sell- ing out actually deserves focused attention of its own, beyond its position as a corollary to the fluidity of authenticity. That audiences, critics, and musicians continue to struggle against the anxieties produced by the fear of selling out testifies to the continued resilience of the concept, and, there- fore, the continued power of modernist means of constructing personal identity. As such, Metallica's example provides an important opportunity for popular music scholars to examine the issue thoroughly.

In particular, I explore the roots of the relationship between creativity and commerce with an eye toward the specific marriage between original genius and legal copyright that occurred in the early nineteenth century. Importantly, Metallica's rhetoric and actions against the Internet-based peer-to-peer service Napster some 200 years later did not differ fundamen- tally from the precepts laid out by European Romantic aestheticians, even if the band's notion of artistic authenticity was influenced more directly by the rock press of Dave Marsh, Lester Bangs, and *Rolling Stone* than by Goethe or Schiller. Thomas Frank's notion of "hip consumerism," which grounds his study of the marketing of a culture of individuality during the 1960s (coincident with the rise of rock criticism), provides an illustrative basis for understanding the continued significance of the terms of rock authenticity. Both fan accusations and Metallica's defense against them were fortified by complex and divergent readings of authenticity, yet I argue that the contradictory nature of mass-mediated culture allows both to co-exist. As such, I treat the concept of musical authenticity as a histori- cally specific phenomenon and as a set of reactions and ways of being that are crucial to the negotiation of meaning in a consumerist society.

Metallica's music from the late 1990s, specifically that on *Load* (1996) and *Reload* (1997), largely eschewed the multipart structures and rhyth- mic complexities of previous albums, musical characteristics that were subsequently repositioned by the rock press as "immature" and even "incomprehensible." Ironically, the *Load* and *Reload* albums featured the appearance of guitar techniques and vocal performance styles quickly heard (and mostly esteemed by critics) as a general "bluesy-ness," the very style the band had been celebrated for avoiding only a few years previ- ous. I explore this issue by framing it with the questions of "whose blues?" and "which blues?" because the genre of the blues, like all genres, is never static; the blues are never simply a "thing," but represent the product of people and their engagement with representations of the musical past. Though the basic note contours of Hetfield's riffs continued in some of the same ways as the riffs from the 1980s, subtle changes in the performance of those notes in the 1990s seem to have provided all that was necessary for the application of a label such as "bluesy." Furthermore, they also allowed what might seem like minor details of performance articulation to balloon into major anxieties about genre and identity. Largely absent from Metallica's later riffs is the distinctiveness of the Phrygian and Locrian modes, and, more significantly, the lack of palm muting as a generic identifier and rhetorical device (as discussed in Chapter 1). While mode may form an important component of understanding popular styles along terms of traditional notation-based analysis, it is also clear that in heavy metal articulation and timbre hold the same level of importance that pitch and harmony do elsewhere.

I analyze the specific ways Metallica's late 1990s riffs can be heard as bluesy, but I also link that analysis to the larger issue of musical identity, most notably the important changes in the way James Hetfield represented himself. The song "Mama Said" (1996) marks a significant change in how he presented the idea of subjectivity in his songs, and the content of this song offers an important perspective on his general self-fashioning after the huge commercial success of the *Metallica* album. Featuring strummed acoustic guitars, a rich baritone singing timbre, and the distinctive presence of a pedal steel guitar, "Mama Said" draws extensively from the imagery of country music, particularly the "hard" or "outlaw" country sounds of George Jones, Merle Haggard, and Waylon Jennings. The song looks back over Hetfield's life in philosophical and metaphorical terms, providing an often-tortured reassessment from the vantage point of many years in the future. Moreover, his reassessments are also marked by the adoption of the specific kind of working-class masculinity contributed by the country music components of Southern Rock.

My overarching methodology in *Damage Incorporated* is to challenge the assumption that musical identity in popular music arises intact and fully formed, just in time for the next photo session or radio interview. The industrial mechanisms of celebrity make such challenges difficult to initiate and sustain, but not impossible. As this approach peels back layers of representation that have served to define "Metallica" since the early 1980s, there emerge a variety of pictures of the band, sometimes contradictory. Yet, each demonstrates the central tenet of this examination: the argument for musical identity as not merely a stable mask, but instead an ever-changing representation, the result of active production and development.

Once exposed, the variety of representations enables the complexities of culture to be further revealed.

CHAPTER 1

Thrashing All Around

Rhythm, the Body, and the Genre of Thrash Metal

[W]hat really blew our mind, the second we heard it, was that
Metallica was the answer to America's prayers. They were the first
band that we heard that really made America look good … they
gave the American headbangers something to hang their hat on.

Jon "Johnny Z" Zazula[1]

Introduction

For the New Jersey music promotion and shopkeeping team of Jon and
Marsha Zazula the arrival of San Francisco-based Metallica in April 1983
may have indeed been the answer to a prayer, even if most of the rest of
America had not exactly felt the need to appeal to the divine on behalf
of homegrown heavy metal. The Zazula's record shop and flea market,
Rock & Roll Heaven, had acquired a copy of Metallica's 1982 demo *No
Life 'Til Leather* via the tape-trading network of the underground metal
scene. Eager to expand their promotion interests, the Zazulas contacted
18-year-old drummer Lars Ulrich, wired $1,500 to him and three other
young men in California, and then prayed, once more, that the band would

actually make it 3,000 miles across the country without killing themselves or each other. Gigs in the New York–New Jersey area had been booked already and the band (which had recently added Cliff Burton on bass) did make it. Barely. In particular, tensions between Metallica's two guitarists, James Hetfield and Dave Mustaine, had reached an alcohol-fueled breaking point on the cross-country trek, and after only two shows on the East Coast, Mustaine was officially kicked out, sent back west to California on a Greyhound bus. At the same time Kirk Hammett, recently drafted out of another San Francisco metal band called Exodus, was quickly making his own trip east to audition as Metallica's new lead guitar player. Hammett's first gig took place exactly one week after Mustaine's last. Following two more shows, and with the band's lineup apparently settled, the Zazulas then took the biggest financial risk of their lives by bankrolling the recording of Metallica's first album, *Kill 'Em All* (in May 1983) and then forming Megaforce Records in order to manage the band and promote the album.

In the received history of thrash metal, the Zazula's gamble paid off exceptionally well for Metallica. For the Zazulas, the episode also turned out to be one of the high points of their professional activities in American metal. The two groups would part company in mid-1984, following the Megaforce release of Metallica's second album, *Ride the Lightning*. At that point the Zazula's promotion efforts proved to be so successful that Michael Alago, head of Artists & Repertoire for Elektra Records, lured away Metallica.[2] Unable to compete with the broad marketing reach of Elektra (or those of the band's new management company, Q-Prime), Megaforce stood little chance of retaining any business association with Metallica. In the face of sticking with a financially troubled independent label (even with the close personal ties that went along with it), the band consciously decided to make a move into the burgeoning major-label metal market and tap into resources that would enable its commercial visibility to expand far beyond its already impressive underground status.[3] Metallica's decision was ultimately a business one, and would be its most significant career decision until the preproduction for the *Metallica* album at the end of the decade aimed, in part, to give their music a broader commercial appeal. For not the last time, moreover, accusations of "selling out" accompanied the label and management decision.

The intense commercial activity surrounding Metallica during 1983 and 1984 offers an illuminating nexus in the discussion of popular music and identity. Intertwined are the emotional impact of heavy and powerful music played to an enthusiastic audience and the desires of a range of individuals to capitalize on that enthusiasm for mutual monetary gain. Moreover, the arrangement with Elektra promised to give the band an unusual amount of authority over the artistic content being released in their name.[4] In other words, Elektra would not force the band to change its writing and recording habits by insisting on a company-chosen producer or company-hired songwriting help. At the same time, the arrangement enabled Metallica to appear as though it was separate from the industrial machinations that seemed to create pop metal bands, even though their relationship with Elektra—also home of Mötley Crüe and Dokken, two of the most successful pop metal bands during the 1980s—meant the band was ensconced in it to some degree.[5]

This chapter investigates some of the details of the music known as thrash metal. I focus, of course, on songs by Metallica, but my aim is neither merely to draw a picture or take a snapshot of the genre, nor to somehow write the book on thrash metal. Rather, I spend this chapter investigating not the question "what is thrash metal?" but the more provocative and compelling "*why* does thrash metal do what it does?" The "what" answers, which those unfamiliar with the music might seek, are hopefully contained within the "why" question, but the "why" questions enable answers with potentially more significance for projects not directly related to Metallica. The sound and musical techniques of thrash metal have been little studied by popular music scholars, and while the style has been examined as part of heavy metal (in general), a detailed investigation of how thrash metal's characteristics are finely deployed provides an important contribution to the study of many issues in popular music studies.

The Genre of Thrash Metal

Formed in late 1981, Metallica emerged as perhaps the single most important group of a heavy metal underground during the 1980s, a musical style variously labeled "thrash metal," "speed metal," and (later in the decade) even "death metal." Based on their reworkings of British metal groups such as Diamond Head, Iron Maiden, and Motörhead, Metallica is usually credited with inventing the thrash metal genre during 1982 and throughout 1983, a process that culminated commercially with the release of *Kill 'Em All* in July 1983. Throughout the 1980s many thrash metal groups followed, taking the sounds of *Kill 'Em All* as an important model and developing the particular aesthetic of shock and intensity that parents' groups would eventually understand as genuine celebrations of violence, mayhem, and Satan worship.

However, when we study the history of genres, we can best look for beginnings rather than origins, as different conversations wherein people come and go, where certain things jump out of previous conversations to be re-articulated in others. Within those conversations the details and elements of a genre regulate the exchange of meanings. In popular music generally, and within genres specifically, Robert Walser notes that "subject positions are constructed and negotiated, social relations are enacted and transgressed, and ideologies are developed and interrogated."[6] Many of these ideas also occur in discussion of literary genres. Russian literary critic and theorist Mikhail Bahktin, writing in the first half of the twentieth century about the nineteenth-century Russian novel, states that language is, at its core, "heteroglot," meaning that it is the product of multiple—but still historically specific—individuals reflecting multiple identities:

> [L]anguage is heteroglot from top to bottom: it represents the co-existence of socio-ideological contradictions between the present and the past, between differing epochs of the past, between different socio-ideological groups in the present, between tendencies, schools, circles and so forth, all given a bodily form.[7]

While the assessment of Metallica's heraldic position is an interesting one in light of the band's great success in later years, Bahktin's ideas dispute the claims that genres are ever fully invented. Rather, as part of larger cultural conversations musical syntaxes become reconfigured, with certain parts emphasized over others. Furthermore, the crucial elements of recognition and response among the participants must be present for any reconfigurations to have meaning. In the case of the thrash metal genre, then, we might clarify the above and say that Metallica drew on the multisectional song structures of New Wave of British Heavy Metal (NWOBHM) groups such as Diamond Head and Venom, foregrounding the speed, the particular harmonic language emphasizing tritones and flatted seconds, dark, fantastic lyrical imagery, and the celebration of a metal musical-cultural identity quite opposed to the glam metal scene in Los Angeles.[8] Throughout the 1980s, numerous bands joined the conversation, notably Megadeth, Slayer, and Anthrax, and each offered further reconfigurations. For instance, Slayer placed less emphasis on the notion of multisection song structures in favor of even more breathtaking speed, even more shocking lyrics, and wildly chaotic guitar solos, while Megadeth's early music focused largely on Dave Mustaine's lead guitar skills.

Moreover, 1983 might be thought of as the origins of a thrash metal "school" simply because some of the most successful bands associated with the style released their first albums that year.[9] In the intersection of commerce and creativity, and due to the necessity of historically situated individuals for the production of musical meaning, the application of the thrash metal label to the 1983 albums represents the distillation of broad notions of musical identity into a linguistic expression. The large-scale commercial infrastructures of the record label system are of course not the sole means by which generic conventions are expanded to new participants, but neither is the label system insignificant in that regard. The understanding of Metallica (or Slayer, or the other 1983 bands) as representative of something called thrash metal took place after *Kill 'Em All* had come out.

By many accounts, thrash metal was not a term used to describe the 1983 bunch before they had connected with record labels, nor did the bands use it in their own promotion efforts.[10] Indeed, Metallica's 1982 business card used the term "power metal" to describe the band, but even that label did not amount to much importance. Accounts of early 1980s metal musicians and fans consistently acknowledge the appearance of the term thrash metal as occurring after they had heard the 1983 bands on purchased recordings and read about them in metal fanzines and other publications. It was in this way that the institutionalization of thrash metal and its application to Metallica's music largely took place. Such a sociolinguistic pattern was not unique to thrash metal, but it does help illustrate part of the dynamic interplay between musical expression and cultural meaning. Thus, while 1983 makes for a tidy origin for thrash metal, it overlooks the complexities of individual identities as well as the complex processes by which meanings are incorporated into new situations. Why, though, is the term thrash metal attached specifically to the 1983 moment? If sheer speed represented the most obvious and remarkable characteristic of the music, what was the difference between up-tempo metal from the late 1970s (for instance) and up-tempo metal from 1983 onwards? When does speedy metal not automatically constitute a distinct generic type called thrash metal? Where do the beginnings lie, and what kinds of utterances and subject positions become reconstituted in order to mark the beginning of a different set of conversations?

The primary musical difference lies in the consistent treatment of tempo in a rhythmically intense manner and as a distinctly aggressive musical element. The speed of thrash metal in the early 1980s was also a reconfiguration of the sonic transgression from two other sources: American hardcore punk bands such as Black Flag, Dead Kennedys, Misfits, and TSOL; and the British metal bands Venom and Motörhead. The relationship between American hardcore and thrash metal was complex, but a large degree of aesthetic influence projected outward from hardcore toward metal in the first half of the 1980s. Indeed, thrash metal giants Slayer and Anthrax (as well as Metal Church) were organized in 1982 by guitarists who had begun their performance careers in otherwise unsuccessful hardcore bands. The frenetic pace of hardcore, driven by loud rock instrumentation and a high-pitched distorted vocal style, stood as perhaps the most direct sonic link between the two styles. Thrash metal also drew on a similar suburban working class audience that characterized the hardcore scenes in Orange County, CA and San Francisco. Moreover, it imported hardcore's mosh pits and its image of independent Do It Yourself (DIY) values.[11] Still, though they shared a common interest in presenting extreme transgression, individual musicians could also be (and were) adamant about either a hardcore or metal identity. Thus, thrash metal's ultimate musical divergence from hardcore involved a conscious move to write more musically involved songs, as well as to embrace some amount of individual virtuosity. Frenetic tempi, according to the early thrash aesthetic, occupied only one element (to be sure, a significant one) of the ideal musical picture.

Lyrically, too, thrash metal musicians were much less ardent in their politics than most hardcore bands, preferring instead to derive their images of power from other sources. To thrash fans and musicians, hardcore seemed too preachy, too concerned about getting a "message" across (and usually a Leftist one at that), and perhaps too real. Dead Kennedys's "California Über Alles" (1980), for instance, opens with the lines "I am Governor Jerry Brown / My aura smiles and never frowns / Soon I will be President ..." and exemplifies the potential for a kind of seriocomic critique largely jettisoned by thrash (even while the underlying harmonic language of these lyrics, with its rhythmic articulation of the tonic chord and reliance on a quasi-Phrygian tension in the riff, could comfortably be found a few years later in thrash metal[12]). Thrash metal ultimately came to present a politics of its own, indeed one that shared some common sociological roots and inquiries with hardcore. As will be discussed in Chapter 3, thrash metal lyrics later in the decade would question injustices related to industrial capitalism, warfare, the environment, as well as the issue of social control. But thrash metal's initial answers to questions of broader social relevance rarely revolved around music as the means for political commentary or direct sociopolitical change. Instead, thrash metal focused on the elevation of the individual, rather than a united underclass of "kids" (represented by bands), as the agent of social struggle. Indeed, its notable reliance on imagery drawn from fantasy and the occult provided the palette for thrash metal's representation of the triumph of the individual.

From Motörhead and Venom came important models of a new heavy metal identity based sonically in the transgression of speed. Since the mid-1970s, but most notably with its 1980 album *Ace of Spades*, Motörhead's approach to tempo operated as a component of a broader aggressive and powerful aesthetic. The lyrics of the song "Ace of Spades" celebrate a devil-may-care attitude that is underlined by a fast drumbeat, a rhythmically insistent single-note riff, and the distorted tone of singer Ian "Lemmy"

Kilmister's bass. While many of Motörhead's songs dealt with sexual conquest, none of the band members presented themselves as sex symbols in the usual sense (the famous large wart on Kilmister's left cheek did not help matters). Instead, Kilmister's theatrically angled microphone, the band members' tattoos and rings, the band's snarling dog-creature logo (fitted with a Kaiser-style spiked motorcycle helmet), as well as the conspicuous umlaut over the second "o" in the band's name, presented a level of iconographical daring that seemed as flippant as punk rock. At the same time, this imagery is drawn more from the fantastic and perceptions of the gothic as mysterious and powerful. The band's name evokes the power of the mechanical, but the quasi-Gothic script used to write the name, as well as the umlaut, tell us the machinery in question is not sleek and futuristic. Rather, it is purposefully dirty, grungy, and visceral.[13]

While Motörhead had courted both punk and metal audiences to some degree in the late 1970s, Venom put forth a distinct conception of metal. Venom operated within the recent upsurge of posturing over the sonic representation of metal during the NWOBHM years. As Steve Waksman has discussed, Venom's role within the NWOBHM was as advocate for metal as sonically extreme and visually transgressive.[14] In Venom's case, this meant obscure stage names for the band members (for example, Abaddon, Chronos, and Mantas) and Satanic visual and lyric imagery to accompany very fast riff-based music. The song "Welcome to Hell" from its first album of the same name (1981), demonstrated the kind of transgression and sociological stance characterizing the version of heavy metal envisioned by Venom:

> Kill, we will kill. Death.
>
> Masturbating on the deeds we have done.
>
> Hell commands death. Kill.
>
> Argue not, feel the death of the sun.

Lyrically, these images are quite a bit more immediate and decadent than the more philosophical musings on the occult and other dark subjects by Ozzy Osbourne and Black Sabbath some years earlier. Furthermore, Venom's refusal to shy away from questions regarding a direct link between the characterizations in their songs and their individual lives only heightened the sense of transgression surrounding the group: the band members never really *denied* being Satanists. Ultimately, journalist Geoff Barton, in his capacity as the metal editor of the British music weekly *Sounds*, worked to claim Venom as part of the NWOBHM movement. Due largely to those efforts, Venom's second album, *Black Metal* (1982), achieved relatively broader recognition, and became a crucial aesthetic statement for the use of transgressive lyrical imagery and frenetic tempi as a component of heavy metal. Neither Venom nor Motörhead wrote especially complex songs, but the riff style of both, coupled with basic visual references such as long hair, introduced new elements into the musical conversation surrounding the development of thrash metal.

A third important British model for the aggressive speed of American thrash metal came from the particular punk/metal approach of Iron Maiden between 1979 and 1981, in particular the band's first two albums, *Iron Maiden* and *Killers*, featuring lead singer Paul Di'Anno. Di'Anno styled himself squarely between the contemporary idealized endpoints of metal and punk: he sported short spiky hair, but wore leather pants; he could sing with a punk shriek in songs such as "Sanctuary" and "Running Free," but also made an effort to "sing" during the band's less intense, more esoteric songs (e.g., "Strange World" and "Remember Tomorrow" from *Iron Maiden*). Nevertheless, Iron Maiden's use of two lead guitarists, who both played solos on most songs, and the technical ability of its bassist and group leader, Steve Harris, worked to secure its identity as a metal band. Harris, who professed very little respect for punks and punk music, also insisted upon an emphatic assertion of Iron Maiden's metal identity. Indeed, as Waksman explores, Iron Maiden ultimately offered another competing claim for heavy metal against both the constructed chaos of Venom and the pop sound of Def Leppard.

Yet, as a genre and a broader category of musical identity and experience, thrash metal should be thought of as more than just fast songs. As I mentioned previously, tempo in thrash metal was a consistent (though not necessarily constant), aggressive presence in the music. Earlier metal songs, such as Judas Priest's "Exciter" (the opening track to the 1978 album *Stained Class*) featured a fast tempo, intense texture, and rapid riffing across a dramatic structure, but they also lacked the particular component of confrontational aggression provided by either hardcore or Venom. Singer Rob Halford's voice was far too trained (in a classical sense), and usually far too beautiful for his vocals to have been considered transgressive in the way Chronos' vocals for Venom (or Motörhead's Kilmister) were. Additionally, within the oeuvre of Judas Priest the musical style of "Exciter" did not represent the band in a general way, competing as it did with delicate ballads like "Before the Dawn" and "Last Rose of Summer," or the mid-tempo hard rock of "Living After Midnight" and "Sinner."[15] As such, "Exciter" may have foregrounded tempo, but in doing so it did not also fundamentally redirect the band's overall musical aesthetic.[16]

Fast songs contribute to a range of possible subject positions, and tempo gains much of its significance from its relationship from song to song. Metallica's approach to aggressive speed differed noticeably from its contemporaries in the Los Angeles heavy metal scene, and the band's first recording, included on the first *Metal Massacre* compilation (1982), illustrates how surrounding context can inform the reception of musical style. The album features songs by nine metal bands with Metallica's "Hit the Lights" positioned last on the album.[17] While "Hit the Lights" has a fast tempo (160 bpm), other songs on the album also have sections of up-tempo rapid riffing such as "Live for the Whip" by Bitch. However, on this album there is a clear difference between fast and up-tempo in that "Hit the Lights" makes *fast* the main point by consistently presenting the idea of fast as distinctly aggressive. In other songs on the compilation fast might also signal intensity, but sections of lesser intensity also seem to negate that sense of drive. "Live for the Whip" begins with a very fast, active riff marked by solid sixteenth notes in the guitar, but the energy falls away completely during the much slower whole-note feel of the song's verse sections (the drumbeat, in particular, falls off considerably). Thrash metal songs might also use tempo as a rhetorical tool to distinguish and characterize individual sections in songs, but never at the level of the whole note.

In "Hit the Lights," on the other hand, Metallica's aesthetic foregrounds consistent speed as a sign of consistent aggression and power.[18] The difference can be heard in the kind of rhythmic atmosphere created by the main riff, as repeated sixteenth-notes in the guitar and the continuous rapid snare hits on offbeat eighth-notes make the song feel twice as fast. The song's lyrics celebrate a heavy metal identity, and, as I will discuss below, it is one of a number of thrash metal songs from the 1983 period that are about thrash metal itself. Hetfield's short opening shriek that coincides with the introduction of the full band texture is also crucial for making the fast tempo sound aggressive: his short, high-pitched, distorted vocalization coming across as a blast of transgressive energy. Indeed, initial vocalizations such as this became a significant stylistic marker for early thrash metal, appearing on the opening tracks of the debut albums by Slayer, Megadeth, and Anthrax. In each instance the shriek launches the proper introduction of the songs and thus serves as both a structural demarcation and a moment of controlled chaos.[19]

Cycles of Energy and Bodily Performance

James Hetfield's opening shriek on "Hit the Lights" also presents the sound of a young voice. Nineteen years old at the time, his voice is thin and comes mostly from his falsetto. As Hetfield has described numerous times since then, his role as Metallica's singer was determined largely by default: some-one had to be the singer in the band. Still, he had never envisioned his voice as his primary instrument, and like many young men he worked to over-come a slight embarrassment about singing in public.[20] At that point, in the early 1980s, the most notable metal role models for Hetfield were the classically trained voices of Judas Priest's Rob Halford and Iron Maiden's Bruce Dickenson, and the glittery camp swagger of Van Halen's David Lee Roth. Hetfield's shriek therefore stands as something of an act of defiance, as a statement that if he was going to be forced to sing he was going to shriek as unbeautifully as possible.[21] The issue of stage chatter between songs, and the need to stoke the audience's energy and excitement during a concert, all of which are the usual purview of a charismatic front man, also needed to be dealt with. Again, Hetfield seems to have approached the role with some trepidation and lead guitarist Dave Mustaine often took on the job of inter-acting with the crowd. With Mustaine out of the band after 1983 though, Hetfield quickly learned the mechanics of stage presence and developed the kinds of routines essential to a rock or metal concert. Importantly, as a "nonsinging" thrash metal vocalist, his voice received little preventative care or attention, and over the course of thousands of concerts the young-sounding voice would be forced downward in register somewhat. Due to that process, as well as to the natural lowering of male voices with age, it also gained a powerful chest presence necessary to create the confident mid-range "bark" that would become the sonic image of Hetfield.[22]

Moreover, the timbre and register of Hetfield's voice were only part of his bodily contribution to thrash metal in the early years. While the devel-opment of Hetfield's vocal identity is to some degree shared by the devel-opment of his bodily identity, there are a number of ways in which thrash metal worked on and with the bodies of performers and audiences.[23] The song "Whiplash," from Kill 'Em All, demonstrates how "cycles of energy," operating on multiple levels, focus power and intensity into bodily expe-rience in the thrash metal style. A range of elements contributes to how musical energy flows through the body in these songs. On one level there are the rhetorical gestures of tempo and rhythmic intensity, wrapped in the sound of a distorted guitar timbre, to assault and affect the bodies of the performers and audience, usually through some sort of headbanging or moshing. At another level lies the physicality of playing riffs with a heavy amount of palm-muting, a guitaristic technique that offers a great amount of timbral shading and control based on slight alterations of the guitarist's right hand during performance (I describe this technique in more detail below). Finally, speed and timbre combine to produce the extra heavy sound of what are often called the "mosh parts" of thrash metal songs, those sections that either cut sixteenth-note intensities into eighth-note intensities; or maintain a sense of continuous rhythm in the guitars but do so accompanied by a halftime drum pattern. It is in the organization of these combinations that I find the idea of cycles of energy to be particularly fitting.

The affective realm of the verse music in "Whiplash" represents one part of an energy cycle: a very fast drum beat (164 bpm) and a nearly undifferentiated two-measure stream of sixteenth-notes on Low E.[24] The stream stops only at the very end of the second measure—indeed at perhaps the last practical moment within the measure—by an eighth-note blip on G, on the "&" of beat four. Because it lasts for so short a time, the quick change to G functions less like a harmonic point than as a rhythmic one: it is almost as though the G chord is less important by itself than the disruptive rhythmic effect it creates. Even as the rhythmic hit on G seems to demarcate the end of the verse riff, the speed and presence of the snare drum's offbeat eighth-notes can make this moment sound like it is occurring on the downbeat. While not quite disorienting, the accent nevertheless injects a distinct interruption into the overall rhythmic flow.[25] Moreover, video footage of Metallica's performance of "Whiplash" in early 1983 shows James Hetfield and Dave Mustaine enacting the stream of Low Es with very rigid bodies: they stand straight up essentially but are anchored to the floor by thirty successive sixteenth-notes.[26] Both guitarists stare menacingly out into the crowd during the stream but Mustaine's expression slowly begins to change in anticipation of the upcoming rhythmic hit. Indeed, at the brief hit on G they both provide the first significant bodily response via a quick jerk of their heads before resuming their previous pose. While the sixteenth-notes are of course far too fast and undifferentiated for much reaction, the players' relative inaction signals a sense of the riff's constant power.[27]

If the sound of the repeated Low Es produces a stable affective base, the palm muting of each sixteenth-note greatly helps in the creation of that effect. Palm muting slightly muffles each note with the palm of the guitarist's picking hand (more specifically it is the outer side of the palm). By greatly emphasizing both the lower frequencies and the very high overtones of the sound envelope, as well as cutting out the mid-range, palm muting results in a distortion timbre that generally sounds tighter and more precise. Furthermore, palm muting produces a distinctively percussive timbral variation. In the verse riff of "Whiplash" the rhythmic hit on G is not palm muted, enabling it to stand out further from the background of palm-muted Low Es. Most important here are the aural and performative differences between palm-muted and nonpalm-muted notes, differences which provide important means for rhetorical contrast within a section of music and contribute to the flow of energy across a song.[28]

As a series of synchronic events, the stream of thirty palm-muted sixteenth-notes during the verse music conveys a sense of an unchanging eternity. Contrasting this affect is the vigorous activity of Ulrich's drums, which present a lot of activity in a short amount of time. The drum pattern itself is relatively simple, but much changes on a moment-to-moment basis: kick drum, snare, and high hat all come and go in rapid succession of one another. Thus, we could describe the Low E base in the guitars and the drum pattern as an expression of kinetic energy, or the energy of stable motion: nothing in the verse music itself points us toward the inevitability of a different riff or change of energy. Indeed, the kinetic energy is such that the riff could go on forever and only because of the standard hypermetric repetition scheme of rock does the song move to the chorus.[29] During the chorus, the guitars contrast the previous state by dramatically changing the general accent patterns, and in doing so demonstrate just how powerful that kinetic energy really is. Importantly, the harmonic breakthrough up to the sixth scale degree, C, is specifically not palm muted. This "opening out" to C, followed by a half-step slide to B, functions not only as a harmonic change, but is rhythmic as well: both chords last at least an entire quarter-note, and the entire measure acts as an explosive display of a higher *level* of kinetic energy (see Figure 1.1). The subsequent move to a palm-muted F# for one measure then hauls the energy back under tenuous control and transfers it to a forward-driving galloping rhythm. The new rhythmic pattern, pitch, and palm-muted timbre then reconstitute the energy as a build-up of potential energy, energy released as kinetic by another explosion back to C. Each repetition of the two-measure chorus music increases the overall potential in two ways: F# provides a component of harmonic tension challenging the previous stability of Low E (as well as a tonally jarring jump from the area around C), and the galloping rhythm provides a component of rhythmic tension, challenging the relatively stable bed of sixteenth-notes of the verse music.

Figure 1.1 "Whiplash"—Verse/Chorus Energy.

After three iterations of the chorus pattern the guitars suddenly break off, but the drums overshoot the break for half a measure of offbeat tom fills.[30] The disappearances of both the regular snare-led drumbeat and the steady galloping guitar rhythm of the chorus' F# measure are the initial means for creating the sense of disorientation. The offbeat accents of the fill itself contribute another. In rock music, tom fills generally increase the anticipation of large-scale formal change within a song, and at this moment in "Whiplash" all of these things combine to push the overall tension to a brief but dizzying extreme. Hetfield's vocal exclamation "Whiplash!" seems to arrive out of nowhere due to the rhythmic disorientation and brings the music to a complete halt for a split second. The exclamation functions not only as a tag to the tension created by the tom fill, but it also finally breaks the repetition of the chorus section and leads directly to the return of the "faster" Low E stream of sixteenth-notes and the start of the next verse/chorus energy cycle. In addition, the vocal exclamation exhorts the audience into renewed physical motion and direct physical expression of the kinetic energy in the music, and to acting out the celebrations of bodily experience that are described through lyrics such as:

Bang your head against the stage like you never did before,

Make it ring, make it bleed, make it really sore,

In a frenzied madness with your leathers and your spikes,

Heads are bobbing all around—it's hot as hell tonight.

I will have more to say about these lyrics in the final section of the chapter, and at this point in "Whiplash" the solidly accented return of the entire band resolves both the harmonic and rhythmic tensions introduced by the chorus. Most importantly, however, the return of the verse music and the stream of sixteenth-notes mark the transformation of a general sense of potential energy back into its kinetic counterpart. The cycles of energy between verse and chorus outlined above continue throughout the song, but a wholly new section of music following the third verse introduces a halftime rhythmic texture and illustrates one of the most characteristic rhetorical aspects of thrash metal's musical style. This new section, usually called a bridge in rock music, is sometimes labeled the mosh part on thrash metal album lyric sheets. Even as it shares the same tempo as the verse and chorus sections, the mosh part of "Whiplash" cuts the rhythmic intensity in half such that what had been a lot of frenetic sixteenth-note activity becomes eighth-note based. Moreover, the new one-measure guitar riff treats Low E very differently, using it to fill the metric space following the

Figure 1.2 "Whiplash" mosh part riff.

riff's primary harmonic activity (see Figure 1.2). The four Low E eighth-notes at the end of the measure function as a stabilizing expression of kinetic energy. The Low Es also comprise the most important component in creating a texture that sounds more focused and, because it follows the fast pace of the verse/chorus cycle, distinctly "heavy."

The 1983 video footage of this moment in the song shows Hetfield and Mustaine adopting very different postures than during the verse riff. Standing directly in front of the drum riser, their feet are spread slightly wider than shoulder width. The halftime pulse allows them to play the Low E eighth-notes as palm-muted downstrokes and to headbang on each quarter-note. With their heads facing downward, their bodies seem to absorb the weightiness of the repeated Low Es. Bassist Cliff Burton, on the other hand, enacts the textural change by slowly swinging his thick hair back and forth through the air in rough equivalent to the *half*-notes. Unlike Hetfield and Mustaine, Burton's headbanging does not always coincide strictly with the beat: this and other footage of him illustrate that he often expressed the heaviness at the level of the half note, but also was not restricted to headbanging precisely in time. As such, Burton put forth a very different body image than the other members of the band. Tall and lanky, frequently dressed in a denim jacket and bell-bottomed jeans, and with a very large amount of long hair, Burton engaged with the changing rhythmic intensities of Metallica's music in a very flowing manner. Rarely affecting the same direct engagement with the audience as either Hetfield or Mustaine, his body motions were generally slower than the others, but also more fluid and large-scale.

Perhaps the most noticeable development in Metallica's stage identity during the 1980s, though, was in the presentation of James Hetfield. While he always remained a dynamic performer, particularly during the instrumental sections of songs, his stance at the microphone underwent considerable change between 1983 and 1986, such that by 1986 he had come to the particular way of presenting himself that ultimately served as the cultural image of the on-stage "James Hetfield" for many years afterward. The stage image of Hetfield during the mid-1980s and into the early 1990s (the years during which Metallica's commercial and cultural visibility

Figure 1.3 James Hetfield performance stance c. 1986.

increased rapidly) was one of stability and self-confidence. At the microphone Hetfield's unusual crouched stance enacted a powerful compactness that appeared to be just barely containing a great deal of energy.

As illustrated in Figure 1.3 for example (taken from a 1986 performance of the song "Master of Puppets"), the classic stance might be described as follows: feet flat, shoulder-width apart, right foot backset a few inches and turned slightly outward; knees bent slightly for a lower center of gravity; torso hunched forward slightly, singing *down into* the mike (though the eyes look out to the audience); head often slightly tilted right allowing his hair to fall forward and drape the right side of his face. In addition, Hetfield used an Explorer-style guitar almost exclusively during these years. The Explorer guitar shape is a "tall" guitar in that the bridge end is a long line from an elevated point at the top down to a point at the bottom (spanning some eighteen inches), and distributes its width dimension fairly evenly such that the guitar body lies squarely in front of the pelvis. Overall, therefore, Hetfield's body appears very well balanced, solid, and anchored for the delivery of lyrics, while the drape of his hair and downward angle of his face convey a kind of confident menace. However, the energy that seems barely contained by his stance is in fact released many times in "Master of Puppets" via a quick backward thrust of his head and torso at the end of most lyrical phrases (see Figure 1.4). The headbanging thrust also has the

Figure 1.4 James Hetfield hair toss c. 1986.

effect of tossing his hair with a certain theatrical flair that shows off its length and volume.

That flair, though, was not exactly possible in 1983. Not only did Hetfield style his hair differently then (longish, but layered, with noticeable bangs that did not really get in his face), but also he had not yet settled into the crouch. Instead, like most singer/instrumentalists he stood more or less straight up, with the microphone at mouth level, eyes looking out over the crowd. In hindsight, Hetfield in this stance seems much less confident, less powerful, and more vulnerable to an errant gust of wind than in the image of powerful compactness he arrived at only a few years later (see Figure 1.5).

Video footage from a European tour in late 1984, though, shows that elements of the crouch had begun to materialize. Still using the Flying-V style guitar he had used since Metallica formed, Hetfield's lower body had found its component of the crouch. Still to develop were the upper body hunch and the downward angle of the face. Finally, footage from Metallica's August 1985 performance at the Day on the Green Festival in San Francisco shows Hetfield with the Explorer guitar and with both the hunch and crouch in place, all three of the main components of the classic stance. The Day on the Green show was Metallica's penultimate show before starting production on its third album, *Master of Puppets*, in Denmark, and it was not until March 1986 that the band toured again (opening for Ozzy Osbourne).[31] Importantly, it was with that tour that Metallica first played arena-size venues and in the process gained a great deal of commercial exposure. As such,

Figure 1.5 James Hetfield performance stance c. 1983.

the performance practice of James Hetfield, his own response to the music enacted via the powerful, confident, and barely contained crouch, entered into a more complex web of reification and collective memory.

It has been necessary to step through the details of stage presentation in order to emphasize the produced nature of musical identity. The most culturally significant image of James Hetfield is based on his late 1980s presentation, but we must not overlook the fact that we are studying a body in the process of being represented. That Hetfield's most well-known image did not emerge fully formed coincident with Metallica's first concerts, but was actively produced in the course of hundreds of performances illustrates the significance of understanding identity diachronically. There are certainly other components to musical identity that deserve our attention, and neither is my claim that this component of Hetfield's (or any other member of Metallica) identity was consciously planned so as to arrive just in time for the band's greatest moment of cultural visibility in March 1986. At the same time, Hetfield's performance presentation is the result of choices, some practical (he perhaps recognized some comfort advantages to the crouch or it would have been discarded) and some aesthetic (enacting the power and heaviness of the music), as indeed all identity presentations are. Ultimately what we gain by looking at these details, though, are insights into the bodily contributions to the recognition of musical genres.

Modular Structures and Formal Dialectics

In addition to thrash metal's lyrical strategy of focused intensity, the extreme tempo of many songs outweighed other musical characteristics of the style, and pure speed became central to the musical identity of the thrash metal genre. In short, people noticed the particular transgressive quality of the speed. Yet, as I have discussed above, tempo in thrash metal operates within a relational system that involves the primarily visceral transformations of energy across multiple sections of a song. David Lidov theorizes a distinct relationship between the intensity of pulse (here understood as tempo) and different somatic effects of music. He notes that "speed is exciting" and "intensity is involving," and the relationship between speed and intensity produces different states of perception.[32] Thus, one type of rhythmic contrast in thrash metal, such as the sixteenth-note-dominated verses of "Whiplash," gains much of its intensity when surrounded by musical sections that emphasize eighth-notes (especially repeated Low Es, as in the mosh part of "Whiplash") or a halftime drum pattern, and is experienced through the layered levels of intensity in the music. Similarly, a doubling of the drum pattern against a rhythmically unchanging guitar riff, a hallmark of thrash metal's rhythmic language, functions within the same relational approach.[33]

The last two musical sections of Metallica's "Seek and Destroy" (beginning at 5:50 on the *Kill 'Em All* recording) demonstrate the idea concisely. Following the final statement of the song's chorus (accented by the drums on alternating quarter notes), the guitars introduce a four-measure eighth-note-based riff that is at first accented by the drums on alternating half notes. Like the mosh part riff in "Whiplash," this riff uses palm-muted Low Es as rhythmic "glue" between the individual harmonic gestures, with a string of Low Es then filling out the two halves of the riff. After two iterations of the guitar riff (constituting one repetition group), the drums double their accents to alternating quarter notes, adding crash cymbal hits on beats two and four (see Figure 1.6). Next, the guitars introduce the second new riff, accented even more irregularly by the drums before a similar change to alternating quarter notes during the second repetition group (see Figure 1.7). As is illustrated in the examples, the kick drum patterns in the first repetition group of both riffs generate most of the plodding and labored feel, while the second repetition groups sound more confident and forward-driving precisely because of that initial quality. Indeed, the drums' change to regular quarter note accents seems to repair a distinct rhythmic disassociation between guitar and drums, but one that is felt primarily in retrospect: we remember the first repetition group was labored because the second group, the musical "present," is not.

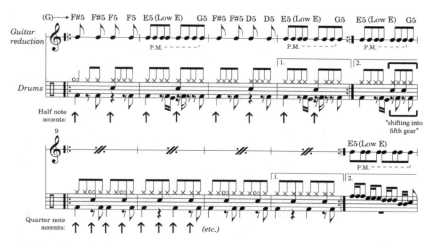

Figure 1.6 "Seek and Destroy"—Coda, 1st riff (mm. 1–16).

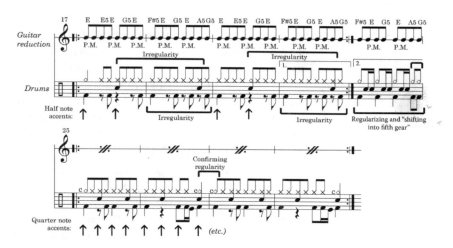

Figure 1.7 "Seek and Destroy"—Coda, 2nd riff (mm. 17–32).

In phenomenological terms, the experience of the rhythmic shift occurs as part of the temporal "thickness" of subjectivity. As Harris Berger discusses with respect to tonality, "musical experience is composed of protended sound, sound in the now-point, and retained sound." These ideas can easily be applied to rhythm, however, such that when we experience the drums' quarter-note change as an injection of smooth regularity we are simultaneously holding on to protended anticipation of the regularity as well as retaining something of the previous labored feel.[34] The drum fills at the tail end of the first repetition groups function as the crucial experiential bridge between the two temporal realms. The two quarter-note snare hits at the end of measure (m.) 8 in Figure 1.6 point us to the larger quarter-note organization of the second repetition group. Similarly, the measure-long fill in m. 24 of Figure 1.7 actually counts in four solid quarter notes amidst a cymbal/snare-drum flurry and again anticipates the ensuing quarter-note pattern. Moreover, the heavier and labored feel of the first repetition groups gradually but quickly fades from our experience as the more regularized and focused grove of the second group assumes full importance in the now-point of that experience.

In terms of energy, too, the metaphorical effect of both doublings resembles shifting a transmission into fifth gear after building up speed while in fourth: the action transforms the work done in the lower gear (climbing a steep hill, passing, and so on) into the cruising efficiency of the higher one. In thrash metal songs, this sort of shift represents another type of energy cycle, as the labored introduction of a riff builds potential energy, which then becomes the expression of kinetic energy at the entrance of a stable quarter-note drumbeat. Thus, rhythmic intensities do not signify nearly as strongly by themselves, rather the *changes* in intensity provide the crucial context for their signification. Part of the impetus for thrash metal's emphasis on a riff-based style of composition therefore lies in the process of creating different rhythmic intensities (each one powerful in its own way) while still maintaining an overall sense of energy across an entire song. The various contexts then create the cycles of energy that make songs like "Whiplash" and "Seek and Destroy" so effective.

Although the elements of speed and energy certainly contributed to Metallica's early identification within the thrash metal genre, it was the approach to form that consistently distinguished thrash metal over the course of the 1980s. Conceptually, the style of composition used by Metallica and other bands (notably Megadeth) can perhaps best be thought of as "modular" because it uses independent riffs strung together into largely foursquare sections. The individual riffs are typically based in E and feature the same general grammar as those in "Whiplash," but there are more of them in one song. Moreover, when the energy transformations occur from riff to riff, rather than from within individual riffs, we have one of the primary elements of the modular aesthetic. Investigating the topic of formal structure in thrash metal does not mean that I am attempting to prove that this music is complex and thus significant. Rather, I am interested in what is at stake, in terms of genre and musical identity, *because* Metallica's music is formally involved. Indeed, one of the main components in the critical reception of Metallica centers on the relationship between complexity and aesthetic success (many rock critics conflated the two, as I will discuss in Chapter 3). My goal is not to pass judgment on whether the formal style characteristic of their music during the 1980s was "successful" or "overindulgent." In the following discussion I aim instead to uncover what those kinds of descriptions mean in larger musico-cultural contexts.

Richard Middleton and others have suggested that one way to escape the trap of analytical formalism in the study of large-scale musical development (the emphasis on form as the essential feature of music) is to understand "form" not as a hardened shape or mold, but to see it as process. Viewing form as process in popular music allows one to examine the internal qualities of musical flow without getting hung up on the importance of an external cast. In this way, Middleton points out, the emphasis remains on "the 'internal' qualities of the musical flow, in all their detail, rather than on the 'external' mold into which they may have been poured."[35] As such, content—the stuff people actually care about when listening to music—can be understood across the length of a given song.

The distinction between form and content so important throughout musicology's history has typically understood the value of a work in terms of its relationship to ideal structural types, and from this ideology the chronology of music history has often been rendered as a parade of formal developments. In the case of nineteenth-century instrumental music, for example, analytical high points revolve around instances of form, with details of interpretation often depending greatly on how a piece uses sonata form: such-and-so piece introduces a new theme during the development; another piece begins the recapitulation in the wrong key; this piece does not repeat the exposition, etc.[36] Analysis of popular music, particularly Tin Pan Alley song from the first half of the twentieth century, has proceeded along much the same lines, for instance placing primary historical significance on the standardization of the 32-bar AABA form.[37] Lost (or at least easily subsumed) in all of this is the discussion of content, the moment-to-moment actions taking place in a piece of music. With the realization of the standardization of the 32-bar form comes little interest in examining how the actual content presented by that form creates meaning.

Importantly, Middleton does not simply argue for doing away with form as a topic of study, for he sees musicologists as being in the ideal position to provide important large-scale observations by their ability to connect different sections of a song together.[38] However, diminishing the distinction between form and content through the understanding of form as process produces a way of studying the relationships between different moments in a song as experience and *as content*. Viewing the structural characteristics of the modular aesthetic of thrash metal, for example, as a process enables us to see how the changes from module to module create meaning in a song and serve as important generic markers across a range of songs. The importance of process also provides a way of grasping the significance behind the sometimes lengthy series of modules used in a thrash metal song (as I will discuss). Indeed, the presence of a large number of modules represents by itself a specific kind of content in thrash metal, where length functions in a similar way as melody might for another genre. Still, the series of modules in a thrash metal song is also a formal sequence of events, and while the character of the riffs in each module certainly has a lot to do with fans' reception of a song, the presence of an extended formal structure remains just as important.

Charles Keil theorizes the concept of form-as-process further by postulating two kinds of process: *closed* and *open*. Keil also inserts a historical component into the understanding of form, for he positions score-based classical music (with its extended structure and goal-oriented development) as the paradigmatic example of a closed type. Afro-diasporic practices, on the other hand, which became much more significant across the twentieth century, are more representative of open processes. Such processes deploy formal divisions as large-scale backgrounds that are then extended through less rigid patterns of repetition and the constantly shifting inflection of those backgrounds.[39] The modular aesthetic of thrash metal (like form in most rock at some level) occupies a kind of middle ground between these two archetypes. Though the series of modules is tightly regimented, it is not goal-directed according to a preexisting set of criteria. In other words, the movement from one module to the next, while it does produce important meaning, typically does not represent stages of development in any large-scale sense, even if some kind of development does occur within the module itself.[40] In this way, the modular aesthetic appears as an open process, and as was noted above, the modules achieve their significance in the overall process through repetition.

Overwhelmingly set into hypermetric patterns of four (or its multiples), repetition of a solitary riff or filled-out texture is of fundamental importance to the modular aesthetic.[41] Nevertheless, individual modules in thrash metal do not undergo any variation whatsoever during repetition. Because the content of a module is fixed once it has been constructed, Keil's notion of an open process does not quite apply to thrash metal's modular concept. Repetition of materials certainly is important to the modular aesthetic, but, significantly, those materials are not also treated as frameworks upon which other things develop (except for the obvious case of guitar solos). Rather, the strict regularization and extreme predictability in the repetition of a module injects a distinctly closed sense of order into an open structural process quite different than that found in styles such as jazz and many types of electronic dance music (EDM).

A third way of understanding the modular concept's contribution to form in thrash metal is through the comparison of "vertical" and "horizontal" schema: in other words, the role of musical texture over time. Closely related to Keil's formulation, the ideas of vertical and horizontal forms are also related to repetition. In the same way that Keil theorizes Afro-diasporic popular music as an open formal process for the way it uses repetition, so too can much of that music be understood as relying on a vertical structure. The dynamic changes that are part of a repeated background are more important than the change of complete backgrounds through time. In other words, the various kinds of rap and EDM depend on the construction of a "perpetual present." The idea is to set up a single groove and then maintain that groove essentially for much of a song. In sticking with one musical groove, rap and EDM can be thought of as vertical: a significant musical texture is created that comprises many individual lines stacked on top of one another. That textural block is then repeated many times and becomes subject to Keil's open process. Most rock-based music, on the other hand, can be thought of as horizontal because whatever perpetual present is created through repetition of a riff or chord sequence is comparatively short-lived. As such, rock styles typically contain at least three different musical textures (harmonic sequences, drum patterns, instrumentation) that appear across a single song. The overall effect of this organizational method can be a determining factor in the length of the song, and as the progressive rock of the 1970s made clear, the horizontal approach could result in some very long songs.

The extended formal structure of "The Four Horsemen" (also from *Kill 'Em All*) illustrates the formal characteristics that would play a significant role in Metallica's reception throughout the 1980s. The song lasts a little over seven minutes and is the longest song on *Kill 'Em All*. It does not feature a frantically fast tempo as in "Whiplash," but some of the main guitar figures (during the verses, for example) are marked by quick, palm-muted bursts of rhythmic intensity on Low E. These short bursts also contrast with the longer whole-note chords of the song's chorus, and it is this idea of rhythmic contrast that will be very important for the entire song. Eight discrete musical sections (modules) appear throughout, with an extended sequence of bridge sections contributing greatly to this number (see Figure 1.8). The section labeled "pentatonic transition" in Figure 1.8 is just that, a transition marked by a descending pentatonic-based figure, and it is the only part of the bridge sequence not presented via a standard foursquare repetition scheme. Its short length and lack of immediate repetition also disqualify it as a true module. Each of the other bridge sections is presented that way, and, more importantly (because of the repetition scheme) each of these sections assumes an independent character even as that character also depends on the context of the surrounding modules. Indeed, the character of each bridge group (labeled A-A′, B-B′, Chorus′ in the example) contrasts dramatically with the others in terms of tempo, rhythmic structure, and mood even though they are all based solidly in an E modality. In other words, these sections are not organically related to each other, but stand as discrete modules, a series of perpetual presents, and are independent to the degree that one could pull any of them out of "The Four Horsemen" and use it to duplicate the same formal approach in a new song.[42]

1. Intro. riff
2. Verse 1
3. Chorus
   ****
   Intro. riff
   Verse 2
   Chorus
   ****
4. Bridge A (repeated Low E)
5. Bridge A′
   Pentatonic transition
6. Bridge B
7. Bridge B′ (with lyrics)
   Pentatonic transition
8. Chorus′ (w/ "lyrical" guitar solo)
   Bridge A′
   Pentatonic transition
   ****
   Intro. riff
   Verse 3
   Chorus
   ****
   Intro. riff
   Bridge A′ (w/ "frenetic" guitar solo)
   Intro. riff (one iteration)

Figure 1. 8 "The Four Horsemen"—Modular Structure.

For thrash metal in the 1980s the value of the modular style lies within a cultural system that values musical "complexity" and "musicianship" as a particular way of distinguishing certain content as artistic. In Metallica's case, the modular style draws heavily on turn-of-the-decade British bands of the NWOBHM, in particular the music on the album *Lightning to the Nations* by Diamond Head, released in 1980. In turn, Diamond Head guitarist Brian Tatler remarked that his band was inspired in their own style by lengthy multisectional songs such as "Xanadu" by Rush and "Kashmir" by Led Zeppelin: "We liked epicness; we wanted things to be grand."[43] James Hetfield recalled the influence of the NWOBHM as "[teaching] us that there were more than three parts to a song—that you could have a song with different parts, each of which could almost be its own song."[44] Yet Metallica's musical relationship to bands such as Diamond Head was not just one of straightforward artistic inspiration.

Indeed, Metallica included cover versions of Diamond Head songs in their own set during shows throughout 1982 and 1983, and Ulrich has often joked that Metallica began its career as a Diamond Head cover band. Of the nine songs performed at its first gig on March 14, 1982, only two were original songs ("Hit the Lights" and "Jump in the Fire"). The other seven were covers of NWOBHM songs, and *five* of those were Diamond Head covers. Moreover, Metallica opened its early sets (and the *Kill 'Em All* album) with "Hit the Lights," a song that begins with a noisy two-chord flourish meant to evoke the opening of a concert. However, in a further illustration of the NWOBHM's important role, the opening flourish—drum fills and all—seems to have been lifted straight from the beginning of "Set the Stage Alight," a 1980 B-side by the band Weapon.[45] In no case is there evidence that Metallica ever announced the cover songs as being covers, and this obfuscation amounted to a bold move on the part of the band.[46] Its strategy of passing off NWOBHM songs as its own not only made up for a lack of original tunes, but because of Diamond Head's relative obscurity to American audiences, it also circumvented a "no covers" rule apparently in place at many Los Angeles-area clubs.[47] This close relationship to early-eighties British metal, as well as the continued obscurity of the original artists, also eventually had the effect of transforming those covers into Metallica "originals." As such, fans today generally identify "Am I Evil?" first with Metallica rather than simply as a cover of a Diamond Head song.

Similarly, Metallica consciously described their sound as "European," and consistently contrasted it with an "American" hard rock sound that supposedly characterized most every other rock group. By the mid-1980s Ulrich (who was born in Denmark) had even linked the thrash metal genre itself to a restrictive American sound, and claimed that Metallica had "always looked beyond such limitations [of the style] and were better defined as an American outfit with European attitudes to Metal," a distinction which casts the "American" sound as somehow less interesting or even banal.[48] As quoted at the top of the chapter, Jon and Marsha Zazula remember the band's initial impact in 1983 somewhat differently, as a distinctly American answer to the successes of NWOBHM groups such as Iron Maiden, Saxon, and Def Leppard.

As it so often does in American culture, the term European here acts as a marker of cultural tension, indicating appropriated sensibilities of elevated refinement and intelligence, of interiority and artistic merit. It has been a constant component in discussions about American culture that it has always been somehow less refined or significant than that found in Europe (or, grossly, that America simply lacks culture). The history of American classical music, particularly since the late nineteenth century when the rise of industrialism renewed the belief in the importance and singularity of national cultures, is rife with anxieties about how to sound "American" while still creating music worthy enough to be considered respectable classical music.[49]

That tension is present in the competing explanations for Metallica's early position in the thrash metal genre given by Ulrich and the Zazulas: the Zazulas clearly heard any European-ness in Metallica as a positive component of their American-ness, while Ulrich describes the band's American biography as less significant than its European musical leanings. Thus, throughout the 1980s Metallica used modular composition (without calling it such) to foreground and publicize their difference within thrash metal and to insert themselves into a particular ideological tradition: songs with multisectional forms were "better" than "just 'open E' riffing for five minutes as fast as you can go." Obviously overlooking the blistering "open E riffing" of a song like "Whiplash," Ulrich remarked that "[W]e try and arrange and structure [the songs] with good breaks, tempo changes and choruses with melody lines."[50] He may as well have been talking about "The Four Horsemen" in that comment. Moreover, he is talking about writing Music (with a capital M), and his statement also reflects a specific negotiation of metal's reception by mainstream culture. Often viewed as superficial and mindless, metal in the 1980s (on the whole) had few influential defenders against attacks from social conservatives and others who could not accept metal even as music. Ulrich nonetheless recognizes that by highlighting Metallica's efforts as "compositional," specifically expressed through complexities of structure, he can then make a claim for a higher form of cultural prestige than would otherwise be available to him.[51]

Thus, Metallica's compositional approach, through the use of discrete modules to augment the middle section of a song, had two interrelated results. First, it complicated their position within the early thrash metal milieu, and, second, it became one of the aesthetic elements that would garner the band high praise from rock critics until the release of *Metallica* in 1991. After 1991, much of the commentary regarding this particular aesthetic turns decidedly negative, and I will have much more to say about this and about other meanings of the modular aesthetic and its reception history in later chapters.

Community, Violence, and the Edges of Immediacy

Lyrics like those from "Whiplash," quoted previously, gain their significance in a discussion about energy from the direct, visceral imagery contained within them. Each phrase in the "Whiplash" excerpt relies on short punches of imagery to foreground and complement the sense of immediacy found in the accompanying music. Importantly, "Whiplash" is a song about the experience of an early 1980s thrash metal show, where the metaphor of whiplash represents the physicality of headbanging taken to an extreme level. The lyrics also constantly acknowledge that experience as one of community and identity. Within "Whiplash" Metallica positions itself in a role akin to chroniclers, but it is also important that they be seen as participants in the community. The band's presence on stage, elevated above the audience, would seem to make such equality illusory, but the direct imagery in these lyrics also acts to minimize that distance. According to the lyrics, moreover, the most attractive elements of the thrash metal experience are those that are also the most physically transgressive. The exhortation in "Whiplash" to "make it ring, make it bleed, make it really sore" is but one example signaling how pain and violence represent visceral experience. Rather than merely foregrounding a blind celebration of mutilation, the lyrical phrases surrounding that line contextualize it as part of a general sensory excitement and energy.

Songs about musical experience and music cultures are an unusual genre within rock, more so in the years since the term "rock" entered popular music taxonomy in the 1960s. Indeed, such songs have appeared far more often in dance-oriented styles of popular music, like disco and hip hop. Musical styles which have generally resided on the so-called margins of mainstream pop-music culture use these kinds of songs in a number of ways, and they are fundamental to asserting some sort of musical identity. "The Twist," recorded by Chubby Checker in 1960, is a notable example in this regard, as a song designed to create a new dance craze. Likewise, the many songs about dance and expressive musical physicality by James Brown (1965's "Papa's Got a Brand New Bag," for instance) fore-grounded a distinct conception of "soul." Sugar Hill Gang's "Rapper's Delight" (1980) expanded on the function of genre songs in an effort to "introduce" rap to white audiences: the song explicitly takes the uniniti-ated listener on a musical tour of rap and, moreover, works very hard to present a nonthreatening image of the music's inner-city black origins.

Within rock, genre songs turn up most frequently in styles that place a good deal of importance on defining themselves as being about resistance to the mainstream as anything else. Punk and hardcore have traditionally offered such musical sustenance to those alienated from mainstream rock culture. As a style of rock, thrash metal in the early 1980s modeled its own genre songs after the examples in those other styles. In addition to "Hit the Lights" and "Whiplash," Metallica's "Metal Militia" joined songs like Anthrax's "Metal Thrashing Mad" and "Soldiers of Metal," and Exodus' "Bonded By Blood" and "Metal Command" to draw on the identity powers of the genre song, celebrating and reinforcing thrash metal's oppositional identity with respect to competing styles of heavy metal.[52]

Musically, these genre songs were among each band's fastest and most frenetic examples of thrash metal. They were also overwhelmingly rejected as suitable material for subsequent albums. Indeed, it could be argued that once the thrash metal style had been established to some degree there remained little point in continuing to advocate for the lifestyle and musical values of thrash metal with another genre song: the point had been made and anything else could come across as a stagnant cliché. With knowl-edge of the lyrical topics actually present on later thrash albums, the value placed on the belief that vital music and musicians develop continuously in some way significantly informs that view. To be sure, the critical reaction to Metallica's later albums in terms of artistic progress and development depended heavily on rhetorically repositioning songs like "Hit the Lights" and "Metal Militia" as the product of inexperienced, immature, and aes-thetically limited songwriters.[53] Nevertheless, we must not overlook how the experience of thrash metal most likely represented one of the first sig-nificant musical identities for many of its fans and musicians. That the lyrical imagery and physical experience of those songs are often couched in terms of violence was not only a transgressive shock tactic, but, as men-tioned above, linked individuals into some sort of community.

Such a reading is not meant simply to highlight that element and down-play the visibility of violence contained in the "Whiplash" lyrics. Rather, I am interested in how the physicality that characterizes the concert experi-ence is represented by aggressive immediacy in those lyrics. Indeed, the visceral experience, in these cases manifested as violent experiences, can be understood as part of the place of violence in popular culture more generally. Sociologist John Fiske argues that violence is a frequent component in popular culture because of its ability to give expression to broader social conflict.[54] Specifically, the concrete representation of conflict produced by violence operates as a metaphor for the conflicts raised by social domination and subordination and the distribution of power in society. To dismiss the violence in the "Whiplash" lyrics as simply the product of individual baseness ignores the complex ways those lyrics offer an outlet for individual rage. At the same time, the enactment of such violence (like all violence in popular culture) functions as a resistance to that subordination. Thus, the imagery of physical pain as visceral experience can be transgressive on multiple levels: its shock value enables an energetic physical knowledge at the same time that it functions as a tangible method of confronting larger social structures.

The notion of transgressive immediacy as a central characteristic of thrash metal also arises in the form of macabre lyrics about death and war, as well as the dark fantasy of the occult. Just as "Whiplash" constantly foregrounds the intense experience of a thrash metal show through its frenetic music and direct lyrical imagery, Slayer's "Necrophobic" (1986) uses a similar strategy to evoke a particularly grisly experience of death:

Strangulation, mutilation, cancer of the brain,

Limb dissection, amputation, from a mind deranged.

...

Sliced incision, zero vision, loss of vital signs,

Skin contortion, bone erosion, life becomes your fine.

The list of images here is not meant to be internally consistent in an organic or developing sense. Instead, the continuous assault of graphic imagery forms the central strategy in these lyrics. Even more compressed than those found in "Whiplash," the images in "Necrophobic" focus darkness and destruction to such a degree that there can be no release or escape for the victim of this particular death, or for the listener.[55] Slayer emphasizes the focused intensity of these lyrics with a song form lasting only 98 seconds, but which nevertheless employs a recognizable series of verse/chorus sections, a short mosh-part riff, and two chaotic guitar solos. In other words, the intensity of the thrash metal accompaniment directly mirrors the compressed immediacy of the lyrical imagery. Indeed, Slayer's entire *Reign in Blood* album (where "Necrophobic" appears) operates this way, presenting ten songs in a constant stream of power and immediacy, lasting just under thirty minutes.

Walser theorizes the general use of this type of imagery in heavy metal lyrics as being about the cultural power that such images carry with them. He argues that by drawing from a broad range of historical, mythological, and occultist imagery, metal musicians and fans create spaces for the appropriation of power to contest the cultural uncertainties that surround them. In the specific case of thrash metal, it is clear that the particular style of delivery of these images is also of crucial importance: the sense of transgression in thrash metal is distinctly highlighted by the intense musical and vocal immediacy used to deliver that transgression. But if the celebration of transgression through rhetorical directness enables thrash metal songs to represent and appropriate images of power, that same tactic of transgressive directness in the service of musical identity can overstep other important social boundaries and be used to represent ignorance and hate. Indeed, in any of these songs it is important to ask: what kind of "power" are we talking about here?

The immediacy and refusal to evoke anything resembling contemplative interiority in songs like "Whiplash" and "Necrophobic" can be argued as ultimately resulting in a powerful (if relatively harmless) experience. However, the immediacy found in the lyrics to "Speak English or Die," by the band Stormtroopers of Death (S.O.D.), depicts a much more sinister form of that effect. Created in 1985 as a side project by two members of Anthrax, S.O.D. also featured New York hardcore vocalist Billy Milano. The group's first album (and for fifteen years, its only studio recording), *Speak English or Die* (1985), became a cult classic among American thrash metal fans due to the over-the-top character of the lyrics and the intensity of the thrash metal-styled music. Importantly, the band members envisioned S.O.D. as primarily a self-mocking parody lampooning the intense aggression ascribed to thrash metal by writing silly songs about, for example, not having any milk for one's morning cereal. The frustrated immediacy of a lack-of-milk experience is certainly humorous in the guise of thrash metal, as is the album's series of extremely short epigram-like interludes about Jimi Hendrix and procrastination (among others).[56] Yet, most of what passes as humorous immediacy on the rest of the album relies on a distinctly misanthropic form of shock value to provide the laughs.

Like "Speak English or Die," the songs "Pre-Menstrual Princess Blues" and "Fuck the Middle East" find fault with others through the raging rants of the supposedly normal viewpoint of a young white male.[57] According to guitarist Scott Ian, the impetus for the particular aesthetic of S.O.D. was an imaginary character named Sergeant D who simply hated everything and everybody. Still, while there are moments on the album where other participants in the underground metal scene get knocked for being poseurs or wannabes, nowhere does the insult comedy really reach back onto the band itself. This is perhaps not surprising since the Sergeant D's rage is designed to radiate outward in the form of unadulterated frustration. Nevertheless, the strategy of parody makes S.O.D.'s humor quite different from other instances of wide-ranging parody such as the television show *The Simpsons*, where there is a much clearer sense of *everyone* being eligible for ridicule (even the show's creators).[58]

Perhaps the least-theorized component in an examination of the imagery of "Speak English or Die" and even "Whiplash" is the relationship between that imagery and the age of the performers. Regarding "Speak English or Die," S.O.D. bassist Dan Lilker remarked in 2001 "when we wrote the lyrics for the first album we were a little younger than we are now, and I can see how people would take them the wrong way ..." Along the same lines, Lilker added that on the band's second album (released in 2001) "we don't go after nationalities because we realize that that is kinda tasteless."[59] Lilker's comments recognize that there remains a fundamental difference between the shock value of fantastic Satanic imagery (however macabre the final result) and the histrionics of intolerance. Because of how songs like "Speak English or Die" easily tap into a much larger historical narrative of oppression and violence, the song's subject matter revisits attitudes that have held (and continue to hold) very real day-to-day positions of influence in American society. Thus, what makes the broadly-based racism found in "Speak English or Die" most significant (and most troubling) is the normalization of this imagery: the fact that these kinds of lyrical topics did not constitute taking things "too far" for all involved.

As I've been noting with respect to much of Metallica's aesthetic in the early 1980s, the music and surrounding cultural scene are the product of people in their late teens and very early twenties. As such, a transgressive expression such as that in "Speak English or Die" should perhaps not seem all that surprising. At the same time, thrash metal musicians did not invent the kind of impulse expressed (however jokingly) in "Speak English or Die" *ex nihilo*, and simply dismissing the intolerance that crept into S.O.D.'s parodist aesthetic as merely the misguided acts of youth does not allow us to account for its presence in the first place. Ultimately, thrash metal performers walked a thin line when it came to the immediacy of shocking imagery, both musical and lyrical, and the potential for conflicting cultural expressions—the tensions in the presentation of power, aggression, and intensity—was particularly acute in the early moments of the genre. In this way, the forging of thrash metal's aesthetic represents an important cultural snapshot of the mechanisms of musical identity in America.

CHAPTER 2

Death Greets Me Warm

The Fade to Black Paradigm

The word "metal" is real wide—five years ago, Journey was metal. Now, there are all sorts of stereotypes: speedcore, thrash, or fuckin'-death-super-Satan metal. It's really ridiculous, and I don't see us fitting into any of that shit. Someone who listens to "Dyers Eve" might say we're speedcore. But put on "Fade to Black" or "Sanitarium"—they're a whole different thing.

James Hetfield, 1989[1]

Introduction

When I was an impressionable ninth grader, an older kid told me that I should listen to Megadeth rather than Metallica because, as he put it, "Megadeth [was] like Metallica but without that 'Fade to Black' shit." That incident occurred in 1985 when my interest in Metallica's music was still new, having really begun about a year earlier. In addition to Metallica, during the mid-1980s when heavy metal's popularity was increasing, bands such as Mötley Crüe, Ratt, Iron Maiden, and Dio spent considerable time on my cassette boombox. Metallica, then, formed only a part of

33

the listening habits I shared with my (white, suburban) friends. Of course Metallica's music differed significantly from the sounds of my other favorite groups and, importantly, all the so-called bad kids touted them, along with other bands associated with the nascent thrash metal genre, as the newest best thing. The speed and sonic aggression displayed on Metallica's first two albums, *Kill 'Em All* and *Ride the Lightning*, were certainly extreme and definitely pushed the envelope of noisy transgression in ways that the *faux*-Satanism of Mötley Crüe's *Shout at the Devil* and the gory sexuality of W.A.S.P. did not. Musically, thrash metal was outside stuff, and you made a statement by listening to bands like Metallica.

My only problem with my schoolmate's suggestion was that I liked "Fade to Black." A lot. And at that moment I realized that Metallica was not always that far out, that listening to and liking "Fade to Black" somehow pulled me back into the arms of social respectability, if only a little bit. I could still enact some amount of rebellion by listening to Metallica (and therefore have some cred with the real metalheads), but could also avoid the extra conflicts with my parents, coaches, and teachers that would arise from a complete embrace of the genre. Indeed, that older kid's insinuation represented, among other things, an instance of tension in the discourse over musical genre and ideas about personal identity. For my schoolmate, "Fade to Black" stood outside of what he took to be several Truths about metal. The song's quietly arpeggiated chords, moderate tempo, and more reserved singing style could not be reconciled in his mind with what he heard in other Metallica songs such as the frenetic intensity of "Metal Militia" or "Fight Fire with Fire." Perhaps he heard in "Fade to Black" a weakness that had crept into Metallica's music, and the recent emergence of Megadeth neutralized and sealed off that weakness. Perhaps he knew about Dave Mustaine's prior relationship with Metallica (I certainly did not) and believed Mustaine's new band represented what Metallica *should* have been sounding like had it not made the "mistake" of firing him in 1983.

With the concepts of thrash metal that were outlined previously serving as background, this chapter looks at "Fade to Black" (1984) as the primary example of a group of Metallica songs that appropriate musical codes from outside thrash metal to create a sound that also contextualizes and problematizes the discourse of thrash metal itself. In addition to "Fade to Black," "Welcome Home (Sanitarium)" (1986), "One" (1988), and to some extent "The Unforgiven" (1991) together constitute a group of songs that I refer to as the "Fade to Black Paradigm."[2] Downplaying the aggressive tempo and chromaticism characteristic of thrash metal, they inject a dramatically diatonic element into Metallica's music, an element virtually nonexistent in music by other thrash metal bands like Slayer, Anthrax, or Megadeth. Such songs also continue the concept of energy cycles so important to the aesthetic on *Kill 'Em All*, but whereas cycles of rhythmic energy guided songs like "Whiplash," the songs of the Fade to Black Paradigm rely significantly on cycles of guitar timbre to create tension and desire. Effects created through the juxtaposition of distorted and clean guitar timbres shape the presentation of expression. As I will discuss, rhythmic energy cycles still have a place in this approach, but within the Fade to Black Paradigm guitar timbre clearly functions as the most significant element.

Moreover, Metallica's success with the Fade to Black Paradigm has also provided a fairly accessible introduction for audiences who might otherwise avoid the aggressive tendencies of the rest of the band's music. For instance, when Metallica chose the song "One" for its entrance into the mainstream video market in 1988, a Grammy Award nomination for the album *...And Justice for All* in 1989 followed. The success of that video also contributed to the band's winning a Grammy for best heavy metal performance the next year. The release of the video for "The Unforgiven" in 1991 was given significant exposure by MTV in the form of coveted "World Premiere" hype. The Paradigm songs also received the most radio airplay of any Metallica songs by a wide margin and clearly provided a strong crossover appeal for the band during the 1990s. Songs such as "Fade to Black" have therefore provided much of the wider interest in Metallica in the years since 1984, and they have continued to occupy significant places in the band's reception history. From the perspective of thrash metal fans, "Fade to Black" represents an important divergence offered by an otherwise recognizable thrash metal band. Seen from the outside, though, the song offers a way for people to experience identities that might not otherwise appeal to them.

The central content of this chapter is a detailed discussion of the mechanics and meanings of "Fade to Black." In addition to the questions regarding genre and musical identity raised by the song, I use the song to put forth some analytic ideas involving the relationship between the physicality of metal guitar performance and interpretive meaning. Indeed, the fret-based nature of the guitar and the significance of discrete expressive registers offer valuable avenues of inquiry for interpretative work. Finally, at the core of my analysis lies the importance of the lyrical subject in "Fade to Black." The lyrics deal with the topic of suicide, here presented as interior images experienced by one who has decided to commit suicide, and I argue the song actually forces the listener to witness the narrator's suicidal moment. In this way, "Fade to Black" is ultimately a bleak song, a rare statement of powerlessness within a genre seemingly obsessed with assertions of independence, self-definition, and survival. However, in confronting the topic of suicide so directly the song emphasizes thrash metal's willingness to explore and deal with difficult issues in a direct manner. I am ultimately interested, therefore, in how "Fade to Black" creates meanings and negotiates the cultural processes related to musical identity through the codes of musical genre.

Myths of Progress and Stylistic Trilogies

"Fade to Black" appears on Metallica's second album, *Ride the Lightning*, first released by Megaforce in August 1984 and rereleased by Elektra in November of that year. However, the significance of "Fade to Black" is inextricably linked with the aesthetic developments present throughout the entire album. In many ways *Ride the Lightning* moved away from the generic conversations that had informed *Kill 'Em All* a year earlier. Metallica's identification as a thrash metal band remained quite constant, but overall speed played a different role in the new album's aesthetic. Instead, speed gave way to the possibilities of the modular aesthetic, which assumed a more heightened significance. The average song length still hovered around six minutes, with the last song (an instrumental) lasting almost nine minutes. Along with the idea of extended formal structures came the notion of lyrical literacy, as the topics on *Ride the Lightning* largely eschewed the dark fantasy and genre songs of the previous album in favor of real issues and learned subjects: the threat of nuclear war, capital punishment, and so forth. Additionally, Metallica's occasional interest in writing songs inspired by or complementary to various pieces of literature begins at this time.[3] Moreover, many fans (and critics during the 1980s) have ascribed to *Ride the Lightning* another distinction as the beginning of a distinguished trilogy of albums. According to the Trilogy concept, *Ride the Lightning* not only marked Metallica's first serious heavy metal album, but also led to two others, *Master of Puppets* (1986) and *...And Justice for All* (1988), each seen to display an increasing sense of musical sophistication.

In order for *Ride the Lightning* to be seen as serious, though, *Kill 'Em All* is usually repositioned aesthetically as somehow less serious. Accordingly, *Kill 'Em All* suddenly represents naïve amateurism and rowdy fun, and as one writer put it in 1987, "*Kill 'Em All* was the work of an immature outfit whose technical choices and topics (drinking, going to a show) were far more limited than its passion."[4] For later writers, then, *Ride the Lightning* signals the point at which Metallica's music becomes distinctly composed and complex. Wolf Marshall, long one of the central pedagogical theorists and commentators on heavy metal guitar, writes of *Ride the Lightning* in his introduction to the guitar transcription folio of the album:

Displaying a richness of compositional/arrangemental [sic] technique and a well-honed command of the complexities of the music in all its facets, it is a clearly more evolved (and involved) work, signaling an important transitional point between their early style (as heard on 1983's *Kill 'Em All*) and the *shape of things to come* (like the monumental *Master of Puppets*, 1986).[5]

In somewhat elaborate and flowery analytical language, Marshall goes on to list many of the ways in which Metallica seem to have developed musically. He mentions the development of their "manipulation of structural density," and how "they have even seen fit to include a superb instrumental piece, 'The Call of Ktulu,' in this offering." Later on, he remarks "counterpoint and timbral shadings are more thoughtful and plentiful than ever before." Metallica, Marshall continues, have also "refined the technique of overdubbing to a science," as "harmony guitar sections ... grace virtually every track on *Ride the Lightning*."[6] Similarly, in his 1993 biography of Metallica, journalist Chris Crocker characterizes this album as Metallica's "first flush-of-freedom experimentation," leading inevitably onward to *Master of Puppets*, which itself "would have to be a bit more mature ... a *premeditated* act of metal."[7] In addition to the presence of "Fade to Black," I would argue that the reception of *Ride the Lightning* by Marshall, Crocker, and others as more advanced musically than *Kill 'Em All* stems largely from two other elements: the opening prelude of "Fight Fire with Fire" and the length and instrumental nature of "The Call of Ktulu." Though the short sections of harmonized lead guitar in "Ride the Lightning" and "Creeping Death," for example, do illustrate Marshall's observation of the significance of guitar harmonies, the opening of "Fight Fire with Fire" is a far more dramatic development.[8]

Whereas *Kill 'Em All* opens with a noisy flourish of distorted guitars and cymbal rolls, the first sounds of *Ride the Lightning* immediately resonate in terms of studied refinement. Using a clean timbre, Hetfield begins "Fight Fire with Fire" with a short prelude that employs classical-style finger picking and a variety of triadic harmonies. Starting and ending on C major chords, the prelude briefly forays to relatively distant chords such as E major, D major, and B minor. The abrupt arrivals of these chords are not prepared in any traditional sense, but result more from a chord-melody approach that harmonizes notes without regard to usual chord relationships. For instance, after setting up the initial C major key area, the melody outlines an E major chord in the third measure. Following from this, the melody line lands on F#, which is immediately interpreted as the bass of a first-inversion D major chord (Figure 2.1). The first phrase of the prelude ends with this chord before abruptly starting over with the initial

Figure 2.1 Prelude to "Fight Fire with Fire," opening phrase. Harmony notes reduced to emphasize main melody.

two-measure opening. Importantly, Hetfield's decision to interpret F# in terms of D major is not predetermined by the shape of the line, and it is equally conceivable for the F# to have been part of a B major or F# minor chord (or parallels of those). In fact, there is no musical-theoretical basis for D major following E major here, except that each chord is internally and triadically stable. After four instances of the opening two measures, the prelude concludes with a short three-voice overdubbed counterpoint in which the melody lands on a high c while the bass arrives a thirteenth below, on E. This final 6-3 inversion, approached via the upper half step F, is an imperfect cadence, but E nevertheless provides a smoother transition into the distorted Low E that gradually fades in at this point than would a bass note on C.

Marshall describes the prelude as a "mutated Renaissance lute consort," and while that description is certainly evocative, his point is mainly to highlight the striking quality of the prelude within the context of existing thrash metal conventions. Indeed, with this prelude Metallica set an important precedent for the opening of thrash metal albums throughout the 1980s. Not only does a triadic prelude also open *Master of Puppets*, but Dave Mustaine included a classical-sounding piano/electric guitar piece called "Last Rites" on Megadeth's first album (1985).[9] In addition, a more ambitiously orchestrated prelude, including synthesized horns, winds, and percussion, called "Into the Lungs of Hell" opens Megadeth's third album. In some respects the prelude phenomenon mirrors the importance of studied soloistic virtuosity among metal lead guitarists during the same period, but the preludes, aside from their lack of virtuosity, function primarily as contrast.[10] Their importance is textural more than it is linear, with the elements of orchestration and counterpoint standing out against the aggressive thrash metal that typically follows. Still, as I discussed in the previous chapter, the desire on the part of thrash musicians to be seen in some way as "real" musicians was a defensive mechanism against the overriding image of metal as simply noise made by degenerate burnouts, and in this the preludes do serve a similar purpose as soloistic virtuosity. As such, the presence of clean timbres and tertian harmony operate as a way of asserting a more intellectual musical image without appearing unnecessarily pretentious.[11]

The construction of the Trilogy concept and its foundational place in Metallica's artistic career subjects the band to the powerful myth of "progress." Invoking the Trilogy in stylistic histories of the band means invoking the powerful musicological tradition of stylistic periods, and it indicates the continued larger cultural importance of the ideologies of compositional evolution. Furthermore, the notion of a three-album grouping operates as an outgrowth of the ontological shift that occurred during the 1960s via the distinction between "rock" and "rock 'n 'roll." Specifically, during that time an entire album began assuming the central unit of artistic value in rock music, replacing individual singles. At the same time, one can argue that during the years of the Trilogy, Metallica helped to create and perpetuate that organization because the three albums do demonstrate a striking coherence, particularly with respect to organization: eight or nine songs per album, brutally fast opening song, title track second, slow song fourth, long instrumental song toward the end, etc.

As such, the attractiveness of the Trilogy, and the understanding of *Ride the Lightning* as progress from the "immaturity" of *Kill 'Em All*, resided partly in how the music on *Ride the Lightning was* different: complexity *was* foregrounded, the lyrics *were* broader in their scope. The changes in *Ride the Lightning* form obvious developments in the conversation over what is thrash metal, but the notion of the Trilogy depends on style, rather than genre, for its rhetorical force. The band's own resistance to the thrash metal label was also based on their implicit view of style as the better descriptive system. Indeed, Ulrich's comments about Metallica's difference within thrash metal (discussed in the previous chapter) frame the band's songs from the standpoint of style. Obviously, style and genre both deal with the meaning of expressive language, but Hetfield's quote at the beginning of this chapter also reflects a concern with acknowledging the different styles found in Metallica's songs. Similar to Ulrich, it is based on highlighting style over traditional conceptions of genre. In other words, to talk about a thrash metal genre can indeed be helpful at times, but it is not the most informative way of explaining the presence and influence of certain songs.

Along the same lines as Charles Rosen's well-known discussion of a classical "style" (with respect to Haydn, Mozart, and Beethoven), music theorist Allan Moore goes so far as to dispense with genre as an analytic concept and instead relies on style as an organizing principle. In Moore's taxonomy, thrash metal or punk are not genres at all, but styles (substyles, perhaps) of rock. "Protest songs," "power ballads," or "up-tempo dance numbers" represent genres of popular music for Moore in much the same way symphonies, piano sonatas, and string quartets are frequently referred to as primary genres of classical music. The distinction between genre and style therefore allows those writers to account for the impact of individual songs on the understanding of the artist's oeuvre as a whole. Style also helps illuminate the significance of seemingly anomalous songs or pieces within an artist's oeuvre on a more intimate level. As will be discussed in more detail below, "Fade to Black" hardly sounds anything like "Whiplash" (or even "Seek and Destroy"), and it would be foolish to talk about "Fade to Black" as a "thrash metal" song. Indeed, Moore's main point is that individual songs contribute to a sense of style far more than artist-oriented genre labels. He writes, "[S]tyles are *formed through* ... individual songs, and the concept of style is properly a grouping together of the common pertinent features of like songs: style is a virtual quality which has no material existence except in the minds of listeners."[12] In his statement above, Hetfield seems to have been thinking the same thing. He first notes that Journey (a band) was considered metal at some point, but he then focuses on two individual Metallica songs in order to reframe the categorization question in terms of style. With individual songs such as "Fade to Black" as the focus, broad genre labels such as metal or thrash metal become less helpful and more difficult to defend, a situation seemingly preferred by Hetfield.

Mikhail Bahktin's concept of the speech genre, on the other hand, offers to make up for the deficiencies Moore finds with genre as a whole.[13] Like style, speech genres are rooted in discrete instances. For example, legal documents are, according to Bahktin's formulation, a speech genre based on a set of linguistic and stylistic conventions (what we usually call "legalese") that characterize those documents in much the same way distortion, sustain, two-handed tapping, sweep picking, and whammy bar dives signal the speech genre of the metal guitar solo. Speech genres constitute, essentially, the linguistic codes that are then interpreted as part of the overall production of meaning. For instance, Eddie Van Halen's guitar solo on Michael Jackson's "Beat It" lends the tough streetwise talk of the lyrics a particular edge drawn from the musical imagery of metal. The hypothetical absence of Van Halen's solo (or the substitution of blues guitarist Stevie Ray Vaughan) would shape the lyrics quite differently. Inserted into a dance-pop texture, the speech genre of the metal guitar solo brings with it the extra musical images of metal's depictions of aggressive independence and transgression. Thus, if we conceive of the stylistic elements of thrash metal, not in terms of genre but as speech genre, we can maintain its

important historical distinction vis-à-vis heavy metal while also account-
ing for the musical language of individual songs.

Listening through the Fade: The Music of Suicide

'Fade to Black' is about someone who gives up on life.

Lars Ulrich, June 1984[14]

Through a series of affective "presents," which over their course complete a
fateful circle, "Fade to Black" carefully constructs an inward-looking psychological journey in which a narrator describes his decision to commit suicide. From the beginning of the lyrics it is clear that this decision has been
made some time in the past, and that there can be no reconsideration:

Life seems will fade away, drifting farther every day
Getting lost within myself, nothing matters, no one else
I have lost the will to live, simply nothing more to give
There is nothing more for me—need the end to set me free.

Later lyrics signal that suicide represents the only option, and a welcome
one at that, from undisclosed troubles. Importantly, nowhere in the lyrics
does the narrator provide the circumstances that have led to such a drastic
decision. No reasons are presented, and we are not given any reasoning to
gain our sympathy. As such, the lyrics seem closer to a suicide note than
a cry for help, and they cast the listener into the role of eavesdropper, not
really addressed by the narrator—there is no sense of any direct type of
"you"—but only allowed to observe.[15] We observe a bleak snapshot of interiority, of abject withdrawal from the world, and of single-minded desire
for release from life's remaining confines via suicide. Even by itself, this
kind of presentation of subjectivity marks a crucial statement for a thrash
metal band. Compared to the discourse of self-celebration and power in
many other thrash metal songs (in fact, in most rock songs), a cynical listener might understand the lyrical sentiment in "Fade to Black" as down-
right wimpy, full of "woe is me" angst and unproductive anguish: suicide
as the act of quitters. Furthermore, in contrast to the aggressive and fantastic imagery more typical of the genre, the imagery in "Fade to Black"
introduces lyrical elements found in other styles of popular music that do
not foreground aggressive energy, but elements that do, on the other hand,
foreground the significance of personal "feelings."

Still, the lyrics maintain some identifiable traits that make them at least
recognizable to a thrash metal audience. The direct exploration of the taboo

topic of suicide itself is perhaps the most telling, as is the larger subject of death. The "I" in the song also does not come across as an explicit self-identification matched to the "I" of singer James Hetfield for two reasons. First, because the mechanisms of empowerment in most metal lyrics work from depersonalized, collective settings, songs about a singer's day-to-day experience appear extremely rarely and even less so in thrash metal.[16] The second reason, more broadly speaking, is that, again, we perceive no specific reasons for the suicide decision. While it is obvious that the lyrics are about suicide, there is nothing concrete for a listener to latch on to, no experience that can link the singer-as-Self to them. Such ambiguity is certainly not unusual in songs about suicide, and that openness makes it easier for any listener to map his or her own troubles onto this song. Even as "Fade to Black" traces a dark path toward eventual suicide, fans have repeatedly found the song to offer a way to work through suicidal depression, and many have credited it with saving their lives.[17]

Along with the multivalency of the lyrics, the music in "Fade to Black" also functions within and against generic norms. In the opening section, played at a moderate pace (116 bpm), Hetfield uses a clean guitar timbre to present a repeated figure that moves within a B minor tonal area. With the exception of the final measure, the primary characteristic of this figure is the steady downbeat of the bass line's alternation between B and A in support of a three-note group (F#-G-F#). The simple and repetitive structure acts like a drone, creating a stable background that has the appearance of timelessness. The ostinato pattern also supports an introductory guitar solo that features the warm tone of the neck-position pickup. Completely diatonic within B minor and limited largely to slower rhythmic values, Kirk Hammett's solo evokes an atmosphere of contemplation and repose. Other songs within the Fade to Black Paradigm, such as "Sanitarium" and "One," also use this kind of introductory texture of clean-timbrelled diatonicism accompanying a restrained and diatonic solo.[18] While the second half of the solo does reach into a higher and brighter register, and includes short flurries of faster notes, it nevertheless remains a part of the overall affect: expressive but restrained. Notably lacking from the texture is a regular drumbeat. Instead, the drums provide single accents at the beginning of each return of the ostinato. Significantly, specific elements of this opening ostinato will return in varied form in the fourth and final section of the song, their return marking the completion of the circle.

Hammett's solo concludes with a simple rising A minor scale, harmonized via F major and E major chords, that modulates the song to A minor, and this modulation marks the entrance into the second large section of the song: the verse/chorus area. A number of characteristics distinguish this section even as the previous atmosphere of restraint largely continues: there is no grand entrance of a powerful drumbeat or distorted power chords, no release of energy or transformation of effect. Rather, the timbre of the rhythm guitar remains clean and devoid of outward intensity during the initial presentation of the Am-CM-GM-Em chord progression that accompanies the verse lyrics. The particular *articulation* of that progression also operates within the atmosphere of understatement so important thus far. Specifically, the individual chords are voiced using simple "open-faced" shapes, and played in an arpeggiated fashion (with guitaristic embellishments).[19] Not only do open-faced chords utilize different physical shapes from power chords, but arpeggiating open-faced chords brings out the third of each chord, something impossible through the power chord shape.[20] The use of these guitar chord shapes and their accompanying triadic sounds are also very unusual musical traits in metal and instead typically characterize acoustic styles of popular music. Furthermore, on the studio version of "Fade to Black" Hetfield plays a traditional steel string acoustic guitar, perhaps *the* archetypal instrument of solo singer/songwriter folk music, and as such the song taps into many of the associations that particular instrumentation conveys about direct expression and connection with an audience. In live performances, however, he uses an electric guitar on a clean setting, but because he configures his primary electric guitar to sound best with a distorted timbre, a clean setting consequently sounds very thin and comparatively empty. This timbral quality is particularly noticeable during concerts because "Fade to Black" is surrounded in the set by energetic thrash metal songs that feature a lot of palm-muted distortion.

Even though the shift to A minor occurs without a dramatic change in affect, the drop from the B minor area does produce a guitaristic change. On the guitar, the key of A minor is easier to play in than B minor, as the availability of open strings in the verse progression adds to the uncomplicated sound of the progression. In "Fade to Black" this change in tonal center also evokes an image of simplicity, and it has the effect of reinforcing the narrator's lyrical images. This is not to say that suicide is in any way "simple," but the musical change reaffirms that the psychological conflicts have largely been resolved already. The sense of calm and resolution demonstrated within those images now stand out against a musical background, which for many thrash metal fans, sounds largely indistinguishable from most other popular music styles. Finally, Hetfield's vocal timbre eschews a rough, distorted growl for the most part in favor of a cleaner sound. In this case, his clean vocal timbre codes as unmediated and distinctly "natural," and we are meant to hear this timbre as Hetfield's "real" voice, so much so that one commentator specifically praised the song for allowing Hetfield "to actually sing for the first time on a Metallica song."[21] In this way, the presence of a clean vocal timbre in "Fade to Black" enhances the notion of simplicity via the introduction of certain musical codes that not only reside outside the typical metal or thrash metal musical style, but also, more broadly, indicate quite different constructions of identity.

In line with the lyrics' mood of interiority and despair, "Fade to Black" has no vocal chorus hook that would otherwise serve to draw its audience into collective experience. Instead, distorted power chords assume the rhetorical duties of verbal and poetic expression, providing a moment of aggressive commentary on the emotions of the verse. These power chords also mark the next turn in the timbral cycle of the song. Harmonically, the chorus chords play off the progression of the verse, but where the verse music emphasized the treble parts of the open-faced chords with small guitaristic embellishments, the chorus deliberately accents the bass notes of each chord. Rhythmic figures play an important role by stressing both a sense of forward motion and a sense of harmonic arrival at every measure. In particular, frequent anticipatory eighth-notes, as well as a recurring upbeat figure, either reinforce a particular harmony or push the music toward the next harmonic downbeat.

Not surprisingly, the A-C-A-E power chord progression cycles through four statements, but the chorus arrives at the E chord, and expresses that chord, in two alternating manners, each with different meanings.[22] It is first played as a fretted power chord at the seventh fret on the A string (after being "launched" by a quarter-note-upbeat of the D chord at the fifth fret)—the highest position on the fretboard yet reached in the song. Coupled with the subtle addition of a *major* third and the not-so-subtle motion of the bass guitar into a parallel range, in this higher register the E chord almost begins to sound transcendent. Indeed, because the rest of the song has occurred within the area encompassed by the first three frets of the guitar, a physical reach up to the seventh fret produces a powerful phenomenological gesture, one that literally enters a whole new expressive realm when combined with the distortion timbre. During the repetitions of the chorus, however, the breakthrough is a short-lived experience, for the music must fall back to A to begin the sequence again. Importantly, the alternate instance of the E chord settles in quite the opposite register: a power chord on Low E, the absolute lowest-sounding pitch on the instrument, and at this half cadence the music pauses on Low E, without any rearticulation, before returning to A.

Thus far "Fade to Black" has presented some notable challenges to how music written by a thrash metal group should sound. Indeed, after four minutes almost nothing in this song appears to indicate any relationship to the generic conventions basic to *Kill 'Em All*. The codes are all wrong, from timbre to tempo. However grim and haunting the narrator's apparent determination may strike some listeners, it was perhaps these two sections of "Fade to Black" that most offended my schoolmate many years ago. The identity of a thrash metal fan in the 1980s depended so heavily on the transgressive nature of the genre that this song, with its "feelings," acoustic guitars, and plaintive diatonicism, seemed to violate how real thrash metal was supposed to operate.

The idea of timbral cycles central to the music of the Fade to Black Paradigm has a prominent role in the third section of the song. Played at a slightly faster tempo (144 bpm), the drums briefly drop out of the texture as the guitars introduce a new riff and make a clean break with what had transpired previously. With this riff the song shifts rhythmically, timbrally, as well as tonally, and develops more fully the higher register achieved briefly in the chorus: distortion takes over entirely, the harmonic anchor of the song drops from A to Low E, and all of the activity now centers on power chords based around the seventh fret on the A string, ranging from the fifth through the tenth fret. While this last point may seem important only from a performance perspective, the sound of these particular power chords—as well as their rhythmic construction in this section—marks a crucial change of affect from the somber demeanor of the song's first two sections. Moreover, as I will discuss, the upbeat-articulating rhythm of the first part of this new section supplants the steady downbeat quality of the previous sections and introduces a similar framework of temporal thickness described previously with respect to the two coda riffs in "Seek and Destroy."

In the physical register from around the seventh to the twelfth fret on the guitar neck, fretted power chords have a distinctly intense sound. Not only do they sound brighter because of characteristics of the sound envelope at higher string tensions, but also in this register the physical shape of the chords usually includes the octave that is sometimes omitted from power chords played in lower registers. Furthermore, this register marks the practical upper boundary of power chords.[23] Of particular significance for the present discussion is the way the music again reaches for these higher chords in the first part of the third section of "Fade to Black." Note in Figure 2.2 the movement throughout the second measure as the upbeat rhythm propels the harmonies from the fifth fret, D, all the way up to the tenth, G, before falling back, on an offbeat, to the ninth fret, F#. Again, given the distinctive timbre of these power chords and the preceding rhetorical context for this motion, these are relatively extreme ranges. Thus,

Figure 2.2 "Fade to Black," third section, first part with lines one and four of bridge lyrics.

at this point in "Fade to Black" the general contrast with the preceding registers and clean timbres amplifies the intensity of these higher-pitched power chords even more, making the affect provided by the distortion sound more insistent.

A new group of lyrics also appears in the first iteration of the third section. The large-scale musical shift to a more intense register and rhythmic setting also raises the emotional intensity of these lyrics. Marked by a higher vocal tessitura, the melody line matches the rhythms and chord roots of the underlying riff, and the combination increases the overall sense of urgency. As illustrated in Figure 2.2, Hetfield sings "No one but me" as "*No one* [rest] but me," a rhythmic presentation that emphasizes the individuality of the narrator's psychological mindset and adds to the sense of determination in the words. The embrace of death in the last line of text is also foregrounded rhythmically as "Death greets me *warm*," and Hetfield even "warms" the word itself with a slight touch of vocal distortion.

The final phrase of the lyrics—"now I will just say goodbye"—trails out across almost two measures and leads directly to the shorter second half of the third formal section.[24] The drums, which thus far in this section have been providing a very restrained and plodding accompaniment accenting every half note, suddenly begin accenting every quarter note at this moment. Much like the final two riffs in "Seek and Destroy," this particular musical strategy always dramatically increases the forward drive and energy of a song, and the change in "Fade to Black" is no exception. Indeed, in "Fade to Black" the change in energy finally arrives almost five minutes into the song and as such is therefore all the more viscerally effective. Four solidly palm-muted Low Es smooth out the pointed upbeat rhythms of the first section's riff and create a preparatory sense of rhythmic stability that propels the music through the same sequence of structural harmonies as in the first part (Figure 2.3). The very introduction of repeated Low Es also

Figure 2.3 "Fade to Black," third section, second part.

functions as an important generic identifier, gesturing toward a musical code recognizable at least as "metal," if not uniquely as "thrash metal."[25] From this point onward "Fade to Black" works primarily within that general language even as it forgoes any further verbal expression (this section and the final large section of the song are purely instrumental), a rhetorical decision indicating that only the characteristics of heavy metal, and not those of other popular music styles, can adequately express the severe emotions of the song's subject matter.

In general, then, the two parts of the third formal section illustrated in Figure 2.2 and Figure 2.3 function very much according to a cycle of energy—within a larger process of timbre—creating and building up potential energy in the first part before releasing it as a driving and seemingly endless kinetic energy in the second half variation. At this point in the song, moreover, the turn of the energy cycle transforms the narrator's feelings of despair into determined self-assertion to the point that words can no longer convey any explanation behind his action. Indeed, I would argue that it is at this very moment that the narrator reaffirms one last time his decision of suicide. From this point forward there will be no turning back—there *cannot* be any turning back because we are now in a wholly different expressive realm, one that has not only transported us too far away from where we started, but, as I will explain, one that is so powerfully self-perpetuating in terms of *its own* energy cycle that only the actual act of suicide remains.

The fourth and final large section of "Fade to Black" concludes the narrator's psychological journey. However, the move from the third section into the fourth provides an interesting realization of the form-as-process characteristic of the modular aesthetic: the fourth section feels like a continuation of the previous section because it enters after only two iterations of the second part of the third section (the module illustrated in Figure 2.3). How that occurs, and what it means, is worth a more detailed look because of the fourth section's crucial importance to the overall unfolding of the narrative. The affective relationship between the end of the third section and the beginning of the fourth—the process guiding the move between large structural sections—is essentially rhythmic, with the specific changes that occur in Figure 2.3 setting up the rhythmic qualities of the fourth section. While the harmonic contents of both parts of the third section are certainly related, the overall rhythmic character of the second part and the fourth section share the same general sense of stability. As I noted above, the repeated Low Es in the variation create a driving kinetic energy, smoothing out the pointed upbeats of the first part, and consequently positioning that part as relatively unstable in our rhythmic memory. Yet, the variation's softening of the upbeat rhythms also enables a smoother change into the rhythmic character of the fourth section. The dual structural identity of Figure 2.3 therefore transforms it into something of a "bridge within a bridge" between the third and fourth sections as large units, linking the narrator's final texted moments to what will become his final earthly moments.

Even as the new music retains a distorted timbre, wordless character, and quarter-note drumbeat, the fourth section moves away from power chord harmonies and into single-note figuration in the guitars, and in so doing represents a divergent path within the same affective realm. Perhaps most significant, the fourth section returns us directly to the song's initial B minor harmonic region (with important variations), at once closing a large harmonic circle while still indicating an apparently endless continuation of the emotional state bounded by that circle. Initially, the underlying motion in the guitar figure B-F#-G || A-F#-G || B-F#-G had formed the main musical material of an ostinato, its consistent eighth-notes constituting a base for a contemplative and restrained guitar solo. Here, though, the fourth section draws out individual pitches of that motion and expands them from eighth-notes into dotted quarter-notes (Figure 2.4). The triple feel of the guitars creates a hemiola and seems to float, somewhat independently, above the drums' resolute duple pattern rather than clashing with it. This section of the song makes another important change: instead of merely alternating between two harmonic roots, B and A, the fourth section extends the harmonic pattern downward to G before returning through A to the begin-

Figure 2.4 "Fade to Black." Closing rhythm guitar figure, highlighting structural bass notes and internal rhythmic expansion.

Figure 2.5 Reduction of closing rhythm guitar figure representing a stretched-out circle.

ning of the cycle. Represented visually, the undulating sine wave of bass notes represents a circle that has been stretched out (Figure 2.5), a recognizable musical depiction of fate since the fifteenth century.[26]

Combined with the floating effect created by the dotted quarter-note rhythm, the harmonic motion in this section creates a series of tensions and releases that removes us from the larger teleology of the song. As such, the internal order demonstrated in the perpetual repetition of this riff, and its effect on the understanding of this section in the song, acts phenomenologically according to what could be understood as "virtual time." As theorized by John Blacking, music is especially good at playing with our perception of time, and often creates a clean break with what we experience as "everyday time."[27] Our experience of virtual time is also a completely interior psychological experience, and in this case meshes nicely with the sense of interiority found in the repetitions of the final section of "Fade to Black."

Susan Fast also provides a thorough discussion of various ways of theorizing the relationship between musical experience and the body as it applies to the music of Led Zeppelin, paying explicit attention to experience of guitar riffs. In her discussion of certain riffs by Led Zeppelin, Fast explores Mark Johnson's concept of the "cycle schema," one of several image schema Johnson posits for understanding the body in culture, as offering a framework for explaining the effect of repetition *within* riffs as well as repetitions *of* riffs. Significantly, Johnson proposes the sine wave as the graphic representation of the cycle schemata, an image that is best able to account for the overlapping of the many cycles we constantly experience in our lives.[28] After three turns of the final B minor circle in "Fade to Black," rolling double-kick sixteenth-notes begin in the drums, introducing a new source of momentum, but one that, in the end, only powers the perpetual present of the cycle's motion. Throughout the conclusion of the song, then, the effect created by this cycle will continue obstinately the mainly downward motion further symbolizing a bleak and relentless oppression—a twentieth-century *fortuna desperata*—that only suicide can transcend.

Against this background of fateful certainty, a final guitar solo tentatively begins. Hammett begins his solo not at a strong metric point, but at one of the most unstable hypermetric positions possible: halfway through the second measure of the second iteration of the final ostinato (indeed, at G, the very bottom of the harmonic circle). The metric imbalance of this entry point only reinforces the timeless quality of the cycle, as the solo seems to arrive from out of nowhere. In addition, most of the musical material of the solo itself seems ungrounded, wandering across the surface of the cycle in a series of relatively unconnected and aimless melodic ideas and guitaristic techniques: long descending sequences of scalar triplets interspersed with flurries of double-stopped bends, all occurring largely within a narrow physical range from the seventh through the tenth fret. Most of the solo avoids any large-scale goals or teleological trajectories typical of metal guitar solos, which in "Fade to Black" would perhaps signal an escape from the cycle's trap. However, when played over the background of the cycle, the solo's figurations only amplify the omnipresence of the cycle's repetition. In a crucial sense, therefore, nothing is really happening here—the chord progression is cycling, the guitar solo wanders through that without really affecting it or being affected by it, and we are immersed in an unending present. It is a powerfully ominous effect, this creation of unending nothingness.

However, after what amounts to five turns of the pattern and thirty-plus measures of disoriented soloing, a dramatic rhetorical change suddenly occurs. Abruptly energized by snare drum accents on every quarter-note, Hammett actively pushes against the weight of the harmonic repetition and introduces a new surge of potential energy. In a torrent of sixteenth-notes located in a register an octave higher than before and strictly organized into four two-measure patterns, the solo climbs resolutely and concertedly (see Figure 2.6). Paradoxically, the same elements that have been providing the perpetual kinetic energy of the harmonic cycle now seem to contribute to this new momentum, pushing the solo's patterns higher up the guitar fretboard every two bars: 15th position moves to 17th, moves to 19th, moves to 21st. Indeed, the entire texture of the song's final moments

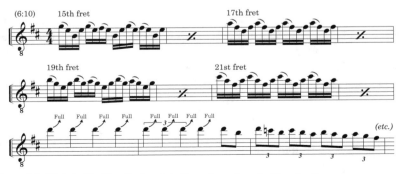

Figure 2.6 "Fade to Black"—Final push by the guitar solo and withered collapse.

seems to push the narrator toward *his* final moment. At last, everything culminates into a brilliant and ecstatic breakthrough on high, high e (e‴), a release followed by *eight* rearticulations in an accelerating rhythm that repeatedly pierces into another experiential realm and seems to push ever higher to announce the arrival of transcendence (this would seem to be *the* moment). The "goal" thus achieved, the solo falls, withered, in a tumbling collapse through two octaves of descending triplets, reclaimed once more into the affective folds of the timeless and ever-present circles of the B minor harmonic cycle.

This interpretation is not typical in discussions of "Fade to Black." Most other reactions to the song, such as those noted above by fans, point ultimately to its deterrent effect and testify to how it actually has the power to keep kids from killing themselves. Ulrich's comment (given at the top of my discussion of "Fade to Black") notwithstanding, the members of Metallica also broadly cite those testimonials as defense against those who would accuse them of urging kids to commit suicide. Sociologist Donna Gaines, in her book *Teenage Wasteland*, provides a similar explanation of the song and the question of suicide. She writes that "Fade to Black" is "a beautiful song, so morbid, insidious. The hour-of-darkness lamentations of a dying human soul. Alone, defeated, depleted, hopeless and stranded but for one last exit."[29] Nevertheless, Gaines finds a redemptive quality in the song, specifically in the final guitar solo:

> [W]hen I play the song, in the last minute, after almost six minutes of morphine agony, the rescue guitars come in. This song goes to the bottom, but *comes back up*. It gives you the will to power, to triumph; it's cathartic, it's killer.[30]

Gaines's image of "rescue guitars" no doubt refers to the solo's final push, but she views that moment in quite the opposite manner from the interpretation presented here. It is possible to hear the end of the solo as the "will to power" she postulates: the resolute and regimented upward motion breaks out of the previously moribund soloistic atmosphere, and the content of the final push relies on a specific musical grammar recognizably associated with assertions of empowerment in metal.[31] The rapid arpeggios and the very high register signal perhaps the quintessence of the metal guitar solo's expression of individual determination and escape from obstacles of oppressive society. Hammett's precise and flawless performance only adds to the possibility of hearing the end of the solo as some sort of triumph. However, the solo does not actually end with the high Es, and I suspect one reason for Gaines hearing it as an ultimately triumphant expression is that she stopped actively listening once that moment had been played.

This response is not necessarily surprising or unusual though. The studio version of "Fade to Black" literally ends with a fade-out, and in certain listening circumstances in popular music the beginning of the fade-out signals "the end" of the song, and thus the end of our direct attention. The gradual lowering of the volume causes the music to recede from our focused perception, and we usually use the fade-out for brief reflection on the experience of the song as well as anticipating the start of another song. The fade in "Fade to Black" begins shortly after the long collapse that follows the high Es, and the content of the remaining solo music immediately resumes the mid-range pentatonic wandering of earlier. Simply put, the climax of the high Es is so powerful that what follows cannot hold our attention in quite the same way. The solo's climax effectively makes Gaines's point about its "rescuing" qualities, such that everything following it essentially represented *denouement*, hardly worth paying attention to.

Fade-outs are often overlooked as sites for possible musical meaning in popular song, but in the instance of "Fade to Black" I would argue that we need to listen *through* the fade, for that is where much of the evidence behind my claim for the solo as a depiction of suicide resides. As but one solution to the ending of a song, fade-outs are actively chosen by artists. As an active aesthetic choice they therefore need to be considered with the same degree of attention as any other aspect of the rhetorical mechanics of a song. Specifically, the change of volume level that occurs in a fade-out often creates a sense of timeless continuation or functions as a metaphor for spatial or temporal distance, ultimately representing a kind of indeterminacy. Thus, only by listening through the fade of "Fade to Black" and considering its role in the unfolding of the song do we get a more complete picture: the stable B minor progression spins out apparently forever at the end of the song, unchanged in the wake of the solo's moment of transcendence. The final guitar solo fails to affect the bass, drums, and rhythm guitar even as it reaches a higher register and rhythmic velocity. Through its repeating cycle, the progression is omnipresent, and the recording's fade-out serves as a powerful reinforcement of that quality. It is as if the underlying progression had not even noticed the intense expression of the solo and simply absorbs it back into the cyclic schema.

In some ways Gaines needs to save "Fade to Black," to read it as ultimately positive and regenerative, because her overall project in *Teenage Wasteland* is social justice. Her work tells the stories of and gives voice to a segment of society much maligned and discarded as "losers" or "burnouts." Most media images of her research participants throughout the 1980s were decidedly one-way and decidedly negative, and she rightly challenges the misconceptions and stereotypes that informed those images. Gaines is also right to celebrate the fact that one of the reasons for thrash metal's success lies in its willingness to explore topics that other popular music styles rarely touch and to engage those topics with a degree of bluntness found almost nowhere else. Walser, writing more generally about heavy metal, agrees: "[E]ven when it models musical despair, heavy metal confronts issues that cannot simply be dismissed or repressed."[32] But, Gaines's claim that the rhetorical strategies in "Fade to Black" at once signal rescue from suicidal despair and are thus cathartic, is, in my opinion, misguided. "Fade to Black" can be cathartic and powerful precisely because *there is no rescue*, because it models a vision of suicide so completely, because it goes all the way.

The Fade to Black Paradigm

Within the larger progress myth of the Trilogy, "Fade to Black" marks the most significant development of this stage of Metallica's generic negotiations within the Fade to Black Paradigm. The song's slow tempo, quiet arpeggios, and "open-chord" diatonicism deliberately pushed against the aesthetic identities that had driven Metallica on *Kill 'Em All*. The decidedly introspective tone of the lyrics, characterized by a distinct sense of despair and inner turmoil, also bespoke an important divergence from previous lyrical strategies. Yet the song's combination of more acoustic-timbred verses with powerful distortion-laden commentary standing in for vocal choruses (as well as a soaring, transcendent guitar solo) still works along the broad outlines relating to cycles of energy.

"Sanitarium" and "One" largely duplicate the characteristics of "Fade to Black." As was mentioned earlier, the three Trilogy albums rely on a very similar song layout, and the stylistic success of "Fade to Black" directly influenced the composition and inclusion of those songs on the latter two albums. Both songs utilize clean-timbred opening chord figures that are complemented by restrained lyrical diatonic solos in their introductions. As in "Fade to Black," distortion appears during the choruses to intensify the verbal images (Hetfield employs vocal distortion in these sections as well). Indeed, in 1991 Hetfield described "Sanitarium" as addressing the band's conscious desire to replicate the aesthetic feel of "Fade to Black" but with an explicitly sung chorus.[33] And, like "Fade to Black," the final sections of "Sanitarium" and "One" make decisive textural breaks from previous sections through musical gestures such as repeated Low Es and rolling double-kick passages. However, the breaks in these two songs are much more distinct than in "Fade to Black." Rather than returning to some version of earlier material, as in the final section of "Fade to Black," both "Sanitarium" and "One" introduce completely new musical atmospheres following their second choruses. Hetfield's cry, "Just leave me alone!" at the opening of this section in "Sanitarium" may indeed mirror the same kind of cry leading into the final section of "Fade to Black," but the ensuing music of "Sanitarium" is faster and far more aggressive.[34]

Likewise, Ulrich's drumbeat that begins the new section in "One" features a flurry of triplet-sixteenth-notes in the kick drums on beats one and three that is soon taken up by the bass and guitars on palm-muted Low E. The lyrics of this section, which present the narrator's desperate isolation and claustrophobia due to the loss of all sensory abilities, exist only within those beats. The snare hits on beats two and four function here as rigid barriers to the narrator's expressions of inner anguish, providing a layer of musical claustrophobia and hemming his thoughts into the space of a single metric pulse.[35] "One" expands even further, turning this section into a *tour de force* example of thrash metal by developing the triplet-sixteenth rhythm on different pitches, adding a series of harmonized guitar sections, and featuring a highly technical and virtuosic solo by Hammett.

The similarities between the "Fade to Black" songs and the sound of the eighties pop-metal power ballad provide one potential explanation for the relative appeal of the former group of songs, though on the surface the two groups may seem irreconcilably different. Still, like the Fade to Black Paradigm, power ballads such as Skid Row's "I Remember You" (1988), "Alone Again" by Dokken (1985), or Poison's "Every Rose Has Its Thorn" (1988), deploy a cycle of guitar timbre to mark off and emphasize the chorus or to signal a particularly expressive moment elsewhere in the song. The power ballad also offers a very different form of masculinity from that found in most other metal songs, albeit one that exists almost exclusively within the power ballad aesthetic.[36] The lyrical topic of most power ballads—the ups and downs of romantic love—finds no place in Metallica's Fade to Black Paradigm, even as the presence of a less-aggressive male interiority nonetheless goes some way toward linking the two. Commercially, the pop-metal power ballad played a crucial role in the success of bands like Skid Row and Poison in the 1980s by appearing to set aside for a moment the bravado and hedonism of the rest of those bands' music. The Fade to Black Paradigm also shifts focus to a very different set of lyrical concerns than were otherwise typical for the band. Structurally, the power ballad's proclivity for constantly repeating its main chorus hook as the concluding musical gesture is a not a structure duplicated by the Fade to Black Paradigm. Rather, the Paradigm songs essentially resist being turned into power ballads by the conscious use of new material in their final sections, material that often reasserts some notion of "thrash metal."[37]

In general, the presentation of interiority stands as the primary aesthetic characteristic in songs of the Fade to Black Paradigm. The willingness to explore emotional states far removed from transgressive occultism, violence, or celebrations of generic identity has been a contentious aspect of these songs' reception—it has been both praised as right-thinking artistic development as well as used as evidence of softness, weakness, and of having "sold out" (as I will discuss at length in later chapters). The prominent choice of acoustic-timbred diatonic chord progressions, as well as a relationship between acoustic and distorted guitar timbres, intensifies that interiority. On a deeper level, however, these songs' incorporation of musical and affective traits from other styles of popular music recontextualizes those traits (for example, open-faced chords and clear diatonicism) in order to express emotions that the aggressive sounds of thrash metal cannot. However, because musical elements do not exist in a social vacuum, but are crucially dependent on the constant construction of personal identities for much of their meaning, the process of appropriation is inextricably linked to notions of identity.

Along those lines, I want to close this chapter and point the way toward the next with a brief look at a final example. Perhaps the best-known song related to the Fade to Black Paradigm is "Nothing Else Matters," from Metallica's most commercially successful album *Metallica* (1991). Though it operates within the larger proscriptions of the Paradigm, "Nothing Else Matters" departs significantly from the earlier songs by presenting the lyrics in ways we are to understand as coming directly from the singer. Lyrics such as "Never opened myself this way" are perhaps the most obvious sign that a different kind of subjectivity is present here, one in which the "I" is meant to be identified quite closely with the "real" James Hetfield. Indeed, most interpretations of the lyrics have focused on a subtext of romantic love, but the lyrics present that notion in a rhetorical style that purposefully obscures such dramatic content. Written away from the Metallica collective but recorded on *Metallica* at the urging of the rest of the band, "Nothing Else Matters" is quietly reflective, its finger-picked E minor harmonic progression simple and straightforward. Unlike "Fade to Black" or "One," there is no distortion-filled commentary in dialogue with the verses. Instead, clean-toned electric guitars dominate throughout, and though there are more active ensemble choruses, the clean timbre maintains a kind of focus on the overall sentiment of the song. Only toward the very end of the song does the music break out of this introspective space. But the release is wordless. Following an emphatic "yeah! yeah!" Hetfield contributes a brief distortion-filled guitar solo featuring bluesy double-stop bends designed to be heard as distinctly "expressive" over the slow chord changes underneath it.

Ultimately, Hetfield resists explaining "Nothing Else Matters" as a love song, preferring instead to offer it as an expression of closeness between people. There are important reasons for his reticence: embracing the idea of a love song involves the embrace of a significantly different kind of masculinity, and even a different kind of white masculinity. Although Metallica included the song on *Metallica*, and played it regularly on the lengthy tours supporting that album (and regularly since then), "Nothing Else Matters" continually threatened the version of faceless masculinity centered on depersonalized lyrics and structural complexity that the band had constructed around itself to that point. Still, it is the quieter songs of the Fade to Black Paradigm (when they were not being derided as wimpy by my school friends) that also contributed to Metallica's desire not to be seen as just another thrash metal band but to be thought of as a distinctly "intelligent" metal band. How that image of intelligence was shaped and what it meant in the context of 1980s American society is the topic of the next chapter.

CHAPTER 3

Thinking-Man's Metal

*Whiteness, Detachment, and the
Performance of Musical Complexity*

> People always categorize us as this new conscientious band or
> whatever, but fuck that shit! I hate whiners and I certainly don't
> want to be labeled as one of them ... I don't want to be labeled as
> hippies of the '90s, political activists—I don't like that shit.

> **James Hetfield, 1990**[1]

Introduction

As rap music moved into white America at the end of the 1980s and concerns
were raised about how albums such as Public Enemy's *It Takes a Nation of
Millions to Hold Us Back* and N.W.A.'s *Straight Outta Compton* threatened
the calm existence of my suburban San Diego adolescence, Metallica's
political concerns remained well below controversial limits. Indeed, in a
conservative military city like San Diego (home of the U.S. Navy's Seventh
Fleet and, at the time, the Top Gun fighter school) firebrand exhortations
of any sort would have been read as Left-wing "whining" and definitely
would have clashed with local values. Although Metallica's invectives on

aspects of American society could certainly be pointed and aggressive, the band pursued a rhetorical strategy throughout the 1980s that largely avoided didacticism and direct confrontation in the staging of important social questions. And while the lyrical views of chief songwriter James Hetfield often espoused a philosophy that critiqued the injustices of late capitalism and challenged social institutions such as organized religion by emphasizing freedom of choice, self-reliance, and personal independence, he and the other members of the group always vigorously downplayed any direct political consequences of those views. Instead, between 1984 and 1990 Metallica continually employed a strategy of critical detachment in the presentation of a range of issues dealing with personal control. During those years, the band's frequent assertions that their pointed critiques merely represented "things we're interested in" stood as a clear alternative to other styles of popular music.

The broader subject of this chapter involves a discussion of the implicit political aspects inherent in both the critical reception of Metallica's music in the late 1980s and the consequences for musical identity in the aesthetic of detachment. Importantly I do not mean to suggest by the word "detachment" that Metallica presented an image of ponderous withdrawal from society or one of nineteenth-century Romantic interiority; rather, their engagement with serious social issues remained constant. Lacking from such engagements, however, was the kind of topical and direct populist/ activist praxis seemingly central to the ideology of rock and fundamental to the political invectives of the most socially conscious rap of the 1980s. Instead, Metallica displayed an almost pathological aversion toward any representation that might position them according to any variety of politics. I want to highlight this image of nonpopulism as something very unusual in rock music (though it illustrates the general contradictory nature of communal individuality in popular culture[2]) and yet highly successful in Metallica's case. Indeed, the avoidance of politically charged activism worked both with and against the general rise in political activities that characterized the 1980s pop music world. Even as they reflected a certain naiveté and at times a contradictory outcome, the decade's mega-events, such as "We Are the World," Live Aid, the Sun City recording, and the many Farm Aid concerts refocused the explicit political possibilities of popular music.[3] Thrash metal bands also developed a more politically confrontational tone in song lyrics, but that tone was rarely transformed into any act of political action, and never with the cultural visibility of a mega-event. However, as will be discussed, rock critics tended to celebrate the denials of a spectacular image and the quasi-Libertarian sentiments of thrash metal lyrics (specifically those of Metallica) as an antidote to what they viewed as an otherwise embarrassing heavy metal scene during the 1980s.

The relative cultural value of musical complexity occupies a central position in this reception, but specific understandings of how race and gender can be represented through complexity greatly informed critics' views. For those metal musicians seeking (however implicitly) cultural validation in the 1980s, the performance of musically complex and virtuosic music seemed to further that goal. Robert Walser's work on the uses some metal guitarists found for rhetorical devices borrowed from eighteenth-century classical music rightly points out how those guitarists translated not only the musical techniques and sounds used in that music but also the "historical" quality of certain Baroque musics into twentieth-century indicators of mystery and power. Walser argues that musical characteristics associated with composers such as J.S. Bach largely overshadowed any real desire on their part to "refer to a prestigious discourse and thus to bask in reflected glory."[4] Nevertheless, it is also clear that metal fans have understood the achievements of Eddie Van Halen, Randy Rhoads, Yngwie Malmsteen, and others as enabled by the social prestige of music theory, a concept, which is itself only a small step from a type of complexity. Those musicians' intent may not always have been to position themselves as classically trained musicians, but for better or for worse they could (and did) find that knowledge useful in terms of validation as musicians in ways that other guitarists, who avoided focus on technical training, could not (and did not). Moreover, by continually occupying an important position in contemporary cultural power hierarchies, the specific kind of music theory learned by metal musicians (basic tertian harmony, scales and modes, notational literacy) still serves as an indication of intelligence and "complexity," even if it is not linked explicitly to classical music genres. As has been discussed in previous chapters, the specter of music theory certainly served as a sign of stylistic difference for the members of Metallica and their fans during the 1980s, one in which complexity played a significant role.

Part of the goal in this chapter, then, is to problematize and examine the ways in which musical complexity acts as a component of musical identity in popular music. My discussions of the songs "Master of Puppets" and "Eye of the Beholder" illustrate an argument for the need to explore the performance of musical complexity as a political act on many levels, since the prominence of complexity and virtuosity in Metallica's music during the 1980s played a key role in the success of the band's aesthetic. Indeed, musical complexity must be understood as more than simply formal complexity. It needs to be approached via the interlocking complexities contributed by broader cultural forces, and to ignore the avenues of inquiry enabled by considerations of such things as race and gender reduces the study of musical complexity to ahistorical formalism, effectively ceding the delineation of what counts as complexity in music (and the language used to analyze it) to formalist music theory. Describing a song as "complex" is not, of course, a bad thing by itself since the discussion of formal complexity can be used as an important relational tool for illuminating meaning in music. However, fundamental to any understanding of complexity are important intersections of race and gender as historically contingent markers of meaning. Placing the reception of Metallica's musical complexity along these lines allows it to be viewed as the historical actions of people. As such, the very concept of "thinking-man's metal" immediately poses important questions about the construction and representation of masculinity that accompany the construction and representation of formally complex heavy metal. Also, as the critical reception discussed below demonstrates, understanding Metallica's music of the 1980s as thinking-man's metal means conceiving of the relationship between lyrical substance and formal complexity as the product of a particular kind of white masculinity.

Importantly, complexity occupies one corner of a triangular set of relationships that also includes detachment and control, and discussing one corner means interacting with the other two. In other words, detachment and control are not separable from complexity, nor do they occupy slots in any sort of linear or hierarchical progression. In what follows, I constantly juggle these three concepts because they are never wholly independent. While detachment and control are by no means the only configurations that could be useful in a study of complexity, I use these particular relationships for the purpose of illuminating the conceptions of masculinity and whiteness that lay behind the band's production of identity through musical complexity. The responses of fans and critics to Metallica's aesthetic during the 1980s consistently demonstrate how what I describe as complexity is always informed by larger cultural forces, and they are interested in how components such as the band's lyrics about personal freedom and control are represented by music that is understood to be equally intelligent.

Finally, two kinds of control are specifically relevant to Metallica during the 1980s: (1) Control by others, typically institutional forces in society or other influential segments of society, directed at individuals; and (2) An individual's ability to resist those types of control for the explicit purpose of maintaining personal independence. The two angles share the recognition of the ever-present struggle over the power to define selfhood. Concerns over control and freedom are by no means limited to heavy metal (or to Metallica's style of metal), though metal's modeling of the relationships between control and power have constituted some of its most distinctive moments, and the details of Metallica's music in the 1980s make it very clear that control is a central theme. Moreover, the band worked very hard to put forth a public image that did not contradict the essential issues characterizing their music, and during the 1980s Metallica successfully avoided anything remotely approaching a scandal typical of out-of-control rock stars: there were no paternity lawsuits, drug overdoses, or wrecked Ferraris for rock journalists or the tabloid press to have a field day with. This is by no means a claim that Metallica served somehow as a model of puritanical abstinence within thrash metal. Indeed in the late 1990s Ulrich publicly discussed having constantly dabbled in cocaine since the mid-1980s, and Hammett admitted to a more serious addiction to the drug until the early 1990s. Neither am I denying what must have been obvious marijuana and/or opium use by the members. Cliff Burton in particular made no effort to hide his recreational use of those substances. Of course the absence of titillating scandal involving Metallica may have been due to the lack of such issues ever coming up in the course of interviews at the time. In the case of Burton, too, his death just before the band's public presence became relatively widespread meant he experienced fewer opportunities for the subject to come up, and thus for the possibility of serious scandal. Nevertheless, Metallica's only public vice seemed to be alcohol, which in American society is generally no vice at all. The nickname "Alcoholica," coined by a journalist in the early 1980s, became a badge of pride, but, more significantly, it also operated very clearly as a familiar and apparently reassuring reminder that not only will boys be boys, but also that personal independence was apparently for real men.[5]

Situating "Master of Puppets"

Metallica's concert tours during 1998 and 1999 had as their centerpiece a performance of the complete eight-minute version of the song "Master of Puppets" from the album of the same name. These tours also featured three other songs from that album that had also not been played consistently in at least ten years, "Battery," "The Thing That Should Not Be," and "Damage, Inc." Those three tunes specifically gave the concerts a nostalgic tinge, a nostalgia for Metallica's much-revered 1980s past. As I discussed in Chapter 2, the albums *Ride the Lightning, Master of Puppets*, and *...And Justice for All* together occupy a significant place in Metallica's reception history, and are often understood by fans and critics in terms of a distinct progression, and as a Trilogy. The reception history of Metallica's 1980s music rarely fails to position these albums into a sequence of ever-increasing maturity or forward thinking. To be sure, the band had frequently included in its 1990s set list three songs from *Ride the Lightning*: "For Whom the Bell Tolls," "Creeping Death," and "Fade to Black," and in some ways the performance of those songs had always constituted a nod to the band's 1980s career. However, the constancy of those songs within the set list also obscured their status as distinct markers of Metallica's past. In other words, their performance throughout the 1990s did not mark them with a sense of "past" because they were constantly carried forward into the present.

Crucially, then, it was the performance of the songs from the *Master of Puppets* album that specifically represented the band's past.[6] Thus, I take the song "Master of Puppets" as my musical starting point and examine how it has achieved such a vaunted status over any other song from the *Master of Puppets* album, and even any other Metallica song from that period in their career. What is it saying to fans? How does it seem to embody, musically and otherwise, such a significant musical representation of Metallica? In short, "Master of Puppets" offers fans competing experiences of personal control: precise ensemble playing across a lengthy and complicated musical structure serve as powerful metaphors for staying *in* control, whereas the lyrics' topic of drug abuse represents but one means of complete submission and the *loss* of control.

Following the formal aesthetic presented throughout *Kill 'Em All* and *Ride the Lightning*, "Master of Puppets" features a well-developed modular compositional style and shares many structural aspects with an example from Chapter 1, "The Four Horsemen."[7] Like that song, "Master of Puppets" is organized according to a basic formal template of two verse-chorus cycles followed by a lengthy interlude before a final verse-chorus cycle. Each of the large sections also contains a number of subsections that, in this case, amount to nine unique modules (see Figure 3.1). Metallica purposefully highlights the element of complexity in this song through the use of multiple sections of music and lengthy arrangements, foregrounding the high degree of ensemble precision, control, and virtuosity required for its performance.

Most of the song is aggressive heavy metal, with pointed chromatic stabs punctuating streams of Low Es. It moves along briskly at 220 bpm, but the complete absence of any sixteenth-note motion during the introduction or in the verse-chorus cycles keeps the music (and therefore most of the song) from sounding frenetic; instead, at this tempo the nearly constant eighth-note motion presents a feeling of driving intensity and complete focus. While the chorus has quite a different feel, the music of the introduction and the verse/prechorus sections do not disengage from the eighth-note motion except for occasional quarter-note accents at the ends

(1) Introduction I
(2) Introduction II–IIa
* * *

(3) Verse Music I–Ia
(4) Prechorus
(5) Chorus
* * *

Introduction IIa
* * *

Verse Music I–Ia
Prechorus
Chorus, followed by Grand Pause
* * *

Interlude:
• (6) Clean-timbre chord progression (diatonic E minor)
• (6a) Clean-timbre chord progression with harmonized guitar figure
• Clean-timbre chord progression with lyrical guitar solo (Hetfield)
• Clean-timbre chord progression with harmonized guitar figure
• (6b) Distorted-timbre version of chord progression
• (7) Power chord riff I (F#-G with C# accents)
• Verse Music I and Ia with virtuosic guitar solo (Hammett)
• (8) Power chord riff II (E-F♮ with B♭ accents [variation of Intro. IIa])
• (9) Scale-based riff (E natural minor)
* * *

Introduction IIa
* * *

Verse Music I–Ia
Prechorus
Chorus
* * *

Verse Music I (music only)

Figure 3.1 Modular structure of "Master of Puppets."

Figure 3.2 "Master of Puppets," Verse I module.

of phrases. Moreover, each repetition of the verse module specifically avoids starting with a quarter-note before resuming the eighth-note motion. In other words, the verse module always begins with a rhythm, ♫♫♫♫ maintaining the intense affect, and never falls back on a slightly more relaxed ♩ ♫♫♫ rhythm. Avoiding the quarter-note beginning requires complete attention and precision on the part of the performer because of the huge sense of arrival following the two emphatic accents at the end of the verse riff and the overall tempo of the music (see Figure 3.2). Hetfield contributes yet another layer to this intensity and focus by playing these streams of eighth-notes using only palm-muted downstrokes rather than alternating between up- and down-strokes.[8] At the tempo of this song, constant downpicking represents a significant challenge requiring the development of wrist strength over time and the achievement of precise control in order to move the wrist only as much and as fast as necessary. Thus, the sheer physicality of this technique grants these sections of "Master of Puppets" a kind of power very different from that found, for example, in the speedy alternate-picked sixteenth-notes of "Whiplash."

The musical atmosphere created by this solid eighth-note texture makes the song's lyrics seem all the more intense. As I mentioned above, the topic is drug addiction, but the lyrics assume the first-person subjectivity of Addiction itself. Addiction is presented here as powerful and in complete control of the addict: during the first verse module it gloats over its power with lines such as "I'm your source of self-destruction," "Chop your breakfast on a mirror," and "Now your life is out of season." The aggressive accents at the end of the 5/8 measure further augment the power of Addiction. Because of its asymmetrical layout, a measure of 5/8 might seem instead to destabilize the general affect by breaking up the streamlined quarter-note pulse of the previous three measures (4+4+4). Concluding the riff with a measure of 2 1/2 quarter-notes should also create something of a rhythmic stumble or brief disorientation as the riff returns to its beginning, as is generally the case in rock music when odd meters are used. Here, however, the 5/8 measure (based on the sliding figuration of the riff's second bar) consists of two accented hits that are placed metrically so as to *predict* the quarter-note pulse of the ensuing measure, thus maintaining some sort of flow from one repetition to the next. Any sense of "stumble" occurs at the beginning of the 5/8 measure by the delayed sense of downbeat. Yet, the stumble is forcefully covered up by the heavy accents on the second and fourth eighth-notes of the measure. The effect of these two powerful hits is that of a quick burst of energy that seems to anticipate the downbeat of the next repetition without creating a disjointed feeling.[9]

A variation of the verse transposes the music a full step higher, from Low E to Low F#, and also ratchets up the intensity of the Addiction's images of control that go along with that section: "Taste me you will see, more is all you need / You're dedicated to, how I'm killing you." The following prechorus module increases the energy level still further by shifting the music up an octave from the Low E of the verses. In this higher register the power chords sound tighter and are marked by quarter-note accents, the first true quarter-note rhythms of the song. A prominent D# accent on the sixth fret also explicitly bounds the seventh-fret E, and at this point the Addiction goads the addict, beckons the addict to "Come crawling faster," and commands it to "Obey your master," before finally arriving at the unambiguous exclamations, "Master! Master!" The two exclamations, one accompanied by a Low E power chord and the other up a half step on Low F, forcefully break the perpetual motion of the music and begin the chorus module.

The rhythms during the chorus contrast greatly with the solid eighth-notes of earlier modules as half notes and whole notes expand the music spatially and provide the lyrics with a distinctly declarative power. Harmonically, the chorus slowly spirals upward from Low E through the octave, with arrival-like steps on G, C, A, D, B, and finally E. With the exception of the Low F during the return of the "Master!" exclamation, the harmonic progression here is quite stable within the minor mode, but the presence of intermittent bars of 2/4 and irregular periods of 4/4 create jarring lyrical interruptions ("Just call my name, 'cause I'll hear you scream") as well as moments of anticipation (as in the six-beat hold before the final statement of "Master! Master!").

The exclamations of "Master!" have become one of the most recognizable moments in all of Metallica's music, and the phrase serves as the focal point and the epitome of the song's topic of control.[10] Within the narrative flow of the song, "Master!" stands as the culmination of all the previous statements of control made by Addiction, but the repetition of "Master" in the first phrase of the song's chorus, "Master of puppets / I'm pulling your strings," allows for the power underlying that control to be appropriated by fans in a way that the previous lyrics do not. Indeed, the exclamation is so powerfully focused that it forcibly shifts the song's subject position from a faceless Addiction to the fans themselves. Tens of thousands of fans shouting "Master!" are not merely singing along with the controlling Addiction, but are experiencing its power for themselves. Importantly, the exclamation and the subjective shift it entails offer the experiences of being powerful and being in control, a quality previously characteristic of the Addiction.[11]

A three-minute interlude follows the second turn of the verse-chorus cycle (beginning at 3:34 on the *Master of Puppets* recording), and as a whole, the interlude provides an abrupt contrast to the driving energy that had characterized the introduction and the two verse-chorus cycles. Moreover, it is the most important section of "Master of Puppets" in terms of the reception of Metallica's music as displaying qualities of musical complexity, and the specific inclusion of this section of the song on the 1998–1999 tours made those performances so significant.[12] The presentation of a completely different aesthetic begins this section of the song (marked as module 6 in Figure 3.1): an arpeggiated chord progression squarely in E minor, played at half the previous tempo, and using a clean guitar timbre. The clean timbre, and its associations with acoustic instruments and generally more pensive expression, combined with solid diatonicism, marks a general sound most familiar from "Fade to Black," and as in that song, "Master of Puppets" features an expressive guitar solo over the chord progression (marked as module 6a). Hetfield's solo in "Master of Puppets" is also positioned between two statements of a descending melodic figure harmonized in sweet thirds.[13] Furthermore, the whole section floats gently, slightly off-balance and quietly dreamlike, over an irregular phrase length (five measures) and a shifting metric landscape: 2/4, 4/4, 4/4, 4/4, 2/4. In particular, Ulrich's drum pattern during the two statements of the harmonized melodic figure uses a half-time feel, and he frequently accents weaker beats within the 4/4 measures rather than strictly emphasizing the harmonic downbeats of the chord progression.

This, then, is a moment of repose, with the specific qualities of diatonicism and instrumental lyricism signaling the representation of some sort of interiority after the outward aggression and intensity up to this point. Yet, even as it draws on the musical techniques of contemplation and thoughtfulness, to cast it fully in the introspective tradition championed by the singer/songwriter aesthetic would be to misread the meaning of this section. Instead, Metallica presents here a very detached subjectivity, one that presents emotionality without seeming to admit to it consciously. No other thrash metal group in the 1980s utilized the kind of clean-timbred diatonicism heard in "Master of Puppets," and for Metallica fans the sense of contrast provided by this sound within the larger context of the energy of "Master of Puppets," while reminiscent of the Fade to Black Paradigm, signals artistic breadth and craft. The quality of contrast, by itself, quickly became part of the rubric of "complexity" on the level of both music and emotion.

A principal component in this particular understanding of the interlude in "Master of Puppets" comes from the presence of similar sections in other Metallica songs from the 1980s such as "Orion" and "To Live Is to Die." The much-revered presence of Cliff Burton, bassist on Metallica's first three albums, also guides this understanding of complexity. In "Orion" (also from *Master of Puppets*) Burton's bass figurations lead the guitars' diatonicism during the song's middle section, eventually building up the music into a three-part contrapuntal texture. "To Live Is to Die," written and recorded after his death for ...*And Justice for All*, includes a short section of spoken lyrics written by him as part of its sprawling 9′45″ length. Burton's death, in a tour bus accident in Sweden in 1986, remains a powerful turning point in the histories of Metallica as told by fans and journalists.[14] Accordingly, he stands as the musical guide for the other members of the group during the first few albums, and many see the kind of complexity in Metallica's music, particularly the sections of lyrical diatonicism under discussion here, as coming from his quasi-mentorship of Hetfield and Ulrich as songwriters. Commentators also revel in the apparent contradiction between his distorted bass tone and virtuosic "lead bass" improvisations, and his understanding of basic tertian music theory and laid-back personality.[15] So important has Burton been in the reception of the group's mid-1980s music that his replacement, Jason Newsted, never really shed the nickname "New Kid," despite playing in Metallica for almost thirteen years (compared with Burton's three years in the band). Above all, Burton's image contributes an important component to the reception of Metallica's music in terms of the relationship between personal independence and freedom, and particular connections to musical complexity.

The significance of these interludes as models of complexity relies on more than just a contrast between distortion and clean timbres, or between heavy and quiet. Rather, Metallica's specific contrast of aggressive heavy metal with lyrical and diatonic music grounds the interpretation of and claim for complexity. Were these types of interludes to use clean timbres to present more chromatic music (even something as "simple" as a chord progression featuring a ♭V or Phrygian second) the understanding of complexity would be quite different. At a basic level, a chromatic or otherwise foreboding clean-timbred interlude would increase the structural density of a song, and therefore could provide some basis for complexity. Still, I would argue that such an interlude would sound less like a contrast than a development of the surrounding affect of the song: foreboding distortion and a foreboding interlude are both foreboding on some level even if the interlude uses a clean guitar timbre. By the fact of their lyrical diatonicism, though, Metallica's interludes explore harmonic and expressive realms perceived as antithetical to the more "visible" image of thrash metal's noisy transgression. Thus, the coexistence of two extremes of musical expression in one song may be read as part of the overall modular aesthetic, but it is the presence of lyrical diatonicism that contributes to Metallica fans' understanding of this music as "complex."

Drugs are bad and we're going after them.

Ronald Reagan, 1982[16]

The cultural context within which the musical complexity of "Master of Puppets" operated provides an important interpretive angle in a discussion about the broader relationships among complexity, control, and detachment for musical identity. The decade of the 1980s marked a significant effort by the United States government to enter directly into the lives of America's young people in ways that differed dramatically from previous decades. At the core of this intervention were two interconnected strategies: the War on Drugs and the Parents' Music Resource Center (PMRC). While the tradition of invoking "children" or "youth" as the source of future stability and prosperity has, of course, a long history in American politics, during the Reagan era (as well as into later decades) such invocations became increasingly hysterical in the way they up-ended the optimistic visions of earlier eras. There was a visceral fear among adults that the generation of children growing up during those years faced dangerous threats to their well being (and posed dangerous threats to society) that children of the 1970s weren't subject to or somehow avoided. Moreover, as Mitchell Morris makes clear with respect to conservative Christian organizations in the early 1980s, a great deal of concern at this time centered on controlling the intersection of popular culture and children.[17] As had occurred in the past, popular music and other media forms came under intense scrutiny from governmental organizations for offering seductive images of rebellion and chaos.

Yet the actions in the 1980s represented a very different effort than had driven earlier instances of scrutinizing. Behind the alarm bells of the 1980s lay a complex web of so-called crises spun by networks of middle-aged adults (government agencies, business leaders, and parents), themselves products of the turbulent 1960s, that implicated 1980s American youth as, when not explicitly "troublesome," then at least "in trouble." Concepts such as teen pregnancy, teen suicide, teen drug use and abuse, and the impact of mass media on adolescents all gained great emphasis during the decade, with each apparently having reached "epidemic" levels. Sociologist Mike Males specifically assails the creation of those crises as a massive act of scapegoating on the part of adults, viewing both the emotional hysteria and the narrow-minded political remedies that have resulted as indicative of a "war on adolescents."[18] Analyzing the frenzied rhetoric of government officials, parents groups, and religious leaders, Males argues that the problems faced by American youth (and there are real problems to be faced) stem more from disastrous and ignorant social policy than fundamental predispositions to violence and chaos on the part of teenagers. Furthermore, the problems of adolescents have been less indicative of their own reckless behavior than evidence of the harmful actions of adults who, crucially, rarely have to take responsibility for those actions. Indeed, the interventionism that began in the 1980s has had a distinctly moralistic tone and was visibly grounded in the question of values, but the hypocrisy with which adults have acted against their children has, according to Males, seriously backfired, revealing more about a Baby Boom generation in the throes of brutal denial about its own problems instead of actually producing healthy adolescents.

The Federal government's War on Drugs, which received prominent recognition by Richard Nixon in the late 1960s and early 1970s as part of his larger "law and order" agenda, represented the most pervasive form of interventionism during the 1980s. First Lady Nancy Reagan's "Just Say No" campaign, begun in 1984, in turn represented the Reagan administration's most well-developed public relations campaign in the War. That front aimed to protect children, but Reagan, William J. Bennett, and others in the antidrug orthodoxy specifically used the slogan as a way to close off discussion on drugs, drugs abuse, and the War itself. As Dan Baum writes, the "Just Say No" ideology "reduced the debate to a single word. Don't talk about why people are using drugs, the slogan said … Don't talk about the difference between drug use and drug abuse. Don't talk at all. Just say no."[19]

While the War on Drugs had always included some kind of childhood-epidemic angle, previous antidrug messages usually formed part of much broader concerns about the disastrous effects of drugs on American society as a whole. Also, drug education programs existed before the Reagan era, but they focused primarily on the pharmacological aspects of drugs (the biochemical effects on the body), and, most importantly, they were not part of any massive Federal prevention program.[20] The key change came in the early 1980s when drug "education" became synonymous with "prevention," and, most importantly, was accompanied by the clear reassertion of parental authority. Indeed, programs such as these specifically used the public school system as the primary beachhead for the new intervention-ism, introducing distinctly formalized drug education classes and curri-cula. I can remember quite clearly the sense of awkwardness exhibited by my eighth-grade teacher as he worked through his teaching manual's "les-son plan" detailing the ever-escalating hierarchy of danger that marked the major narcotics. Though he certainly did not oppose on fundamental ideological grounds the drug education curriculum used in our class, it did seem as though he had just as little experience with the subject matter as most of us did. In particular, I remember my reaction at being told about hard drugs such as cocaine and heroin, drugs whose image resided in an almost mythological state, as somehow "way out there" and light years away from my secondhand knowledge about marijuana. There certainly was not any evidence that any of my peers were being subjected to an epi-demic of hard drug abuse (we would not have been able to afford cocaine or heroin had we even known where to buy it), but the curriculum's rheto-ric that all drugs and all drug use was equally "bad" was not designed to reflect the nuances of any real public health epidemic.

If the War on Drugs represented one element of an interventionist strat-egy during the 1980s, the establishment and operations of the PMRC rep-resented a far broader set of concerns for the welfare of children. Formed in 1985 by a group of wives of Washington political figures, the PMRC focused on perceived threats posed to children by general mass media, and its primary target was popular music. As the project of the PMRC developed, however, it became clear that heavy metal constituted a spe-cific threat worthy of focused attention. While the PMRC had no direct governmental power of its own, the high-level conjugal connections its members enjoyed aided its reach and visibility. In particular, the group worked to expose the genre of heavy metal as a subversive and "hypoder-mic" influence on America's children. The PMRC's ability to convene con-gressional "fact-finding" hearings, run by the Senate's subcommittee on communications, in September 1985 demonstrated its powerful influence. The hearings, though advertised as an open discussion about rock lyrics and images, ultimately reinforced a kind of siege mentality among those in charge of the proceedings: everywhere its members turned, the PMRC saw an epidemic of morally degrading presentations of sexuality, drug use, Satan worship, and violence in heavy metal. In his larger discussion of the PMRC and censorship controversies involving heavy metal in the 1980s, Walser argues that the PMRC succeeded as well as it did by casting its objections to heavy metal specifically as a threat to youth. Moreover, the threat posed by metal ultimately signaled an erosion of parental control, and placing that control at stake enabled the PMRC to "mobilize parental

hysteria while avoiding the adult word censorship."[21] Protecting parental control via the strategy of protecting "the children" had two results:
(1) it contributed to the general climate of fear about children's lives; and
(2) it allowed the PMRC to present the threats to children as oppositional
to the reproduction of certain cultural values, particularly a system of values rhetorically assumed to be normative and "universal" by the (upper-
class and all-white) PMRC.

It is within the context of the intensified drug war and parental authority that the representations of control and complexity found in Metallica's
"Master of Puppets" resonate. While the entire *Master of Puppets* album
received the direct attention of PMRC representatives, and was listed in
the PMRC's 1986 "report card" as noncompliant regarding the voluntary
placement of warning labels for explicit content,[22] I am primarily interested
in how the song addresses the notion of control through commentary on
the topic of drug abuse: "Master of Puppets" appeared in the middle of
the 1980s, right at a time when so much sociopolitical energy was being
focused on didactic messages and actions directed on behalf of American
youth. That some of those youth were also Metallica fans makes this confluence all the more significant. The specific historical context of this situation matters a great deal and affords a preliminary understanding of how
the band viewed the role of their lyrics generally throughout the 1980s. In
this instance, the avoidance of any pedantic statements about drug use or
the refraining from anything in the lyrics that sounded like a direct "don't
do drugs," "drugs are bad," or "Just Say No" message presents the topic in
a much more subtle manner. Most importantly, the lack of a clear pedantic
message in "Master of Puppets" marks the implicit recognition of the distinction between drug use and drug abuse, the very distinction that was
anathema to the "Just Say No" policy.

The conflation of use and abuse in the public's mind, epitomized by the
concept of marijuana as a "gateway drug," had formed a fundamental basis
of drug war strategies since the 1970s, as well as serving as justification for
the intrusive hysteria of groups like the PMRC.[23] However, "Master of Puppets" focuses specifically on drug abuse, a distinction that allows the topic
of drugs in society to be expanded and to represent more complex issues of
control and individual freedom. Metallica's strategy of flexibility-through-
subtlety also prevents the song from becoming a confrontational political
statement solely about the perils of drug use, and this is a crucial choice on
Metallica's part. The song's music, with its driving intensity and exclama-
tory chorus phrase, does not serve to propel the directedness of a specifically
antidrug message. "Master of Puppets" certainly characterizes the Addiction as an incredibly dangerous and powerful force, but the rhetoric of the

song tells us that the most important struggle is actually the underlying personal control over the Addict. Beneath the surface of this whole topic, then, lies the subject of manipulation, and I would argue that the energy of the music allows fans to experience power first and foremost within the context of personal control and independence. At a more fundamental level the "message," therefore, is not "drugs are bad, just say no," but the more flexible and subtle message that "drug abuse is bad because you are being manipulated and will lose all personal control and all personal identity." Yet, because this kind of nuanced message lacked the focused appeal of an explicit antidrug statement, the PMRC did not see that "Master of Puppets" could perhaps have been a useful tool in a pro-child campaign aimed at keeping teenagers from abusing drugs. Blind to the distinction between drug abuse and drug use, and locked in a desperate struggle for parental and moral authority, the PMRC could only view that absence as evidence of the song's avocation or endorsement of drug use.

Seeing through the Selfish Lie? "Leper Messiah" and "Eye of the Beholder"

The theme of manipulation runs throughout many of the lyrics on *Master of Puppets* with powerful influences ranging from religion to the military to mental illness, all characterized as dangerous threats to the freedom of individuals.[24] Most of the explorations of manipulation employ a similar subjective tack as "Master of Puppets," but the song "Leper Messiah" takes a more confrontational approach to the topic of religious control. While the intensity of the lyrics represents something of an attack on religious institutions, underlying that attack are pointed stabs at those who, in Metallica's view, blindly surrender to the control of such institutions. Indeed, the faithful here are labeled in this song as "spineless from the start" who "marvel at his tricks," and the band delivers a sarcastic command to the faithful in the final line of the chorus: "Bow to Leper Messiah."

The main verse-chorus sections of "Leper Messiah" grind along at a medium tempo of 136 bpm, marked by gnarled syncopations and a chorus consisting of a chromatic descent from E to C# in block chords of half-notes. However, Hetfield reserves his most ardent criticism of the faithful during the song's lengthy middle section. The new module is at a quicker tempo (184 bpm) and the prominence of the rhythmic figure ♫♫♪ ♩ makes it sound even faster. Within this intensity the lyrics proclaim: "Witchery, weakening, sees the sheep are gathering / Set the trap, hypnotize, now you follow." The middle section then concludes with a return to the descending chromatic line of the chorus, but inserts energetic gallops on Low E between the individual harmonies (see Figure 3.3). This new

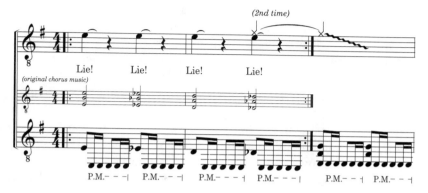

Figure 3.3 "Leper Messiah," chorus variation (5:01).

rhythmic energy fuels eight exclamations of the word "Lie!"—the last of which explodes into a distorted scream that downshifts the motion of the middle section back into the comparably slower verse music.

The aggressive mocking of organized religion and the religious faithful, specifically those belonging to evangelical strains of Christianity, has become a familiar topic in songs by artists from many other genres of popular music and was not infrequent in thrash metal during the 1980s. The transgressive shock of Slayer's "The Antichrist" (1983), wherein lead singer Tom Araya repeatedly screams "I am the antichrist / It's what I was meant to be" and "Jesus Saves" (1986) which belittles the central tenet of born-again Christianity, provide two rhetorical poles for how religion has been addressed by thrash metal groups. The first pole is based on the idea of inversion, specifically the celebration of the images of evil that run throughout Christianity. "The Antichrist" and other quasi-Satanic fantasies combine imagery of the occult with aggressive thrash metal and use the shock value of that combination as one form of commentary. The very public scandals surrounding televangelists Jimmy Swaggart and Jim and Tammy Bakker during the 1980s certainly provided easy ammunition for the sentiments in many of those songs (and in "Leper Messiah"), but thrash metal bands also latched onto the hypocrisy raised by the scandals as a way to talk about control.[25] The second rhetorical pole for addressing religion directly lay in confronting the judgmental approach at the core of much evangelical Christianity in the 1980s: "Jesus Saves" and "Leper Messiah" threw judgment right back. In other words, if Swaggart was going to condemn metalheads to eternal damnation, Slayer and Metallica roared that all Christians were simply brainwashed sheep.

For James Hetfield, the situation was also intensely personal. Raised in a strict Christian Science household until he was 14 when his mother died, his lyrics in "Leper Messiah" are as much about breaking free from that particular background as they are about mocking Swaggart, the Bakkers, and the faithful.[26] Importantly, Hetfield's experience with Christian Science, as it informs the lyrics to "Leper Messiah," makes no distinction between that denomination—which refuses most points of evangelicalism and American Protestantism and is not considered very "Christian" by more mainstream groups—and the rest of non-Catholic Christianity. By collapsing such a range of religious groups, his diatribe against "the faithful" encompasses a much wider segment of society, with the effect that all are viewed as equally detrimental to the individual.

Given the intensity of its attacks against evangelicalism, it is worth noting the structures of religious control thrash metal had very little interest in. Bands like Metallica and Slayer had little if anything to say directly about the powerful control of the Catholic Church, even as singer Sinead O'Conner's spats with Catholicism began to make headlines at the end of the decade. Offering a much less publicized view than evangelical Christianity (at least in America), Catholicism did not rely on the kind of charismatic and media-savvy leaders so central to its Protestant cousins, nor was Catholicism engaged in exactly the same kind of political struggles over morals and values that drove organizations like Jerry Falwell's Moral Majority.[27] Rather, metal bands of many styles generally used the rich historical imagery of Catholicism as raw material for occultist appropriation instead of aggressive derision. Contempt for followers of non-Christian religions such as Judaism and Islam was also rare, at least publicly (and never in the mainstream), and any derision in those cases accompanied explicit racialized fears about the threat from nonwhites and not merely concerns about individual freedom and control. In depicting an image of faithful subservience to and corruption by the hands of religious institutions, Metallica's aggressive tone in "Leper Messiah" therefore presents that image in a more didactic approach to the issue of personal control than appears in "Master of Puppets." As such "Leper Messiah" offers an example of a rhetorical style that confronts topics of social consequence more directly while nevertheless refraining from any call for overt social change. Even as this style can be much more accusatory, it nevertheless couches those accusations in the guise of description. In this way, the scenario illuminated by "Leper Messiah" ultimately stands as the description of a threat to personal control and independent thought that is essentially aligned with the band's other lyrical material.

This rough balance between various strategies of detached social critique falls away most notably on the third album of the 1980s Trilogy, ...*And Justice for All*, released in September 1988. The lyrical topics on this album include the corruption of justice by corporate capitalism, totalitarian blacklisting, and war, but the general tone at first appears to engage the topics on a much more explicit level of confrontation and awareness.[28] For example, the verses to the album's title song warn of "Halls of justice painted green" while the chorus rages "Justice is lost / Justice is raped / Justice is gone." The song "Eye of the Beholder" offers the most overt appraisal of the threat to personal control and independence, but, significantly, it also presents a very concrete set of responses to those threats, responses specifically addressed to the listener:

Do you trust what I trust?
Me, myself, and I
Penetrate the smoke screen, I see through the selfish lie.

The very sound of ...*And Justice for All* also differs from Metallica's previous albums, and does so in ways that have been understood by critics as analogous to the precision and automation of machinery, a reception with important ramifications for the band's strategy of detachment. For example, Simon Reynolds in his review of the album noted, "This isn't thrash, but thresh: mechanized mayhem. There's no blur, no mess, not even at peak velocity, but a rigorous grid of incisions ... Everything depends on utter punctuality and supreme surgical finesse."[29] It is easy to hear why Reynolds' emphasis on a sense of purity delivered by the complexity and precision of this album is so vivid. In particular, the general mix on ...*And Justice for All* provides ample evidence for such an observation: the mix contains almost no discernable bass guitar to provide a full sonic texture. Even during sections of music that feature a clean-timbred guitar sound, Jason Newsted's bass is essentially inaudible, leaving the mix incredibly top-heavy. Moreover, Hetfield used an extremely "scooped" distortion timbre on the recording, an equalization configuration that consists of boosted high and low frequencies and very little mid-range frequencies. While the elevated low frequencies of a scooped sound produce a good distortion timbre, they do so at the expense of the bass guitar within the mix. With the low end boosted in the guitars, the overall sonic spectrum in that range becomes saturated to the point that the simpler harmonic characteristics of the bass guitar simply cannot cut through.[30] What bass there is in the ...*And Justice for All* mix is largely provided by the bass frequencies of the distortion timbre itself, augmented by heavy palm muting. Absent the visceral punch of bass frequencies typically contributed by the bass guitar, only distorted guitars, drums, and vocals can really be heard in the overall mix.

Ulrich's drum set was also recorded in ways that highlight the precision of his parts, and ...*And Justice for All* is the first Metallica album where every piece of percussion is clearly discernable. However, like the rest of the mix, the drums lack a wide frequency range, and noticeably contain very little bottom end and very little ambient decay. The most striking example of this timbral quality can be found in the sound of the kick drums. Obviously recorded in such a way as to spotlight Ulrich's double-kick work, the kick drums have been engineered to the point of sounding mostly like a low-pitched click. Using a gate to cut off the natural decay of the sound, the click-like timbre certainly draws the ear toward that instrument and allows every hit to be heard cleanly.[31] Still, the emphasis on the precision of the sound's attack, without a corresponding decay, results in a very mechanistic timbre, adding to an overall mix that contributes a distinct sonic component to Reynolds' reading of the structural complexity and ensemble virtuosity of the album's music.

Even as it seemed to convey a sense of sterility, the drum sound on ...*And Justice for All* had an important impact on the way heavy-metal drums would be recorded in subsequent years, particularly the attention that would be given to the kick drums. As was the case in the early 1980s for metal guitarists, the increasingly virtuosic abilities of metal drummers in the late 1980s and early 1990s benefited from a focused attention to technology and a careful development of recording techniques. In particular, thrash metal recordings from this time demonstrate that the initial production idea of highlighting the double-kick style so crucial to the genre had been fine-tuned such that the drummer's double-kick work could be heard and emphasized but also produced with a full sound. The music on *Seasons in the Abyss* by Slayer (1990) and *Painkiller* by Judas Priest (1990), for example, focuses less on structural complexity, but both albums achieve an incredibly powerful representation of clarity and precision in the overall sound of the drums. Megadeth's *Rust in Peace* (1990) features ensemble virtuosity and precision every bit as intense as that on ...*And Justice for All*, but does so with a recording that deftly balances the importance of clarity with the power of a very full sonic texture. The sound of Metallica's next album, *Metallica* (1991), while quite different aesthetically from previous albums, even benefited from the attentive approach to precision and clarity developed in those other albums.

Thus, the sonic landscape of ...*And Justice for All*, in all of its mechanized "thresh," casts the specific musical details of the songs and the particular expression of lyrical detachment in a revealing light. The sound of

precision that characterizes the album's production reinforces an important means of hearing the relationship between musical complexity and
personal independence. With these observations in mind, I want to examine the song "Eye of the Beholder" in more detail because it marks the clos-
est Metallica came to an explicit philosophical statement about individual
autonomy and personal control in the 1980s. Unlike the previous songs
discussed to this point, the pronoun "I" used in the "Eye of the Beholder"
lyrics (quoted above) appears to be a distinct portrayal for some form of
the singular "I" of James Hetfield. Whereas the narrating voice, the "I," in
"Master of Puppets" assumed the persona of a fictional Addiction to make
its points about control, "Eye of the Beholder" distinctly lacks that kind of
rhetorical position. The absence of any substantial narrative, metaphorical
character, or easily identifiable external scenario in these lyrics also signals a very different purpose behind the lyrical "I" in this song.[32] Yet, the
trajectory of the lyrics across the verse-chorus cycle nevertheless presents
two competing subjectivities, both named with the pronoun "I." Different
musical affects delineate these two subjectivities, and the word "I" comes
to signify both Hetfield and the adoption by the singer of a persona representing forces of manipulation and control (much like that heard in "Master of Puppets"). Significantly, the outcome of the musical narrative can by
no means be seen as an uncritical celebration of individuality. Rather, "Eye
of the Beholder" ends quite ambiguously: the repeated occurrences of the
manipulative affect, particularly at the final moments of the song, and the
recurring presence of a perilous collapsing riff (discussed below), serve to
warn listeners that the threats posed by such forces remain powerful and
ever-present. Indeed, unlike many other metal songs, which work by offering listeners a sense of empowerment to overcome adversity and a glimpse
of community (a strategy that can have profound real-world implications),
the ambiguity in "Eye of the Beholder" strongly resists our reading it as a
unifying anthem.

Particular combinations of rhythm within a narrow half-step-based
harmonic range distinguish the two affective realms. The Hetfield-ian "I"
appears during the verses of the song while the "I" representing Manipulation occupies a kind of prechorus module. Solidly anchored by a palm-
muted rhythmic ostinato, the verse module contains little harmonic
motion, but the burst of sixteenth notes in the first half of each measure
of this figure creates an intensity not unlike that found in the verse module of "Master of Puppets." However, where that module seemed to "break
out" at the second half of the figure by moving decisively away from Low
E, the palm-muting in the verses of "Eye of the Beholder" builds potential
energy continuously, except for a short, eighth-note accent on beat four (see

Figure 3.4 "Eye of the Beholder," verse module.

Figure 3.4).[33] The harmonic range of this figure spans only a minor third, moving from Low E up to G before sliding down to F#, but the narrowness of this range and, more importantly, the slowness of the harmonic rhythm amplifies further the groundedness of the rhythmic ostinato. Moreover, Hetfield's rough vocal timbre sits in a mid-range tessitura, between B and d, in the middle c octave, and an area among the lowest of any song on …*And Justice for All.* That tessitura enables Hetfield's statements to appear confident and assertive without coming across as shrill. As a whole, the musical elements of the verse module function as a solid projection of stability supporting the pronouncements of the verse lyrics.

As was noted above, the verse lyrics of this song work via a question-and-response format, but one that completely avoids any sense of sloganeering. The responses given in the lyrics do not answer the questions, and are not meant to include the listener in the way a specific call-and-response format would. Instead, each stanza begins with a rhetorical question ("Do you see what I see?" "Do you feel what I feel?" "Do you fear what I fear?") that is then followed by an ideological assertion of the beliefs of the Hetfield-ian "I." Responses such as "Moving back instead of forward seems to me absurd," and "I hunger after independence, strengthen freedom's ring" can certainly be interpreted as slogans, but the context within which they are presented—as indirect answers to the preceding questions—grants them a quality of ambiguity at odds with how slogans are typically organized.

If the music in the verse module conveys the beliefs of the Hetfield-ian "I" in a musically focused and intense fashion, the music for the Manipulation introduces a greatly contrasting and relatively chaotic break from that construction. Rhythm and harmonic range also structure the character of this module, but this time the combination is designed to produce instability. Marked by a meter change to 12/8, the rhythmic action of the guitar part accents alternating eighth notes over the drum's emphasis of the dotted quarter-note pulse. Furthermore, the guitar and vocals begin their accent pattern with the second eighth-note of the measure (see Figure 3.5). Because the basic rhythmic pulse has not changed from the previous module, only the number of subdivisions (that is, $\dotted = \quarter$), the overall effect is all the more jarring. The higher harmonic and vocal register of this module also give the slippery chromatic motion of the Manipulation

Figure 3.5 "Eye of the Beholder," prechorus module.

music a distinctly claustrophobic and paranoid feel, perfectly suited for the module's threatening lyrics:

> Doesn't matter what you see,
> Or into it what you read.
> You can do it your own way,
> If it's done just how I say.

Finally, the chorus of the song echoes much of the general impetus of the verse lyrics, but at the same time it consciously backs away from a decisive culmination of those lyrics. In so doing, the chorus does not urge listeners to actually do anything, whether by action or by thought, regarding the instability presented in the prechorus. Instead, the chorus lyrics directly state a set of social circumstances, stepping back from the ongoing struggle between the verse and prechorus:

> Independence limited,
> Freedom of choice
> Is made for you, my friend.
> Freedom of speech
> Is words that they will bend
> Freedom — with their exception.

Mostly oscillating between two chords, Low F# and G, the harmonic structure of the chorus is primarily responsible for producing this expression of nonaction. While the vocal tessitura moves up to F# (a fifth above its initial range) in an effort to express a sense of urgency about the situation, the guitars nevertheless remain stuck in a half-step seesaw. Indeed, only at the very end of the chorus, on the final statement of the word "Freedom," does the music escape briefly up to A (matched by the vocal line) and provide some sort of complement to the emotion in the lyrics.

For all the emphatic warning expressed by the chorus lyrics (however briefly), the module that follows the chorus, and frames the verse-chorus cycle, continually reintroduces the threat of the perilous collapse of freedom. Built from the pedal of a Low E rhythmic figure, the main motion of the riff is the collapse of a power chord fifth into a tritone, a movement of only one-half step, but which nevertheless holds great significance for the rhetorical structure of the song. The last two measures of this module even extend the collapsing motion across an entire octave via downward-spiraling tritones (see Figure 3.6). On the guitar, the collapse of a power chord fifth into a tritone contains a distinct tactility as the physical space between the root note and the upper note shrinks by one fret. That shrinkage entails a fingering change on the higher note, one that physically closes the gap between the two fingers playing the chord shape. A ubiquitous shape in rock and metal guitar, the power chord fifth typically uses the index finger to hold the root and the third finger to hold the fifth of the chord. For the collapse in "Eye of the Beholder," though, the middle finger is used for the tritone shape, collapsing the space between the fingers. The extended collapse at the end of the riff also has a discrete physical component wherein the left hand moves down the fretboard basically in one-fret increments (fret 8 to 7 to 6 to 2) toward Low E, embellishing each arrival point with a half-step upper-neighbor pull-off. The downward fret-wise motion also entails a move across three strings toward the lowest-sounding string on the guitar, the open Low E string, where the music pauses before returning to the verse music. As such, the notion of collapse (of independence,

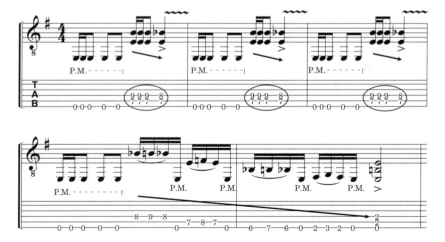

Figure 3.6 "Eye of the Beholder"—collapsing power chord riff.

of freedom) presented throughout "Eye of the Beholder," and represented by the downward spiral of tritones in the framing module is given a clear visceral nudge as Hetfield physically performs that collapse.

The trajectory of the three iterations of the verse-chorus cycle ultimately results in something of a rejection of direct artist-to-audience empowerment. The purposeful character of the verse lyrics, with their unflagging display of individualist ideology, remains a part of the verses only, and does not carry over into the chorus to overcome the opposition posed by the Manipulation's prechorus module. Continually held back by the seesaw harmonic motion, the chorus' attempts at strident warning also fall short. The chorus does not, therefore, adequately provide for the culmination of affect, but remains a detached observer. Lastly, the structural arrangement of "Eye of the Beholder" only deepens this ambiguity by concluding, not with repetitions of the chorus (however noncommittal they may be), but with two complete statements of the chaotic Manipulation module.

We're Only a Rock Band: The Limits of Political Expression

For all the directness in "Eye of the Beholder" and the confrontational tone of ...And Justice for All more generally, Metallica worked very hard to avoid characterizing their lyrics as messages, political or otherwise. The intertwined necessities of detachment and control dictated that they not be presented as such. Indeed, within the context of the commercial success of metal in the 1980s, Metallica's ruminations on control and individual independence attracted many rock critics who pointed to the band's lyrical topics as refreshingly different from what they saw as the trite and macho sexuality of other popular metal bands. Still, in response to such comments, Hetfield was quick to qualify the seriousness and the apparent political edge of their lyrics:

> We're real serious about the words. But we're not trying to push any subject across or do any dictating how people should live. We're just stating an opinion.[34]

Echoing these statements, Lars Ulrich frequently returned to the idea of description and detached observation as the impetus for the band's lyrics. Crucial to his understanding is the belief in the existence of a mode of communication that denies its own existence and is somehow purely objective and "documentary:"

> [W]hen people accuse us of not trying to change the things we sing about I just have to say that I'm not particularly interested in

changing any of it ... I'm just interested in it ... You can just be documentary.[35] ...

... People ask: 'You keep writing about these things, doesn't it make you want to go do something about it?' It's got to be possible to have an interest in writing about the justice system without marching up and down the street in front of the Supreme Court.[36]

The sentiment of such statements, particularly these by Ulrich, highlights a distinctly defensive desperation and illustrates the band's struggle to maintain a clear sense of detached and neutral political interest behind their choice of lyrical topics. That struggle for detachment demonstrates, moreover, another version of the band's concerns about control, because remaining neutral and detached also projects the appearance of control. Here, though, "control" indicates something closer to self-control through self-determination, rather than the version of control discussed previously involving control of an individual by larger social forces. Additionally, detachment in this instance functions as the means by which the members of Metallica avoid calling attention to themselves. "Marching up and down the street," while not exactly out-of-control, is nevertheless a calculated risk. It opens one up to being challenged, to having to argue for one's ideas and to argue against others' ideas, to become part of a vague system of activism and praxis. But most of all, dropping the shield of detachment means relinquishing enough personal control *in order to be read*. The irony of my reading Ulrich's desire not to be read simply punctuates the intensity of Metallica's near-paranoid strategy of detached (that is, "documentary") aesthetics during the 1980s.

Indeed, ...*And Justice for All* and Megadeth's album *Rust in Peace* form a very interesting pair of albums for examining the relationship between structural complexity, virtuosity, and control with thrash metal. Like Metallica's album, *Rust in Peace* relies heavily on multisectional forms with extended instrumental breaks stretched over shifting meters and tempi. Dave Mustaine's riffs are usually much more guitaristically intricate than those heard on ...*And Justice for All*, reflecting his prominence as a lead guitarist in the band, and the long solo sections on *Rust in Peace* trade off between Mustaine's controlled chaos and the technical brilliance of Megadeth's other lead guitarist, Marty Friedman. Furthermore, Mustaine's lyrics cover much of the same general concerns as Hetfield's, but Mustaine is far more sneering and direct in his condemnations of war, environmental degradation, and world politics, and is far less concerned with remaining detached, neutral, or documentary. He also deals candidly with his own personal failings, notably his problems with drug and alcohol addiction. Less precise vocally than Hetfield, Mustaine spits out words in an almost speech-like manner and sings in a high, nasal voice quite different from Hetfield's full-throated aggression. Overshadowed by Metallica's greater commercial and cultural visibility, though, the relationships between complexity, control, and detachment in Megadeth's music are less well documented than for Metallica. However, by the early 1990s, the growth of Mustaine's willingness for political involvement was apparent. In particular, he played minor (but instructive) roles as a spokesperson and commentator for MTV's "Rock the Vote" program, and even walked the floor as a political reporter for MTV at the Democratic Presidential Convention in 1992.

In addition to Megadeth's conscious politics on *Rust in Peace* (as well as on *Peace Sells ... But Who's Buying?* 1986) Metallica's greater awareness of social issues operated as part of a general development of social and/or political awareness within thrash metal. Whereas thrash bands had generally avoided songs about thrash metal and its culture for their second albums in the early 1980s, at the end of the decade they again shifted their lyrical range, this time highlighting social and political topics. Examples by Metallica have already been touched on, but groups such as Testament, Anthrax, and Exodus also began including lyrics on their late 1980s albums easily heard as assertions of political concerns. And, like Megadeth, those assertions went a good way toward linking thrash metal (if not metal broadly conceived) to the tradition of rock music as a vehicle for political expression.

Anthrax's "One World" and Testament's "Greenhouse Effect" are only two of the more obvious examples of thrash metal songs that address contemporary social issues in ways arguably more direct than anything by Metallica. "Greenhouse Effect" (from *Practice What You Preach*, 1989) is a reaction to environmental degradation as a result of the destruction of South American rainforests by wealthy international capitalists. Over a rapid thrash metal beat, the song's prechorus lyrics summarize Testament's warning of impending environmental "holocaust" before emphatically stating the song's call-to-arms sensibility: "It's time to take a stand." Similarly, "One World" (from *Among the Living*, 1987) calls attention to the escalation of tension between the Soviet Union and the United States during the Cold War. Its final verse is the most explicit in this regard, declaring "Russians—they're only people like us / Do you really think they'd blow up the world?" The last part of the verse asserts that Americans should do more to demand then-President Reagan abandon his dream of S.D.I. (a space-based missile defense system) as unproductive toward peace between the two superpowers. In their urging of political action, both songs operate far more clearly as recognizable political expression than Metallica's "And Justice for All" or "Eye of the Beholder."

Accompanying the trend toward political expression were important developments related to musical identity: by the later 1980s the first wave of thrash musicians were in their mid- to late-20s, relatively independent financially, and able to experience American society and other parts of the world (most of them had at least toured Western Europe by this point) as individuals quite different from the ones only a few years previous. The intervening experiences enabled them to develop and incorporate a political voice they had rejected earlier as associated with punk or hardcore and which had resided outside their notion of metal.[37] Why, though, should this new voice, and a willingness to assert a political view, develop at all at this point? Simply noting that it happened does not adequately explore the consequences for musical identity of it happening. What did thrash metal musicians believe they were gaining by including recognizably political lyrics on their albums at this point in their careers? In short, the combination of the "serious" nature of thrash metal music (via the virtuosity and structural complexity) with lyrics on "serious" topics helped shape the image of thrash groups and enable the kind of reception under discussion throughout this chapter. The shift away from songs about thrash metal or the occult and toward topics of social consequence seems to have been recognized by thrash metal musicians as a necessary step in presenting themselves (and metal in general) as culturally significant. Their attention to musical detail, initially functioning as a way to distinguish thrash from punk or hardcore, could now serve to help assert a fuller sense of personal importance and engagement with the world around them. Because of this, any sense of a political awakening by thrash metal musicians should be considered part of larger developments in musical identity. Yet, even with the greater, more direct expression of "Greenhouse Effect" or "One World," thrash metal never became socially active beyond the presence of such songs. This is an important distinction in comparison to the aesthetics of other popular music artists at the time, such as John Mellencamp, U2, REM, or Public Enemy, for whom some sort of conspicuous praxis was an important part of the critique. As such, thrash groups avoided a concerted effort at political visibility through anything resembling Live Aid, Farm Aid, or Sun City that would clearly mark thrash metal as "political" in the wider popular music marketplace.

Indeed, the desire for a detached or documentary approach ultimately remained stronger in metal than in other popular styles. Overwhelming whatever political viewpoints might surface within song lyrics was the importance of maintaining music as the primary purpose of metal. As

Keith Kahn-Harris has discussed, the various "extreme" metal styles to develop during the 1980s and early 1990s, of which thrash metal was one, developed particular strategies to "separate music from politics ... [to] ... render the relations between theory/practice and public/private contingent and disengageable."[38] Kahn-Harris is writing specifically about the issue of racism and black metal in the 1990s, but the idea of disengaging "theory" (understood here as song lyrics about environmental degradation or other social injustices) from "practice" (in other words public action on behalf of theory) provides a useful way of grasping what might seem to be the impotent politics of thrash metal.[39] Indeed, within thrash metal scenes, as with black metal, the essential musicality of the style must always take precedence over anything else. That Metallica and other bands stepped back from embracing political expression as part of a conscious intervention to affect social institutions gave the musicians the impression that they could exert tighter control over their own representation. Ultimately, as will be explored later in this chapter, in doing this thrash metal musicians (and some rock journalists) could appear to carve out a space for the music to be evaluated entirely apart from social structure.

Still, political expression as a concept deserves a little more examination because understanding rock music, and late 1980s thrash metal, as political typically means aligning it with the Left-leaning side of the Western political spectrum. In other words, thrash metal could be considered political only after meeting two criteria: that the lyrics focus on topics of social significance, and that the lyrics' position—implicitly or explicitly—raise awareness or urge action in the service of causes usually ascribed to the Left. Challenging the actions of multinational capital, the power of organized religious institutions, the oppression of the powerless by the powerful, or giving voice to the defense of the natural environment are each examples of critiques levied far more often as part of a Liberal, humanitarian agenda than a conservative one. To be sure, critiques by rock musicians might also be part of an "antiestablishment" view having less to do with neat left/right divisions (the power of mainstream media to shape issues also received criticism in late 1980s thrash). However, the associations of Left-leaning politicians and political groups with rock artists tended to reinforce the perception of a natural connection between the political expression of rock musicians and the political ideologies of the Left. Other than the issues of race, causes typically ascribed to the Right make no appearance in mainstream rock of the 1980s. There were no songs touting the creation of wealth or the rights of business to fuel the engine of progress; other than out-of-the-mainstream white power topics there were no songs celebrating the superiority of one social class over another;

there were no songs urging law-and-order action against communist sympathizers. For reasons too broad to go into here, conservative causes were therefore essentially absent from mainstream rock in the 1980s, and that absence not only allowed Left-wing causes to enjoy greater representation, but also to set the terms by which the notion of political expression could be attached to some rock music.[40]

The cause of personal independence underlies many of the above issues and functions as a concern for both Left and Right, but the reaction to songs ultimately dealing with personal freedom depends on the context through which that freedom is celebrated. Thrash metal's engagement with the topic of war is notable in this regard. Lyrics such as those in Slayer's "Mandatory Suicide" or Metallica's "Disposable Heroes," which rail against the plight of ordinary soldiers ordered "back to the front" in the service of more powerful and influential members of society, present war as against the cause of personal freedom. However, even though Metallica based the song "One" on Dalton Trumbo's antiwar novel *Johnny Got His Gun* (1939), both the song and accompanying video ultimately resist making a clear-cut judgment for or against war.[41] As in "Disposable Heroes," Metallica focuses intently on an individual experience of war in "One," but without the thinly veiled condemnation of large-scale manipulation detectable in "Disposable Heroes." In general, only because the lyrical content seemed to touch on Left-leaning concerns regarding the individual horror of war and lacked a sense of patriotic sympathy for Trumbo's main character, could the music be considered political. Had the content instead seemed to come from a conservative perspective, it might have been understood (and perhaps derided) as propaganda.

Indeed, the question of propaganda is pertinent to the lyrics of Metallica's "Don't Tread on Me" and highlights just how slippery and ambiguous the label "political" can be. "Don't Tread on Me" appears on the band's 1991 eponymous release (often referred to as "The Black Album"), and on the surface it appears to repudiate any sense of Metallica having been disposed toward Left-leaning politics. Anchored by the historical significance of its title phrase, "Don't Tread on Me" presents a clear statement of national pride filtered through the familiar archetypes of individual freedom and personal independence. In addition to the title, Hetfield's lyrics quote phrases and imagery first mentioned in the early days of the American Revolutionary War. A 1775 essay entitled "An American Guesser," likely written by Benjamin Franklin, muses on the symbolism of the rattlesnake that adorned a militia flag seen in Philadelphia (later known as the Gadsden flag).[42] Phrases from Franklin's essay such as "never begins an attack," "once engaged, never surrenders," and "emblem of vigilance" were lifted by Hetfield directly into the lyrics of "Don't Tread on Me." Patrick Henry's famous argument for "liberty or death" also makes an appearance in the song (in fact it is the first lyric). The phrase "Don't tread on me," along with the coiled rattlesnake, was an important symbol of American resolve during the War, and is particularly identified with the Culpeper militia of Virginia, one of the many citizen-soldier militias to take part in the war before the Continental Army was created. Such militaristic images, coupled with the song's quotation of the "America" theme from Leonard Bernstein's *West Side Story*, give "Don't Tread on Me" an unabashedly nationalist sensibility.

Moreover, the general foregrounding of militaristic prowess and national pride in the song swims against the normal criteria of political popular music so that, like celebrations of white racial pride, it was quickly understood as stemming from a generally Right-wing sentiment. Finally, the release of the *Metallica* album soon after the Persian Gulf War—a war believed by some to have at last removed the specter of military failure stemming from Vietnam—led rock critics to hear the imagery in "Don't Tread on Me" as mindless, jingoistic propaganda celebrating a U.S. military victory in which the American homeland and its citizens were never threatened. That Hetfield claimed that the song was not written with that war in mind at all could not downplay the powerful coincidence of its release on *Metallica*. Ultimately, "Don't Tread on Me" takes the subject of politics a step further than even that of "Eye of the Beholder," and by doing so also contributed another component to the development of Hetfield's musical identity.

Following closely on the heels of many of the band's comments about political detachment is a further profession of detachment akin to Ulrich's statement that "[W]e're only a rock band trying to avoid some clichés. Big freaking deal."[43] In the context of detachment and control, clichés are apparently what other bands indulge in. Whether through political activism or a hedonistic rock 'n' roll lifestyle, other popular music groups are not only trapped in a historical predictability, but they have lost a fundamental component of their independence as people. Their very ability to define their own subjectivity, Ulrich's statements seem to contend, has been compromised. Control has been surrendered, and only cheap sound bites and tabloid journalists remain. This kind of sentiment is given an important twist when comments such as the following are thrown in: "A lot of people are surprised when they meet us and find out we're actually fairly normal guys, guys like everyone else." Putting aside for a moment the subtle gender conflation in the last clause, Ulrich's description of Metallica as "only a rock band" contributes a crucial element to the understanding of this particular comment. His choice of words demurely diminishes identifying Metallica as a band, but the words "rock band" even diminishes its identification as a heavy metal band. By rhetorically labeling Metallica as "only a rock band," Ulrich positions the group in an extremely generalized context. As such, he diverts attention away from specific identifying characteristics—politics, thrash metal, heavy metal—because, as the second quote tells us, "we're actually fairly normal guys," and Ulrich understands that being "normal" cannot coexist with specific identifying characteristics.

It is in these comments that we see the first convergence of complexity, control, and detachment. The rest of this chapter therefore takes a deeper look into the complexity of Metallica's portrayal of detachment and considers the public performance of supposedly naturalized social characteristics. Swirling around the triangle of control, complexity, and detachment are broad representations of masculinity and whiteness. Such investigations add not only to our understanding of how musical identities are constructed through social interaction, but also an understanding of how Metallica's specific representations intertwined with the larger tensions surrounding race and genre in popular music during the 1980s.

Three Become Five, Or "Oh Yea! Oh Yea! Yea! Yea! Yea! Yea! Yea! Shit! Fuck! Cunt! Fag! Slut! Yo' Mama!"

The somewhat lengthy title of this section transcribes James Hetfield's call-and-response interaction with the audience at a Metallica concert in 1989, during the band's tour to support ...And Justice for All.[44] Quite sexually explicit when written without the accompanying shouts from the crowd, Hetfield's repeated calls to the audience nevertheless demonstrate a fairly standardized and familiar practice in popular music.[45] But the string of obscenities following the initial statements of generic "yeas" introduces a significant variation from most other versions of a typical concert's audience participation segment. Bound up with a distinctly transgressive energy not unlike S.O.D.'s racialized transgression discussed in Chapter 1, Hetfield's exhortations succinctly represent much of what is important about Metallica's construction of masculine identity. Public swearing, and the extreme manifestation displayed here, carries with it a very specific assertion of independence, a disregard for (or at least a challenge to) common standards of public decency and respectability. My transcription of Hetfield's statements is not meant as mere sensationalism because the choice of obscenities is very significant. Indeed, a great deal is revealed in Hetfield's choosing of words used to denigrate most everyone except straight men. Moreover, one can almost envision the crowd responding each time to the obscenities, not by repeating them, but with the words "not a real man!" "not a real man!"[46] The transgression of these particular obscenities also introduces an important component into my observations on the meaning of Metallica's music from the 1980s: immediately after this interaction, the band starts into the song "And Justice for All," one of the longest and most structurally complex songs to deal with the topics of personal independence and control on the ...*And Justice for All* album.

Ulrich's previous conflation of "everyone" and "guys" into a matter-of-fact statement of normalcy also extends the triangular relationship between control, complexity, and detachment into broader considerations of race and gender. Rather than formally inserting these last two directly into the triangle, I envision race and gender as providing two spheres of influence that orbit around that triangular arrangement. The term "guys" in Ulrich's statement indicates a male gender, but within the context of "everyone else," that male-ness becomes universalized and thus is erased under the mask of Metallica's "normalcy." The ease with which Ulrich makes this statement (note that it is an afterthought) underscores the broad social power of this idea—Ulrich breezes right through the thought without any hint of qualification. Of course, the term "guys" has lost much of its gendered force in American language, but within the context of control Metallica's frequent professions of normalcy also have the effect of turning those expressions into a powerful performance of a specific version of masculinity.

The notion of gender as a process of representation is the theoretical cornerstone upon which cultural studies have created a vast library of work. Feminist scholars have historically been the leaders in this field, as they have had to disassemble the perceived naturalness of gender in order to analyze the social oppression of women and to begin the project of historical recovery of unrecognized female musicians, authors, and political figures. Judith Butler stands as only the best-known feminist philosopher to argue explicitly for understanding gender not as an essence but as a performance. Drawing on the work of Continental philosophers such as Michel Foucault, antiessentialist theories of gender formulated by Butler and others take as an important starting point the questions posed by deconstruction and poststructuralism. In particular, antiessentialism seeks to explore the ways in which gender operates as a historically contingent construction. Suspicious of the notion that identity is a self-contained, knowable, and natural phenomenon, the presentation of gender in society forms part of a continuum that relies on its relationship to other networks of social identity for its power and position. As a nonfixed thing, gender should be understood as contestable and mutable, and the visibility of gender in society, its recognizability, is the result of constant negotiation and change. Teresa de Lauretis writes, "[T]he sex-gender system ... is both a socio-cultural construct and a semiotic apparatus, a system of representation which assigns meaning (identity, value, prestige, location in kinship, status in the social hierarchy, and so forth) to individuals within the society." She goes on to state "[T]he construction of gender is both the product and the process of its representation."[47] Similarly, Susan McClary specifically locates the representation of gender in music with the rise of public opera in the seventeenth century, evidenced most clearly by the mapping onto specific musical techniques the images of "masculinity" and "femininity." Moreover,

> [T]he codes marking gender difference in music are informed by the prevalent attitudes of their time. But they also themselves participate in social formation, inasmuch as individuals *learn how to be gendered beings* through their interactions with cultural discourses such as music.[48]

Yet, we need to look deeper at Metallica's performance of masculinity and extend these ideas: specifically, we need to ask what kind of masculinity is Metallica performing as part of their musical identity? Such choices must have mattered because the band's critical reception during the 1980s consistently praised their image based on what it was not: "braggadocio," "cartoonish, simple-minded bozo-ery," "preening," or relying on lyrics about "fun, escapism or lust."[49] Rather, Metallica was understood to put forth a masculinity that foregrounded things like independence and personal control, intelligence, maturity, and male/female relations implicitly grounded in heavy doses of American Protestantism.[50] In each instance, they act as personal characteristics understood by Metallica to be what everyone should strive for, and to evidence some form of real masculinity. That there is no such thing as a "real man" has fundamentally guided masculinity studies' contribution to the study of gender representation. Still, Walser's blunt metaphor of real masculinity as "passed like a bad check, as a promise that is never kept" does not obviate the need to look any deeper at the production of such a thoroughly dispelled construction.[51] No version of masculinity is natural or authentic, and analyzing representations of "real" masculinity is useful for what being a real man says about other things, most notably the representation and linkage by rock critics of real masculinity as a distinctly white masculinity.

The representation of real masculinity is always the result of the tension between essence and performance, a paradox that is learned by heterosexual men.[52] As part of his inquiry into the relationship between homophobia and masculinity, Patrick D. Hopkins argues that the binary division of gender in society seems to confirm the differences between men and women as a natural, biological given. On top of that structural division are built many other social networks that produce personal identity. As such, social networks (and therefore society) operate by reinforcing and confirming the linkage between gender and "person-hood." However, according to Hopkins, the fundamental flaw in the belief in an essential and natural male-ness is the fact that that male-ness must always be policed and males must guard against losing it. Paradoxically, "the 'naturalness' of being a man, of being masculine, is constantly guarding against the danger of losing itself."[53]

In the 1980s Metallica clearly enacted traits traditionally ascribed to rock masculinity (aggression, transgression, bonding between band members), but they worked very hard to avoid demonstrating those traits *as* masculine. Thus, the band operated within the naturalizing power of masculinity to shape their image such that what constituted the assumed masculinity of the music never required a noticeable and binary demarcation of appropriate feminine traits. In this way, Metallica's version of masculinity resonates very closely with "exscription" of the feminine, of resisting the temptations of pleasurable display for the purpose of solidifying control and maintaining detachment.[54] However, unlike other metal imagery which shielded anxiety over gender behind hardened and armed/armored male bodies, Metallica's masculinity consistently avoided any sort of fantastic or spectacular display: there were no "Iron Men," "Defenders of the Faith," or "Armored Saints" to help defend against such temptations. References to women are also completely absent in Metallica's lyrics (and those of most thrash metal songs), and Walser observes that the avoidance of gendered lyrical references by bands such as Metallica provides an important interpretive opportunity for female fans. To be sure, he notes that "female fans [must be] willing to step outside traditional constrictions of gender identity," and thus active participation in the metal concert experience usually requires that female fans adopt certain masculinizing criteria and behaviors, primarily in terms of attire.[55] The proper costume of T-shirts and (ripped) jeans, though more markedly part of a male subjectivity outside the concert arena, becomes decidedly unmarked inside—it becomes simply "normal."[56] It is this idea of becoming unmarked that gives Metallica's version of masculinity (and indeed all masculinities) its appearance of unquestioned naturalness, an appearance that also grants it a great deal of power.

The long, straight hair favored by thrash metal bands (and fans) also plays a role in the representation of masculinity, but for groups like Metallica, it has served a very different purpose than it did for glam and pop metal bands like Poison, Cinderella, and Bon Jovi. There, long hair was given a particularly spectacular look through elaborate styling, and the styling of the hair (as well as the face makeup) signaled the presence of a specific gender representation in those groups, one that carried with it the enactment of androgyny. In both the glam metal and thrash metal cases, long hair signaled transgression, but thrash metal avoided the uncomfortable linkage of spectacularity with androgyny and femininity, never playing with becoming objects of a gaze in quite the same way as the glam metal bands. For thrash metal bands, long hair was much less flamboyant even as it challenged the role of hair as a marker of gender and engaged with questioning the image of manhood.

Significantly, thrash metal's long hair offered a competing version of manhood grounded not in the ambiguity of androgyny, but in replacing what it meant to be a "real" man. Essentially, having long hair while still being independent, successful, and in control challenged the image of men with socially acceptable short hair who, more often than not, did not seem to be independent or in control. Moreover, the importance of denim jeans as part of the costume of normalcy de-emphasized any latent spectacularity in long hair. For thrash metal, therefore, long hair operated as a symbol of masculine independence, while at the same time the embrace of independence kept the masculinity real. In this way, independence stood as the hallmark of the real man. This costume represents but one version of masculinity—in noticeable opposition to a clean-cut look representative of quite a different masculinity, a difference based on social class—but one that Metallica consciously adopted as a marker of their normalcy. Onstage during the 1980s, Metallica's style of masculinity walked a line between nature and spectacle because the band wore stage clothes that resembled the clothes worn by fans. Denim, T-shirts, and sneakers became the markers of naturalized reality, and that reality gained much of its significance through performance. For all of their attempts at concealing specific identifying characteristics, and at concealing masculinity-as-performance, then, Metallica nevertheless continued to perform masculinity, a masculinity that was reserved and restrained such that it could be understood as "normal."

The characteristic of independence and personal control, in the form of young and stoic white men, figured most prominently in the reception of Metallica's aesthetic. Independence (from overt sexuality and sexual excess, from activist political stances, etc.) was therefore understood as resolutely honest and "real." Journalist Lenny Stoute claimed that "[F]rom day one, Metallica has defied every heavy metal and hardcore tradition in stubborn pursuit of an original groove."[57] Furthermore, Hetfield states, "We do this basically for ourselves ... We're doing it our way, and however many people like it is not up to us. We like it."[58] Ulrich expands the significance of Metallica's independence to include the band's fans: "We do the stuff we like and it's cool that so many people appreciate it. I think they even appreciate that we're doing it for ourselves."[59] Hetfield and Ulrich here foreground detachment so strongly that they come close to erasing fans from the aesthetic. Indeed, rock critic Phil Nicholls seemed so taken by a sense of Metallica's independence that he basically explained the band's aesthetic in terms that removed the band from culture altogether:

> What's far more disturbing about Metallica's counter-cultural thrust is the possibility that, by phonetically mutilating words, wringing them of meaning; by cannibalizing their own racket; by pillaging history, literature, film and philosophy for the sake of sound, they might even be proposing a total break from culture, even "alternative" culture, an absolute otherness, a *completely alternative*, self-sustaining system. Metallica.[60]

Nicholls' remarks explain Metallica in terms that almost sound like postmodernism, focusing on the absence of understood meaning for the sake of expression and the juxtapositioning of apparently unrelated and concrete genres of knowledge. But whereas postmodernism (among its other characteristics) should also be understood to be creating new meanings from such actions, Nicholls understands Metallica's actions as cordoning off the band from anything but its own self-sustaining system. His final grammatical move—"Metallica."—attempts to express a certain kind of unadulterated Truth, and as such, it makes a powerful claim for authenticity. Claims of authenticity such as these are by no means unique to Metallica and remain crucial to the marketing strategies of most popular music, yet the band coupled its claims of personal independence with its more communal "guys like everyone else" image. Not unusually, one of the effects of this balancing act was therefore the construction of a very powerful identity, which, paradoxically, seemed not to be constructed.[61]

Metallica's desire for detached political statements, their arguments for "opinions" and "explorations," and their assertions of independence provided a context for the level of complexity in the music on the three albums of the 1980s, and on ...And Justice for All in particular. Musical complexity was seen as a practical expression of the band's intelligence, as "studied."[62] Along with lyrics which were elevated to the status of the sublime by the description "poetry," critics generally celebrated Metallica's 1980s material specifically for its complexity, almost thankful that *finally* there was a heavy metal band that could write real music. Quite often they referred to Metallica as a distinctly "New Metal" or as "Meta-Metal," a musical style one critic described as "precise instrumental work and tempo and time shifts relating more to King Crimson than, say, AC/DC."[63] In this instance, the specific references to King Crimson, an English progressive rock band, and AC/DC, a white blues-rock band, subtly extend Metallica's independent masculinity along racial and generic lines in very significant ways, ways made more explicit by other commentators.

Perhaps the most direct example of this dichotomy is found in Jonathan Gold's review of a later Metallica album, *Load*, released in 1996. In a mostly negative review of that album, Gold summarizes the band's 1980s style as follows: "Metallica's great technical innovation, the thing that launched thrash metal ... was finally this: they were the band that finally divorced hard rock from the blues."[64] It is hard to miss the understanding of genre-as-race in this statement. Understood by rock critics and rock history as *the* representation of African-American music, the blues are seen in this instance as excess historical baggage carried around by metal. The "divorce," after all these years ("finally") and without any apparent indication of alimony, has allowed the implicitly white hard rock style to shed that baggage, and to appear in its most pure form. In many of the reviews for *...And Justice for All* this same tension between genre and race emerges such that the blues-rock tradition is positioned as backwards, degenerate, and almost slavish in its recycling of blues-based sounds.[65] Simon Reynolds's review of the album calls it "light-years beyond raunch or blues rock,"[66] a way of thinking about Metallica that Erik Davis also uses to condemn the metal band Mötley Crüe as "still tied to the white-blues whipping post."[67]

Of course, African-American blues have constantly had a very romantic image for Western musicians, typically one of primitive and uncontaminated expression. George Lipsitz writes that "the blues are deployed as an antidote to the shallowness of contemporary commercial culture, as an art form precious because it is unapproachable and unknowable, locked in the past but superior to anything we can imagine in the present."[68] Indeed, beginning in the 1960s the blues and blues musicians such as Robert Johnson, Muddy Waters, and Howlin' Wolf have served as spiritual and mystical inspirations for countless white rock musicians from England. Guitarist Eric Clapton stands as perhaps the most notable (and notorious) example of this kind of influence by claiming throughout his career a profound emotional connection with Robert Johnson. As Lipsitz points out, though, Clapton's connection nevertheless neglects the very real sociopolitical circumstances that informed Johnson's music and Clapton's ability to worship it.[69] Moreover, the historical role played by the blues in the history of rock music usually effaces the way it has always been part of the historical and social continuum of African-American music. Nevertheless, as McClary notes, "the way we tell the history of the blues is often shaped by that period of British enthusiasm." As a historical form of expression, the blues had always functioned as a particular expressive option, what McClary describes as "one particular manifestation of a number of deeper elements that live on in other genres."[70] Still, this notion of white musicians' involvement with the blues gets turned around in the genre-as-race dichotomy characterizing Metallica's critical reception.

Walser writes of the general transformation of 1980s metal away from a blues-based influence while retaining certain aesthetic traits of those origins, and it is often difficult to hear how Metallica's metal from the 1980s could be related sonically to the blues. In at least one instance, specific musical techniques illustrate Metallica's separation from the blues-rock tradition. Gold's review, for example, praises Metallica's "astounding rhythmic approach to the heavy-metal riff—based on the drum rudiment rather than on the sloppy blues lick."[71] He is most likely referring here to the song "And Justice for All," and its main instrumental refrain about which Ulrich has explained as having come from a practice session. But, Gold's description, and his particular presentation of etude-like practice as a more "astounding" approach to rhythm, reinforces further the understanding of musical technique ("rudiment" versus "sloppy") along racial lines. Within this very racialized dichotomy, then, critics created a space for Metallica's musical complexity and ensemble virtuosity by shaving away great chunks of American cultural history. In so doing—by separating Metallica from the influence and history of the black blues—critics made the implicit gesture of marking the band as "white." Other thrash metal bands were generally understood in similar ways, and thrash metal's relationship to the blues, coupled with the overwhelming belief in the 1980s that there was in fact no concrete relationship, offer important insight in discussions about musical complexity. In Metallica's case, the band's themes of independence could appear much stronger, and were easier to explain, if they were set outside the blues-rock tradition, set outside any connection to the blues, and set against other heavy metal musicians who seemed merely to continue the appropriation of an African-American musical tradition.[72]

The observations just made with respect to rock critics' evocation of racialized imagery to laud Metallica's 1980s material operate very much within the interpretive paradigm organized around the concept of "whiteness." Importantly, rock critics such as Gold, Reynolds, and Davis never discretely label Metallica as "white." Rather, their language generally inscribes a space that is simply not black. However, in creating a not-black space for Metallica's aesthetic, Gold and the others engage with perhaps the central tactic of whiteness: never naming the thing which is unnamed. Carving such a space for Metallica but never acknowledging the existence or characteristics of that space results in the kind of cultural void so distinctive to whiteness. Indeed it has been the job of a rich web of recent work in American studies to go about naming those tactics, to upend and denaturalize the existence of an unnamed whiteness in American society and its cultural artifacts. Toni Morrison's work in 1992 investigating how the pantheon of white American authors operated according to complex intersections of black and white culture occupies a fundamental position in the drive to "name" the void.[73] For Morrison and other feminist writers of color, the study of the invisibility of whiteness was very much tied to the goal of allowing the contributions of African-American writers to receive equal recognition as fully American authors, and to redress the segregation of those authors in literary writing and university courses. Historians such as David Roediger, Theodore V. Allen, and Eric Lott, as well as George Lipsitz, illustrate a second stream of writing on whiteness by tracing the development of white skin privilege across the history of the United States. In this work, the construction of a white self, specifically a working-class self, against the complex ethnic backdrop of American society marks whiteness as the manifestation of class relations that determined who would be considered "white." Roediger and Lipsitz, moreover, ground their work in a decidedly clear call for what Roediger calls "the abolition of whiteness," a discrete political stance that aims to recognize and remedy the history of social injustice caused by white skin privilege.[74]

Richard Dyer's work on the cultural representation of whiteness as the representation of purity, stability, nobility, normalcy, and (significantly) control, introduces a third aspect of whiteness studies, and the one resonating most closely with my own interpretive goals in this chapter. Like Morrison's literary analyses and Lott's concept of "love and theft," Dyer's close reading of films illuminates the mechanics of depicting whiteness. However (like Lipsitz[75]), Dyer understands whiteness not always to be restricted to the relationship between black and white. Importantly, as a construction whiteness can, to varying degrees, be appropriated by nonwhite people as part of their own assertions of power and privilege, and in Dyer's conception, the working-class white identity described by Roediger and Allen is repositioned as a distinctly middle-class set of values. The Cosby family of the 1980s sitcom stands as a paradigmatic example of the way nonwhites can be invested with the qualities of whiteness usually reserved for white people.[76] Similarly, Colin Powell's popularity among Americans can also be explained by the perception that he does not seem to be "black." Both of these examples highlight not only the constructive potentials of identity, but, as Mike Hill notes, demonstrate how "[T]he relationship between margins and center ... is a mutable agreement. Difference crosses the ontological tracks with astonishing regularity."[77]

With respect to masculinity, Dyer writes of how Western society presents white men as divided, "with more powerful sex drives but also a greater will power." This dual characteristic posits two possible outcomes for white men: "their giving way to darkness [for example, sexuality]" or "the heroism of their channeling or resisting it [sexuality]."[78] In addition, Dyer argues that the development of white identity requires "the attainment of a position of disinterest—abstraction, distance, separation, objectivity—which creates a public sphere that is the mark of civilization, itself the aim of human history."[79] Following on from this, we can better understand rock critics' response to Metallica's 1980s musical aesthetic: celebrate the band in such a way as to deny any connection to the blues. By casting Metallica in the role of the ultimate nonblues rock band, critics like Gold could elevate the band as an example of the kind of detached white subjectivity described above. Ensemble virtuosity, learned musicianship (e.g., "rudiments"), musical complexity and the modular aesthetic powering "Master of Puppets" or the ...And Justice for All album; lyrics discussing political topics and issues of personal control but which emerge in the end as detached "interests" and "explorations"; an image of heterosexuality that resists public display—all of these characteristics can be made to stand as qualities of an ideal type of white masculinity. As part of an ideal, they also contribute to a powerful conception of invisible normalcy.

Thus, for these critics the white blues-rock and pop-metal musicians of the 1980s represented something of a debased whiteness, a whiteness that seemed to have lost some underlying and essential qualities marking true whiteness. Instead, the blues-rock traditions, and blues-based metal especially, continued the marriage too long, to the point that the uncomfortable constructedness of the whole decades-long process had become embarrassingly obvious. Metallica's transformation of metal away from the blues contaminant could not happen fast enough according to rock critics, and they found much of the remaining continued hybridization unnerving.[80] After all, subservience to the blues tradition, for which Mötley Crüe had been castigated, introduced "feelings" and "emotions," both of which had the potential for debilitating "weakness." The representation of black male sexuality constructed by British rockers in the 1960s, mutated into a lopsided "obsession with male sexuality," had been carried forward by 1980s glam metal to the degree that the very assurance of control was at stake.[81] What became embarrassing, therefore, was the perception that metal bands such as AC/DC, Mötley Crüe, Poison, and Ratt had, through their association with the sexuality of black blues (however mutated the final product may have been), demonstrated weakness by failing to resist the temptations of overt sexuality. Most importantly, they had failed to maintain the state of balance to which white men should aspire. This situation, then, formed the debasement that marred the "essential" whiteness of these musicians, and, until Metallica arrived, had threatened the whiteness of metal in general.

The vantage points provided by the interlocking orbits of whiteness and masculinity illuminate much about Metallica's triangulation of control, complexity, and detachment within the multicultural mix of popular music during the 1980s. The label "thinking-man's metal," though first applied to the 1970s group Blue Öyster Cult, remained a useful term at the end of the 1980s (and was applied to other metal groups such as Living Colour and Queensrÿche) because it could quickly encapsulate a broad range of relationships between musical detail and musical identity. Indeed, in the 1990s progressive metal groups such as Dream Theater became the latest metal musicians bestowed with that title. Along with its even greater levels of structural complexity and performance sophistication, progressive metal's substantial Asian and Hispanic participation (as both performers and fans) demonstrates a distinct development in the set of cultural relationships I have been discussing. Still, the application of the phrase "thinking man's metal" to Metallica ultimately does more than just distinguish them from other metal groups. As with every application of the phrase, the implications behind "thinking" and "man's" spread outward to complicate and, in effect, color the desire for detached control. As such, these cases, and many others residing on all sides of the musical landscape, require the continual reinterpretation of what it means to produce musical identity by negotiating the performance of musical complexity.

CHAPTER 4

The Road and the Mode

Musical Tourism and Ethnicity Roaming

And when I'm gone / And at my grave you stand,
Just say God's called home / Your ramblin' man.

Hank Williams, "Ramblin' Man"

Carved upon my stone / My body lie, But still I roam.

Metallica, "Wherever I May Roam"

Introduction

In 1998 Metallica recorded Bob Seger's "Turn the Page" for their compilation of cover songs called *Garage, Inc.*, a self-conscious revisiting both of the band's general history as cover-song artists as well as the specific tone of their 1987 mini-album, *The $5.98 EP: Garage Days Re-Revisited.*[1] Written in the early 1970s, "Turn the Page" has become a classic "road" song, but its particular vision of life on the road with a touring rock 'n' roll band attempts to express a sense of the physical and emotional toil coincident with more traditionally prominent images of hedonism, independence, and popularity. Indeed, the vision in "Turn the Page" is distinctly somber

99

as the lyrics play on the transient nature of place and identity experienced during a tour. Seger's narrator seems able to get a sense of himself only through a series of snapshot-like images: "Here I am ... / There I am ... / Here I go ... / There I go, turn the page." However, the lyrics deny a distinct sense of place by surrounding those snapshots with images that instead convey a feeling of "nowhere": a lonesome highway in Nebraska, no-name restaurants, sixteen hours in a tour bus. Or, the lyrical imagery employs paradox to express the sense of displacement where time and place are constantly in flux while on tour: "Out there in the spotlight, you're a million miles away." The lyrics may alternate images attempting to ground the narrator's specific experiences with others that do not, but the sparse texture of the music presents everything according to a quiet sense of withdrawal that verges on desperation.

For Seger, the wary glances and subtle hostility given off in response to longhaired men in public further contributed to the weariness of being on the road. Historically situated in the 1970s, then, Seger's version of "Turn the Page" resonates both as an understanding of rock's place in society at a given moment as well as a psychological positioning of the road in the life of a touring musician. In the late 1990s, though, Metallica seem to have been primarily attracted to the image of road-weariness as a way of representing a stage in their own career. Recording "Turn the Page" functions as a means of looking back over that career and as a way to shape their level of success as the product of years of tiring work. When they recorded "Turn the Page" the four band members were in their mid-thirties (old by the standards of a youth-oriented industry) and at the pinnacle of success. Moreover, they had spent almost their entire adult lives on the road, often traveling to places much more distant than Nebraska. They had essentially grown up on the road, having been on the move (on tour, traveling to record, and so on) since they were 20—still young by modern standards of personal development. "Turn the Page" and the rest of the *Garage, Inc.* sessions were recorded after a twenty-seven-month period of near-constant touring to support the *Load* and *Reload* albums. While not exactly mourning for time lost to the work of the road, Metallica's cover projects a version of subjectivity that contrasts with the vision of youthful energy from their past. As in the Seger original, much of the emotional impact of Metallica's version depends on identifying the feelings of constant uprootedness and the almost painful lack of a sense of place as important components of the personal histories of the band members. In other words, this song asks us to understand Metallica not as "Metallica," but as James Hetfield, Kirk Hammett, Jason Newsted, and Lars Ulrich.

If "Turn the Page" stands as one vision of the road for Metallica, the group clearly had felt quite differently several years earlier. "Wherever I May Roam," the fourth single from the band's multiplatinum-selling album *Metallica* (1991), envisions the road as the nurturing site for self-knowledge and independence. It too is poetically autobiographical, but its effect is larger than the more narrow focus of "Turn the Page," couched as it is in the huge sound of an up-tempo metal song, with no trace of the anguished interiority found in the later song. Moreover, much of how "Wherever I May Roam" accomplishes its sense of freedom has to do with how we hear the song's central riff, and indeed my interest in this song revolves around tracing the web of meanings which underpin the riff's musical detail and its relationships to surrounding sections of the song. The riff's first presentation, in the guise of a sitar and dripping with Eastern mystery, is perhaps the most striking version, but its reappearance throughout the song as a recognizably metal riff muddies whatever initial questions of Orientalism the sitar-based atmosphere might have raised. Understanding how the analytical details of such a tiny structural element can contain a wealth of cultural context means it is also necessary to examine the tools used in that analysis. In particular, the chief analytical question of this chapter explores the ways the distinct Phrygian sound of the riff, and that sound's function as one of the most common markers of exoticism, frames the imagery of the road in "Wherever I May Roam."

At the same time, the frequency throughout Metallica's general musical style of those musical details which might also be called Phrygian lead me to examine the question of "fit" in the relationship between musical topic and analytical tool. My goal is not to discard completely analytical labels like Phrygian; indeed I think that term is particularly useful in the case of "Wherever I May Roam," and enables an important historical vantage point not addressed by other analytical strategies. My concern, however, is with recognizing what may get lost when our only analytical tools for studying metal's guitar riffs and harmonic patterns are modal ones, and to that end I propose alternate considerations for analyzing the linkage between Phrygian sounds, exoticism, and heavy metal.

The focus in this chapter on "Wherever I May Roam" may strike some readers as odd given the much greater visibility of other songs from the *Metallica* album. "Enter Sandman" and "Nothing Else Matters," for instance, have garnered far more popular attention than "Wherever I May Roam." Indeed, even those critics who do try to say something about this song seem to struggle with how to place it in Metallica's career and figure out what it means. In their exhaustive survey of Metallica's music, journalists Malcolm Dome and Mick Wall can only come up with: "[A] rocker and, on the surface, a serious song about what? Roaming around? Keeping on the move? Staying on your toes? What?"[2] Nevertheless, as part of the issues outlined above, the song is compelling for two other reasons. First, the significance of whiteness and normalcy (in all of their complexities) as important subtexts for Metallica's aesthetic choices in the 1980s remain fully present here. The lyrical subject of "Wherever I May Roam" (reinforced by the video for the song) is a statement about personal freedom and independence as experienced through the complex metaphor of the Road. As was discussed in Chapter 3, the ideas of personal freedom, self-reliance, and an aesthetic of distance guided many aspects of Metallica's music and cultural significance. The desire to be seen simply as four guys, as well as the effort put into constructing that image, also circulates within the affective world of the Road presented in "Wherever I May Roam." In other words, we have to look at Metallica's ideals of normalcy and their distrust of overt politicization within the context of American society, particularly during the second half of the twentieth century; for it is there that the rhetoric in this song finds sympathetic resonances.

Second, in addition to the issues of white masculinity is the obvious element of exoticism introduced by this song. The musical grammar found in "Wherever I May Roam" demands attention because of how it combines general markers of heavy metal musical norms with the demarcations of distinctly non-Western locales. Moreover, the fusion of some generally exotic atmosphere with lyrics celebrating the Road (here meant to be understood in a specifically American context) as a site for personal freedom and identity makes it an important indicator of the means by which the West constructs an image of itself and of its Others. Since the American Road in this case lies outside of Western culture (as I will explain below), questions of musical exoticism and identity, as well as an understanding of the exotic as feminine, crucially inform what follows. I place this song in the complicated historical context of musical exoticism in popular music because of how the song appears unabashedly to continue the long (though historically specific) tradition of Orientalist and exoticist imagery in Western art. Indeed it does this so transparently that the lack of any significant discussion about the song in the rock press or in interviews by Metallica is in itself reason for inquiry.

"Wherever I May Roam" partakes in a kind of musical tourism such as that enabled by what Scott Lash and John Urry theorize as part of a "post-tourist" society, one in which practical geographic boundaries between cultures give way to almost unfettered access through the power of depiction. At the core of posttourism, moreover, is the desire for the Journey, not necessarily the destination as one might think. The confident belief in the

Journey heard in "Wherever I May Roam" reflects the powerful allure of that construct. As musical tourists in America, Metallica engage with both the *flaneur's* technological access to all the world's sounds and the West's concomitant political ability to depict the world. Depiction is thus an exercise in power relations, yet it is also an act of perception and of filtering. Metallica's particular depiction—its act of musical tourism—is of some version of the East, and as such operates according to some kind of Orientalism. As Edward Said has argued so importantly, Orientalism's primary location (since it deals in many important ways with place) is also perceptually based, grounded as it is in the Western imagination.[3] Still, what kind of Orientalism is present within "Wherever I May Roam"? What should cultural critics and historians do with these interactions in the context of postmodern American culture? Are all Orientalist and exoticist practices alike? How should any differences shape our response?

The collision of the Road and the Phrygian mode in "Wherever I May Roam"—to the degree that the freedom of the American Road points *to the East* and not to the West as is usually the case—marks a collision of multivalent meanings and components in the creation of a musical self in late twentieth-century American culture. The following discussion necessarily ranges widely across many aspects of critical study in an attempt to account for the dizzying cultural complexity that lies behind a single metal riff. Such a range is crucial, I believe, because the most significant components of musical detail are illuminated in the contested nature of those details and their part in the negotiation of historical meaning. Furthermore, the sociocultural complexity underscoring a riff like that found in "Wherever I May Roam" leaves little room for neat summarization. Still, this chapter aims for more than an exercise in music criticism; the issues of cultural power and analytical methodology discussed below remain too important, and this song's interaction with issues of Orientalism and exoticism reach into larger areas of significance for the study of popular culture.

The Mode and the Road

"Wherever I May Roam" introduces the Road using musical tropes instantly identifiable as some exotic Other, and it does this through the sound of a sitar at the very beginning. Instantly, we are in "India." More importantly, though, India acts as a stand-in, a quick metaphor used simply to indicate a setting that is definitely outside the West. In other words, there is no evidence that Metallica chose an Indian setting because they had at some point developed a deep spiritual relationship with the music of the East. Rather, the choice to incorporate sounds of the Indian East reveals a complex urge to create a blanket non-Western setting. Even the sitar sound itself is fake, the product of a technological sleight-of-hand sounded on a regular six-string guitar. Like most instances of exotic-sounding music in popular song, the purpose of that music works as a kind of sonic backdrop for the song's lyrics. However, as with much of European opera's exotic music during the nineteenth century, this ethnic backdrop can represent danger or evoke uncertainty and mystery. In France, particularly during the second half of the century, these locales could also be feminized as seductive and sensual, fulfilling Western society's desires.[4]

After an opening gong-like sound (itself frequently a marker of Otherness), the distinctive sitar riff enters, complete with a repeated bass note acting like a drone. The sitar's melody moves through stereotypical motions characterizing the Phrygian mode and is accompanied by softly atmospheric percussion that adds to the overall sense of distance. It is important to reiterate that the sitar sound is a technological contrivance, and, moreover, to note that the sitar timbre is essentially a layer on top of an otherwise standard clean-timbred guitar tone. The drone in this section is also sounded on a clean-timbred guitar, specifically an open Low E string stripped of its low-end frequencies. Nevertheless, the presence of the repeated drone creates a feeling of timelessness while the contour of the melody adds stability: floating above the drone it moves away from its starting pitch, but always pushes back down to it via the pointed resolution of the upper half step. The stark musical landscape created at the opening of "Wherever I May Roam," much like a movie soundtrack, seems to raise the curtain on an overall affect that places the listener somewhere in the "East."

The loud crack of a modern snare drum breaks the heavy atmosphere of the sitar's introduction, transforming the Low E pedal of the sitar texture into a Low E pedal of a distorted guitar reinforced with the additional lower octave of the bass. The guitar assumes the sitar's Phrygian melody, playing it one octave lower than in the introduction (see Figure 4.1). The half-time feel of the drum pattern (a basically straightforward kick-snare alternation on beats one and three[5]) maintains a sense of the initial mood, but clearly that mood is in the process of becoming something quite different. A quick chromatic climb from A to C completes the final stage of the transformation, and at this point the drum pattern doubles (now accenting quarter-notes). With this change, the initial mood of exotic mystery and weighty timelessness largely gives way to a sound and feel quite

Figure 4.1 "Wherever I May Roam," main theme.

recognizable as the forward momentum of hard rock or metal. Indeed, the half-step trill decorating the tonic note of the theme stands as perhaps the sole remaining indication of the previous exotic realm.

The music and lyrics of the verses both illustrate how the distinct representations of East and West, Other and Self that have been created by this point continue back and forth throughout the song. After the heavy metal portion of the introduction, the guitars land solidly on Low E and the drums introduce a new texture, one that is decidedly nonrock but also not the improvisatory accents of the sitar's opening soundscape. Ulrich's drum pattern here avoids a traditional relationship between kick, snare, and high hat, and relies instead on the deep, bass-heavy toms played in a one-measure pattern. The usual signifier of the high hat or ride cymbal as the timekeeping element in rock drumbeats is entirely absent, its function taken up by snare accents on the third beat of each measure. At this point, the tom pattern creates a texture meant to be heard here as some form of "primitivism," one that further emphasizes the overall sense of a non-Western locale. Specifically, the pattern plays on the tropes represented by tom toms, congas, djembe, and dumbeks, all drums from various non-Western cultures. The reliance on the tom pattern in the context of the ethnogeography of "Wherever I May Roam" therefore evokes, at some level, images associated with drumming cultures of the world—and the stereotypes associated with them. Though individually representing very different sets of circumstances, racist images of African savages, the presumed naturalness of indigenous North Americans are, like the sound of a sitar in a commercial jingle, complex metaphors for Western fears and desires. Beat subcultures of the 1950s and counterculture participants during the 1960s and 1970s, as well as modern day drumming circles on university campuses, all turn to access these images through the perceived authenticity of these drums.[6] Thus, the toms—specific drums generally reserved for special accents in most rock and metal drumming styles—are brought to the forefront here to emphasize further the unusual locale of the song.

Above this drum texture, the guitars move through a slow chord progression that emphasizes E, F, B♭, and G. The rate of harmonic change in this section (two measures per chord) serves to continue a sense of the vastness of the song's opening. It is also within this section that the first words are heard. Importantly, they are recited in a low quasi-whisper that augments the sense of strangeness in the new texture surrounding them, as well as foreshadowing things to come. The vocal timbre imbues the text with images of a breathless infinity: "And the road becomes my bride." The manner of this initial presentation signals an expressive distance between the narrator's "real world" and the "authentic world" created by the drum texture. Another powerful blurring of cultural identities takes place when James Hetfield actively joins the drum texture into his own expressive being and *sings* the just-whispered lyrics using a heavy metal vocal style (for example, distorted timbre, louder volume, in a limited melodic range). He continues for the rest of the first verse to sing of how "the Road" stands as the site of his independence and provides for his spiritual health. He possesses nothing but his personal pride and the comfort he derives from the experience of the Road. He confides in the Road, and She gives him all he needs.

The individualist experience of being on the road is quite clearly presented in these lyrics as the province of men. However, when the medium of the Road itself is assigned a specific gender in Western culture and history, it is expressly linked to the feminine. For instance, the ocean (arguably the first Road) always has a female gender, many times represented as a lover. A notable instance of a female Road can found in the novel *The Grapes of Wrath*, wherein John Steinbeck refers to US Highway 66 as "the mother road" for thousands of westward-migrating families during the Great Depression. In both "Wherever I May Roam" and the Steinbeck novel the image of a feminized Road creates a powerful maternal image, connecting as it does to the notions of Mother Nature and the spiritual belief in the sustaining and life-changing forces supplied by the natural environment. Throughout Western history Mother Nature has been represented by the Forest (as distinct from the Desert of early Christianity, for instance[7]), and in American history this has usually meant the great wildernesses of western North America and its associated cultural representation, the American West. The complex ideas of natural purity, bounteous infinity, national birthright, and racial justification represented by these forested lands during the nineteenth century were appropriated during the twentieth after the physical geography had largely been tamed, and in its place lay the endless possibilities of the Road. In both Nature and Road, the feminization creates a maternal replacement that acts as a guide for the traveler. "Wherever I May Roam" does not merely feminize the Road, though: the song's narrator specifically refers to the Road as his "Bride." By investing the Road with the particular symbolic feminine image of the Bride, the lyrics emphasize a specific kind of feminization. Furthermore, in the context of performance the weighty musical texture in which the narrator first introduces the Bride inflects the metaphor with a distinctly mystical significance not unlike the sort found in texts such as the Song of Songs. Indeed, the rich importance of both Nature and the Bride transforms the Road of this song into a very spiritualized center for the narrator.

After a chromatic climb from B♭ to F, the Phrygian riff returns briefly to frame the images in the verse lyrics and the short declamations made during the chromatic climb ("rover, wanderer, nomad, vagabond: call me what you will"). The return of the Phrygian riff at this point reasserts its distinctive character as an important marker of identity in contrast to the slower and more expansive harmonic language of the verses. The riff's distorted guitar timbre (and rock drum texture) combines with its Phrygian melody and the association of that melody with the sitar-based opening to position it as the complex marker of the narrator's selfhood. The rising chromatic tag from A to C again follows this instance of the riff, but instead of returning to Low E, the harmonic area of both the riff itself and the verse music, this time the guitars land solidly one half-step higher, on Low F. The arrival wrenches the narrative out of the stability of the Low E, at once suspending the expectation of Low E while also acting to push the song forward. Moreover, the specific arrival on F (and not, say, F#) is significant in the context of the self/other interactions running throughout this song: the relationship between E and F as the half-step pair most representative of the exoticism of the Phrygian mode is also representative of a multifaceted issue in the theorization of metal's general harmonic language.[8]

The prechorus that follows winds its way through power chords on F, E, and B♭—supporting the freedom to "take my time anywhere," "to speak my mind," and (coinciding with the B♭ harmony) to "redefine anywhere"—and emphasizes each two-measure harmonic point via quick momentum-sustaining rhythmic articulations. In many ways the short chorus which follows, complete with vocal harmonies that inject a transcendent quality, is a four-measure extension of the prechorus. Like the prechorus, the two chords in the chorus (A and G) are held, each for two measures. Further, it is possible to hear the initial arrival on A as the second chord of a half-step parallel harmonic motion: B♭–A mirrors the F–E motion that began the prechorus (see Figure 4.2). At the same time, the A chord functions as the first chord of the chorus, and it is this dual nature of the A chord that gives the chorus its extension-like quality.

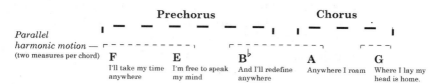

Figure 4.2 Harmonic reduction of "Wherever I May Roam," prechorus and chorus.

The chorus thus states plainly a two-chord affirmation of what has come before: "Anywhere I roam / Where I lay my head is home," and a heavily accented downbeat then returns the music to Low E and the realm of the Phrygian theme. The weight of this accent, though, indicates that the chorus music had not served as a strong enough arrival point in the way most choruses do. Its structural duality limits its effectiveness as a place of constant return and affirmation. Indeed, the return to E requires the addition of the percussive quality of a twelve-string bass guitar to confirm its arrival.[9] Certainly the brief harmonic "roaming" of the prechorus (and the chorus) build some amount of tension, but that tension is emphatically resolved only with the return to Low E. That the chorus *music* lacks sufficient weight to culminate and carry the general lyrical attitude of independence and freedom is also evidenced during the song's outro and fade-out wherein the Phrygian theme repeats through the fade instead of the chorus music as is more typically the case in popular music. The frame provided by the main Phrygian theme therefore contributes a consistent context with which to interpret the lyrical images. By allowing the narrator to "speak" without the restrictions of verbal language and to express the lyrics' ideas in perhaps a more significant way, the theme can emphasize the sentiments of those lyrics by constantly reminding the listener of the essential freedom claimed by the narrator.

Following the second verse/chorus module, a variation of the Phrygian theme itself vividly enacts the idea of "roaming." Ornamented by trills on melodic arrival points, it first climbs an octave, pausing partway on the #3 scale degree (thus inflecting the previously pure Phrygian mode toward a more Phrygian-dominant sound[10]) before continuing upward. The climb is then repeated, but this time the melody overshoots the octave, continuing upward to a G above before leaping down a diminished fourth to D#. The entire process then repeats with an accompanying harmonization in thirds, and the section achieves a roaming quality as the melody seems to break free from its usual contour tying it to Low E. Indeed, it roams into another tactile level as the music literally journeys across the fretboard of the guitar before slamming back down to a Low F power chord for another iteration of the prechorus/chorus combination. "Slamming" is the right word in this case because at the last quarter note of the variation, the guitarist's left hand is up around the thirteenth fret and must be back down at the first fret (Low F) for the ensuing downbeat. Such a large motion cannot be accomplished delicately, and the musical change into the Low F area is given a quite physical reinforcement.

Largely by virtue of the fact that Metallica is an American heavy metal band, the above discussion has assumed that the Road upon which the narrator experiences his independence exists somewhere in America, as the phenomenon has long played a significant role in American culture. For instance, when the Road appears in a country song or a blues song we think we know where we are, geographically speaking. Moreover, as the residue of nineteenth-century Manifest Destiny, the Road in American culture typically heads to the west. Yet, the sitar sound and the particular kind of Phrygian character exhibited in "Wherever I May Roam" evidently does not take place on the roads of America—this Road does not exist in America. Instead, the Road celebrated by Metallica exists somewhere in the Eternal *East*. How does the factor of place change our perception of the Road in this song? How did the American Road get to the East?

As I noted above, throughout much of American cultural history the experience of the Road has served as a tool and a site for the performance of masculinity, as a location for the celebration of individualism, restless energy, and action. However, even if its ties to male activities may strongly imply a masculine gender, we must be careful to distinguish between the *medium* of the Road (be it asphalt, iron, or water) and the *experience* of the Road, or, in other words, the Journey.[11] In her study of the dialectic between Home and Road in American culture as that dialectic operates specifically in country music, Cecilia Tichi notes how Walt Whitman's "Song of the Open Road" (1867) explicitly appeals for experiencing the rugged freedoms of the Road as a rebellion against agrarian conventionality, understood by Whitman as a debilitating femininity. Here, Whitman exhorts the dynamic power of the experience—of the Journey—in opposition to the static experience of domesticity. Before Whitman, Thomas Jefferson had painted in broad strokes the awesome natural features of the Shenandoah Mountains as a geologic Road leading westward across the North American continent.[12] Greil Marcus's depiction of 1950s street musician Harmonica Frank highlights another kind of male road experience: the living-out of the Huck Finn story. Of Frank, Marcus writes "[H]e showed up, made his records, and lit out for the territory ... setting himself free from an oppression he never bothered to define."[13] As American myth, furthermore, the Huck Finn story embodies an impulse to freedom, with Huck "as unsure of his own authority as he is of anyone else's."[14]

If the American Road serves as a place for the experience of personal independence and freedom, it also functions as a site of danger and psychological stress. As in Bob Seger's "Turn the Page," Bon Jovi's song "Wanted Dead or Alive" (1986) presents a panoply of images related to the Road experience that are neither hedonistic nor glamorous. It describes a never-ending sense of weariness and uncertainty, but it also positions the experience as successful male adventure. While that song, like "Wherever

I May Roam," has roots in the lifestyle of a long rock tour, it resonates in important ways with myths in American culture about the Road and the sense of the unknowable that accompanies its true spirit. Moreover, lead singer Jon Bon Jovi infuses those myths with a metaphorical bent centered around images of the American West: as a traveler he is a cowboy carrying "a loaded six string" on his back, and in his travels he has seen "a million faces." Simple open-faced chords played on acoustic guitars only add to the "authentic" imagery of the traveler who has no need for the trappings of modern amplification equipment. On the other hand, those same life-giving sources offered by the Road can also become the site for spiritual and literal death. The mythology of country singer Hank Williams's death in 1953 has the power it does largely because he died literally while on the Road. Furthermore, as Tichi points out, Williams died on the Road after having been disowned by the Nashville establishment, in a sense after having been "exiled" or made "homeless."[15] The poignancy of Hank Williams's story thus begins with the belief that the Road was not simply the site of his musical calling, but that, in the end, it was the only thing he had left.

In remembering Bon Jovi's and Williams's odes to road-weary traveling we must not overlook the tradition of "ramblin' " developed in blues music during the first half of the twentieth century. Songs such as Robert Johnson's "Ramblin' On My Mind" or "Walkin' Blues" are important pieces in this characterization, particularly after Johnson and other Delta blues guitarists became symbols of unfettered male freedom for many British rock musicians in the 1960s. Johnson's ramblin' in particular represents for Marcus "the ultimate American image of flight from homelessness."[16] His travels throughout the eastern portion of America are a defiant laugh at fate, and present ramblin' as "a state of mind that gives no rest at all."[17] The large-scale northward migrations by African-Americans during the 1920s, 1930s, and 1940s were primarily undertaken by men, and the blues frequently present musical representations of ramblin' as largely the prerogative of men. Black women, of course, were directly implicated in those undertakings, and their experiences with respect to the Road are complex. Writing on the various modes of expression in the music of women blues singers of the 1920s, Hazel V. Carby notes that women's responses to migration at once mourn their own loss and imminent loneliness, as well as give voice to the nostalgic desires of the women who had actually been able (or forced) to migrate.[18]

In his review of the album *Metallica*, Robert Palmer singles out "Wherever I May Roam" to observe how Hetfield "echoes, perhaps unconsciously, one of bluesman Robert Johnson's most indelible images."[19] What might otherwise be praise in terms of the sense of time-honored familiarity in traditional rock history comes across as a rather simplistic enjambment in this instance. Linking Hetfield to Johnson via the metaphor of the Road seems to say more about Palmer's inheritance of a version of rock history made standard by years of rock journalism, and serves only to perpetuate the celebratory images of freedom constructed around black bluesmen during the 1960s. Like the linkage of Johnson and Eric Clapton mentioned in Chapter 3, the linkage of Hetfield and Johnson has the unfortunate effect of flattening the very real distinctions of race and historical location between the two men's experiences.[20] It is important to point out that black migration experiences are exactly that: migration experiences, and as such represent a different kind of Journey than the others outlined above. Forced by economic hardship and debilitating racism to flee northward, the meanings underlying the Journey for African-American men early in the twentieth century must not be conflated with the very different reasons presented by touring rock stars and New England poets, the sum rolled into a totalized understanding of the Journey.

Many American "road" films since the late 1960s present the Journey in yet another way: as a Quest, usually taken up by young white men and given over to the task of creating a sense of personal identity.[21] Film scholar David Laderman, surveying the history of those films, discusses the genre as negotiating a tension between "rebellious critique of conservative authority and as a reassertion of a traditional expansionist ideology," and notes that the image of rugged white male individualism drives both the individual narratives as well as their cultural significance.[22] Indeed, in the case of "Wherever I May Roam" such a tension is readily apparent through the way the song's opening sitar soundscape dramatically sets the song in the East. In so doing it foregrounds the narrator's desire to be viewed as independent of a more conservative mainstream American society. At the same time, the song enacts many of the traditional power hierarchies involved in determining and asserting one's identity through its superficial representation of the Other (the technological fakery of the sitar sound described earlier is crucial to this). Laderman summarizes this ideological framework as "freedom to roam for the privileged white male; mobility and opportunism; and glorified individuality and conquest."[23] His discussion of the "freedom to roam" also points toward theories of tourism as a way to understand the meaning of the Quest, a topic I will return to towards the end of this chapter.

Still, unlike classic films such as *Easy Rider* (1969), where two white men set out in search for "America" (and by extension, themselves), "Wherever I May Roam" does not quite represent the Quest, even if it is about the Journey. The distinction is subtle, but the sense that the song's narrator asserts an identity rather than experiences its development seems clear. For instance, the narrator frequently describes a relatively stable sense of self in the verse lyrics rather than describing himself in the midst of a Journey:

> ... And my ties are severed clean
> The less I have the more I gain
> Off the beaten path I reign.

In other words, the Journey (or, in the case of the song's narrator, many tours) has already created his identity. Moreover, the final presentation of the song's chorus includes an extension that shifts the chorus progression suddenly to a power chord on C, the sixth scale degree. The move to C propels the music into yet another location where the narrator's sense of self can be asserted. It is also the chorus' final opportunity to present itself as something more than just a harmonic extension of the prechorus or the anticipation of the powerful Phrygian riff. The lyrics in the extension, quoted in the epigraph of this chapter, insert a specifically transcendent quality into the narrator's vision through their imagery of a tombstone inscription. As these lyrics spin out, the music slowly descends from the C through power chords on B and B♭ before a palm-muted Low E-based flourish conclusively returns everything to the affective world of the Phrygian theme. The appearance of the riff at this point bookends the song, at once reaffirming the sentiments of self-reliant roaming that have carried the song lyrically, as well as beginning the process of ending the song.

Ethnicity Roaming

At this point, I return to a question about "Wherever I May Roam" raised earlier, namely "how did the Road get to the East?" How do we know in this song where we "are?" The relationship between place and identity provides a way into understanding this kind of transformation. The concept of place represents more than the sum of its parts: it usually points to things larger and more symbolic than any physical manifestation of a particular location. Writing about American authors in Paris during the first half of the twentieth century, J. Gerald Kennedy notes how "the uniqueness or difference assumed [about a place] resides not in the material configuration of streets, buildings, trees, or rivers but in an *idea* of place already embodied in consciousness and shaped by cultural forces (art, literature, advertising, journalism), as well as personal fantasy."[24] What is in play, then, is perception, and the dialectic between the positions of an insider and an outsider. The experience of a foreign place calls up subconscious images of the self related to one's original or usual place, and our perception of that foreign place depends very much on how much our insider/outsider status shapes up. Our experience of place does not depend so much on specific geographical features (or geocultural knowledge) as much as it depends on experiential associations. Crucially, however, our understandings of most geographical or ethnographical places need not be based on *firsthand* experiences with them. In fact, most of our experiences with foreign places are not based on any significant firsthand experience. This idea is brought powerfully into focus by contemporary mass media, which relies on bursts of representation designed to convey entire sets of cultural images (that is, entire "places") or, as in the case of advertising, consumer products.

Yet, as George Lipsitz points out, negotiations of place contain intrinsically complex negotiations of political and economic influence. In the postindustrial era, experiences of *displacement* can be, and often are, just as widespread as traditional confirmations of *place-ment*. Lipsitz borrows the phrase *kalfou danjere* ("dangerous crossroads") to conceptualize the mutable relationships between popular music and place, which "transform—but do not erase—attachments to place."[25] While contemporary understandings of place continue to retain some of the contradictory elements carried forward from centuries of racism and colonialism, they also engender new cultural and political energies that are based on new geopolitical and economic realities. In this, Lipsitz argues, place has become "the constitutive problem of the postindustrial era" where the " 'popular' has become a dangerous crossroads, an intersection between the undeniable saturation of commercial culture ... and the emergence of a new public sphere that uses the circuits of commodity production and circulation to envision and activate new social relations."[26]

Lipsitz's work focuses primarily on how the experiences of place have been expressed by various musicians from around the world and from within minority communities in the United States. The multilayered negotiations of place undertaken by those musicians are directed toward the search for collective solutions to problems of global significance, and they deploy the transnational possibilities of place to broaden their critiques. Timothy Taylor's work on the use of so-called "world music" in Western television ads, on the other hand, examines how Western ad agencies have tapped into the commercial visibility of the world music market and incorporate musical styles from outside the West in their ads as signifiers of place for audiences.[27] Taylor's larger project explores new meanings associated with the representation of an elite social/business class through the use of non-Western musics. Whereas the sonic representation of business success could previously be expressed via the prestige of the classical music canon, the current cultural fixation on the benefits of globalism seem to require a different musical accompaniment.[28] Taylor demonstrates how ad agencies create links between globalist business needs and images of successfully attained personal subjectivity, uniformly wrapped in the sounds of world music. Limited typically to thirty seconds, though, ad agency music departments cannot rely on musical largesse to get their point across. Rather, the music for ads selling images of global business and personal success must work almost instantaneously to establish an image in the viewers' minds of some "place." In the case of contemporary business advertising strategies, moreover, that place is usually expanded to encompass the entire world, all of which can be represented in the minds of the audience through thirty seconds of non-Western music. Such music may or may not be from a real tradition somewhere, but its purpose is simply to sound "other." Importantly, this process of representation removes any cultural context so as to create the illusion of infinite timelessness and a kind of global omniscience.

Significantly, however, the music heard in these ads can best be described as a presentation of *timbres* because timbres easily encode a lot of musical information and meaning in a short amount of time. As I discussed with the opening sitar sound in "Wherever I May Roam," the very timbre of that instrument provided much of the information about where we were, and, consequently, how we were supposed to respond. In advertising, it is also the element of timbre that allows the representational process to require no more than a mere thirty seconds. Audiences for modern ads do not require any more time to figure out the place being represented because, according to Taylor, they do not generally rely on a desire for specificity. In other words, they do not wonder: "Is the music in this ad trying to represent western Africa or northern Borneo?" And, as in other examples that construct an image of a location, viewers automatically expand the short hints to include any number of supporting images and details. Thus, small hints of place expand in the listener's mind to become more detailed experiences based on larger sets of collective memory. In many ways, then, this is how we know where we "are."

In the present context, the vagaries of place explain why the opening sitar-based texture of "Wherever I May Roam" can be so short and, moreover, never need return in the course of the song: further authentic presentation simply is not necessary to establish the narrative locale, even if that locale remains largely unspecific. The varied cultural associations and collective memories of the sitar's meaning present in Western society (learned through centuries of deployment, and even more so during the period of mass-mediated recording) are so ingrained that we need only a few seconds of timbre to establish an entire ethnogeographic setting. In this way, "the East" functions according to what Kennedy calls an "encoded landscape," with the sitar serving as a kind of ethnomusical shorthand.[29]

Such a transformation is possible because, like the global images created by advertising agencies, the sitar sound in "Wherever I May Roam" has become a commodity, reified into an image in the way all commodities are under late capitalism. If the sitar can be a commodity, then it must also be consumed in some fashion. Yet, as cultural theorist Frederic Jameson notes, consumption is less about the thing itself than "its abstract idea, capable of the libidinal investments ingeniously arrayed for us by advertising."[30] We hear the sound of the sitar and understand the implication of its presence only because we have heard it before. In a sense, the sitar in this instance operates as a simulacrum: a reproduction of a "copy" for which there is no original. The copy in this case is the sitar sound itself, but its reproduction via Metallica's use of it in "Wherever I May Roam" is the reproduction of its sign—its signification—in contemporary American culture. Like the "world music" created for ads, the sitar sound is also "hyperreal" in the sense theorized by Jean Baudrillard.[31] There is no original because as listeners we depend on a wide set of expectations and meanings *that we have already experienced* to create the locale of the song instead of any "authentic" set of knowledge.

Synthesizer and sampling technology stands as the most visible manifestation of such manufacturable potentialities. Paul Théberge encompasses the complex breadth of that potential with the phrase "any sound you can imagine." Speaking specifically about the availability of ethnic sounds to modern musicians, he notes "[C]ontemporary music-making demands that any musical sound be as available as any other; technological reproduction guarantees availability and, in so doing, contributes to the increasing commodification and industrialization of world music culture."[32] Moreover, Théberge sees the combination of sound developers/creators/scavengers with marketing techniques that position those sounds as exotic and "other" as playing a significant role in the cultural meaning and power dynamic of this process.

Even though there may not be an original, instances of exotic music are nonetheless historically situated, and those meanings we have already experienced have histories as well. For example, the particular social undercurrents that helped to transform "rock 'n' roll" into "rock" during the mid-1960s also introduced a shift in the meaning of the sitar. Sixties rock musicians particularly used the sitar sound as an expression of selfhood within a specific cultural perspective. Jonathan Bellman argues that those musicians' desires for experimentation with cultural otherness went hand-in-hand with their desire to expand the sonic possibilities of rock music generally.[33] In other words, the expansion of textural possibilities in rock via the technological importance of the recording studio carried with it the cultural importance (and technical ability) to construct images of non-Western cultures. Most of these broader representations are specifically Indian though, and they rely prominently on the sound of the sitar for their distinctiveness. This makes reasonable sense given the fact that all of the experimenters Bellman identifies were British and, thus, because of the much greater visibility of Indian communities in Great Britain, would have been somewhat familiar with Indian musical styles. Still, rock musicians approached the incorporation of exotic Indian sounds from a number of different vantage points: The Yardbirds and The Rolling Stones tried it in the spirit of sonic experimentation, separate from any exotic lyrical content; George Harrison's sitar-based music eventually became part of a significant affinity for Indian philosophies, even if the use of the sitar on the Beatles' first Indian song, "Norwegian Wood" (1966), is largely a special effect in an otherwise Dylan-esque folk song; Ray Davies of the Kinks, whom Bellman argues was the first of the 1960s rock musicians to record sitar-aided rock music, uses the instrument in "See My Friends" (1965) to express a sense of the inexpressible (in that case it was Davies's personal crisis about his sexuality), but that song also avoids exotic or mystical imagery in the lyrics.

By the late 1960s the codes of exotic musical otherness in rock, led by the sound of a sitar, had become one component in a series of cultural connections that also included Transcendental Meditation (TM) and hallucinogenic drugs such as LSD. Harrison and the rest of the Beatles may have eventually worked to distance themselves publicly from the LSD portion of those connections, but only in the sense that they then argued for TM as the natural progression in a mature path to elevated consciousness.[34] Musically, all of these associations came crashing together in the form of The Moody Blues' *In Search of the Lost Chord*. That album, released in 1968, represents for Bellman the point at which the mystical infinite, personal journeys of consciousness, and Indian musical elements solidified into a mass of cliché.[35] Whereas the relative unfamiliarity of instruments like the sitar had provided the songs of 1965–1967 with their sense of the slightly forbidden, the aesthetic of *In Search of the Lost Chord* now totally depended on the connections between drugs, meditation, and India.[36] Moreover, this transformation of the sitar into a cliché has important ramifications for an understanding of place. According to Bellman, the consequence of *In Search of the Lost Chord* for subsequent references in popular music has been to "[remind] us more of *us thinking about* the Eternal Orient rather than the Orient itself."[37] In other words, following the period of "Raga Rock," exotic sounds in popular music have often referred to and evoked *earlier homegrown exotica.*

Redefining Anywhere

The element of timbre also enables me to use the analytical term "Phrygian mode" to describe the main riff in "Wherever I May Roam," one that is first presented via the unique timbral markings of the sitar. Terms such as "Phrygian" are by no means disinterested but instead form part of a specific analytic discourse and signal certain desired meanings on the part of the interpreter.[38] In much the same way that notational transcription speaks to a particular understanding of how music "works," the use of analytic terminology can ignore the question of context and, at its worst, carry with it covert strategies of validation. David Brackett warns:

> … if we use musicological discourse to describe the details of a piece of music, we must recognize that the metalanguage of music analysis is not transparent, but that it is a medium that comes with its own ideological and aesthetic baggage which will affect what we can say.[39]

The issue of unquestioned assumptions both about how music works and how it ought to be analyzed is particularly evident as the discipline of music theory has turned toward popular music. While it is not my intention to wholly reopen the debate about analysis and analytical subject, I do want to point out that the debates regarding the appropriate fit between analytical terminologies developed for art musics and their application to popular musics still overlook an important issue: how the particular use of quasi-scientific terminology affects the presentation of a piece of music. For example, in the field of metal guitar pedagogy, established during the 1980s through popular magazines such as *Guitar for the Practicing Musician* and *Guitar World*, modal terminology operates explicitly to position the virtuosity of metal guitar as distinctly studied and learned. Given metal's somewhat controversial *musical* standing among cultural gatekeepers, the discussion of metal virtuosity in terms borrowed from "real" music theory serves as one defense against the perception of metal as mere "noise." However, the use of analytical terminology in metal guitar magazines is not simply proof that metal songs can be harmonically complex.[40] Indeed, the very use of that analytical terminology to discuss metal songs also demonstrates the powerful cultural currency of the analytical terminology itself. My overarching point in this chapter has been to investigate the tensions between musical constructions of Self and Other in a song by

Metallica, and I have been describing this tension in terms of "Phrygian" as an analytical bridge linking the two. How does that label influence our understanding of the Self half of the equation? In other words, what is meant when we say that the Phrygian sound marks an important part of the narrator's selfhood?[41] How well does that term apply, and how does it shape any exoticist goings-on in "Wherever I May Roam?" While much can be revealed about the music by describing it in terms of the Phrygian, what kinds of musical gestures might be overlooked by that term, particularly when it is applied to heavy metal?

> Sometimes it's a real headache. Sometimes you just call certain notes passing tones and ignore them. Sometimes you follow each individual chord as closely as possible … When it comes to chromatic stuff, the minor pentatonic just seems to work. My solos would be quite different if I were playing over straight major progressions.
>
> **Metallica guitarist Kirk Hammett, on writing guitar solos over half-step-based chord progressions**[42]

The term "Phrygian" did not appear in music treatises until the beginning of the sixteenth century, when theorists began to try to classify polyphonic music. Until that time thinkers about music had used a four-point classification system which organized each mode according to its final and range. The basic musical material for the classification system was monophonic chant, and chants with a final on E were placed in the Deuterus category. As part of the larger Humanist project, the Greek names for the modes were reapplied (incorrectly as it turns out), and the modes came to be described in terms of discrete affect. Usually, the Phrygian mode was most often described as suitable for expression of anger and songs about war. Heinrich Glarean, writing in the 1540s, differed somewhat, pointing to the mode's initial half-step as reinforcing his judgment of the Phrygian's suitability for depicting "the sorrowful and the divine, such as threnodies, laments, and burials."[43] Though modal characterizations could certainly be specific with respect to affect, any explicitly exotic description of the Phrygian sound is absent from all of these classifications.[44]

Like all the old modes, Phrygian was gradually absorbed by an emerging major/minor tonal system during the seventeenth century.[45] In the case of the Phrygian mode, the Neapolitan chord mediated the idiosyncratic expressive mechanisms of the old mode for inclusion in a system of functional harmony. In this way, the tonic-supertonic relationship of Phrygian, its most salient characteristic, was often tempered by the insertion of an

Figure 4.3 Giacomo Carissimi, *Jephte* (1650), mm. 289–292.

intermediary dominant chord between the supertonic and the tonic. Figure 4.3 illustrates a typical use of the Neapolitan chord, as found in Giacomo Carissimi's oratorio *Jephte* (1650), usually considered the piece that put the Neapolitan chord on the harmonic map.

Generally speaking, the Neapolitan chord became the mechanism by which composers could exploit the expressive characteristic of the Phrygian half-step. Most significant in the centuries that followed, however, is the history of Phrygian as but one of the many musical representations of the exotic in eighteenth- and nineteenth-century classical music. Indeed, from the use of Janissary instruments to the plaintive sounds of the Spanish guitar, the assimilation of many different non-Western musical characteristics was an important feature of Western art music. The Phrygian sound is no exception, and such instances of musical exoticism occur at the heart of roughly a 200-year shift in the fundamental use of the Phrygian sound. What was once a unique-sounding mode within a fairly consistent musical grammar, and lacking much exotic significance by itself, became a sound that, via the larger historical processes of Orientalism and changing Western musical aesthetics, has become virtually equated with the non-Western world in the minds of Western musicians and audiences. The continued influence of Orientalist and other exotic codes, particularly in nineteenth-century opera, and the appropriations of codes such as the Phrygian mode by Tin Pan Alley in the first half of the twentieth century, remains the most important musical means for recognizing the East today.

During the modern era the Phrygian mode has offered Western ears a means of constructing a vast sense of the Other in regards to both time and space. Its use at the beginning of Giuseppe Verdi's opera *Aïda* (1871) to identify the ceremonial actions of an ancient and mysterious Egyptian society stands as but one example of this. Indeed, throughout the history of opera the purpose behind creating a musical Other has ranged from depictions of that Other as a violent threat to representations of it as the source of tempting pleasure. Moreover, composers have found the mode adaptable for creating soundscapes to represent all sorts of non-Western settings, as it can move easily through ancient Egypt, India, as well as a nonspecific pan-Arabic identity.[46] However, in popular music of the second half of the twentieth century there is an important division in the deployment of non-Western sounds like the Phrygian that has a great impact on how we understand that material in the first place. I have already mentioned how 1960s rock musicians initially approached the incorporation of the sitar from a variety of perspectives. Bellman's argument that the effects contributed by the sitar could be part of a number of different moods means that we must pay attention to how individual instances of the sitar contribute to a range of potential exoticist uses. As he pointed out, the sitar music in "Norwegian Wood" is not nearly of the same kind of exoticism as that found in *In Search of the Lost Chord*.

A similar care should also be taken when looking at how "Phrygian" music operates in popular song. At this point, therefore, I want to stress the difference between the use of the Phrygian mode in songs to augment, or reinforce exotic (or at least exotically topical) lyrical content and its use in songs without particularly exotic lyrical imagery. It may be perfectly reasonable to apply the label Phrygian to both categories, but to do so without taking into account the surrounding musical or lyrical context means we ignore and efface meaningful elements and important differences across individual songs. The Cure's "Killing an Arab" (1979), for example, retells the central moment in Albert Camus's famous novel, *L'Étranger* from 1942. It does so through the explicit use of the Phrygian mode at the opening and closing of the song (modified by an augmented second between scale degrees 3 and 4 as in the bridge section of "Wherever I May Roam"). Cymbal crashes announce each phrase of the Phrygian music, and we know we are in a non-Western setting because the cymbal crashes are not supported by bass drum hits (as they would be if we were still in the land of Western rock music). The cymbal crashes also allow the listener to register and take in each phrase of the Phrygian music, as successive phrases not only demonstrate their general Phrygian-ness but also reemphasize the overall Otherness of the music.

While the lyrics used by The Cure are not the sort of mystically transcendental poetry found some ten years earlier in *In Search of the Lost Chord*, they nevertheless describe events that take place in a non-Western setting and involve, by the very title alone, a non-Western Other. Ellie Hisama argues in her study of this song that The Cure seems aware of the Orientalist politics of Camus's book, and the rest of the song is involved with negotiating the relationship between the narrator and the nameless Arab victim (a negotiation absent from the book).[47] The use of some kind of exoticist musical trapping is by no means surprising in "Killing an Arab" even though The Cure could have chosen anything to represent the setting. Indeed, it is so unremarkable that it seems natural to us that a song about an Arab should be accompanied by stereotypical musical devices that have long signaled pan-Arab settings to Western audiences. As such, The Cure's use of the Phrygian sound serves some basic need for "Arabic"-sounding music to accompany the lyrics. Significantly, the lack of these musical gestures in other songs by The Cure (anything remotely Phrygian) matters a great deal for the meaning of this particular example of the Phrygian in popular song. There are plenty of strange and esoteric lyrics in the group's *oeuvre*, but the band is better known for presenting those lyrics in a gloomy, diatonic minor and synthesizer-driven manner. In other words, the Phrygian sound operates in "Killing an Arab" as the most obvious kind of set dressing or prop, a musical tool used solely to provide a distinctive aural accompaniment to a song about an Arab, but never allowed to become a consistent part of the band's long-term artistic identity.[48]

In heavy metal the sound of Phrygian is not typically wrapped in a non-Western culture; rather, it is wrapped in a distorted electric guitar timbre with much broader uses than representing the exotic. Still, the use of the Phrygian sound in metal songs to accompany lyrics set outside contemporary Western society can operate in the same way as for other styles of pop music. For example, the main riff in Iron Maiden's "Powerslave" (1984) employs a distinct occurrence of the Phrygian dominant (with its characteristic augmented second played as a turn) as a signal for the mystical power of ancient Egypt and the God of the Dead, Osiris. In this song, the Phrygian sound functions very much like that heard in "Killing an Arab," as a sonic backdrop that is ultimately not unexpected. At the same time, "Powerslave" demonstrates how the topic of ancient Egypt can be made to sound exotic by virtue of the fact that the practice of exoticism always renders its subjects as timeless and unchanging. Thus, anything having to do with "Egypt" is thus always exotic in the traditional sense.

However, *ancient* Egypt also functions here as part of a familiar range of imagery in metal lyrics that explores power through the occult and other precapitalist forms of mysticism, the Book of Revelation, the occult, horror, war, and so on. Certainly one could argue for such topics as perhaps exotic compared to the general imagery found in most other popular music styles, but by themselves these kinds of images have nothing to do with exoticism, *per se*, and are instead linked with broader philosophical explorations of life, death, and power. Mercyful Fate's "Curse of the Pharaohs" (1983), for instance, also deals with ancient Egyptian imagery, but the music lacks any distinctively exotic sounds like those heard in "Powerslave" and relies instead on wide-ranging chromaticism and lead singer King Diamond's piercing falsetto to project the idea of the pharaoh's power. The appearance of a stereotypical Phrygian backdrop in "Powerslave" is therefore double-edged: unsurprising because the lyrics are, after all, about some idea of "Egypt," but remarkable because that clichéd soundscape is not universal within the context of other metal songs dealing with similar imagery.[49]

In order to examine how the notion of "Phrygian" operates in "Wherever I May Roam," it will be helpful to expand my scope and look briefly at other riffs by Metallica that carry with them some type of "Phrygian-ness." While there are a number of songs in which the harmonic material of a riff relies on the half-step between scale degrees 1 and ♭2 for rhetorical power, many of those riffs also suggest that, beyond this relationship, the analytical label Phrygian should be applied with caution.[50] As I will argue, the 1/♭2 relationship only partially indicates the larger presence of the Phrygian mode in metal, and, more importantly, there are multiple kinds of 1/♭2 relationships that cannot be adequately encompassed in a strictly linear form of analysis. In particular, I want to propose hearing the relationship between 1 and ♭2 in terms of a phenomenology between the most common 1/♭2 pair in heavy metal: the pitches E and F. Though I am not interested in doing away with the Phrygian label as an analytical concept, I do want to concentrate on some characteristics of performance and composition surrounding those two pitches that fundamentally inform the creation of affect, as well as take into account the essential fact of these riffs' guitar-based realization. Doing so attempts to hold multiple analytic strategies in tension in order to provide a fuller picture of the musical and generic context surrounding the main riff for "Wherever I May Roam."

In those riffs featuring significant harmonic motion through chords other than 1 or ♭2—such as 7, 3, or 4—the Phrygian label can be applied with some degree of confidence.[51] Though the mere label should not be the ultimate goal of the analysis, in these cases there is simply more material with which to get a sense of the particular musical contour being articulated by the riff. For instance, the bridge section from "Creeping Death" moves deliberately through 7 and 3, two important pitches defining the contour of the Phrygian mode (see Figure 4.4).[52]

The bridge section in "(Welcome Home) Sanitarium" (from *Master of Puppets*) also moves through more than just 1 and ♭2, and even concludes its harmonic cycle with a basic V–I cadential gesture (see Figure 4.5).

Figure 4.4 "Creeping Death," bridge section.

Figure 4.5 "(Welcome Home) Sanitarium," bridge section.

Figure 4.6 "And Justice for All," chorus.

Figure 4.7 "To Live Is to Die," main riff.

Using broad whole-note power chords, the chorus music in "And Justice for All" dramatically accents the consistent return to Low E with a deliberate punch from Low F (see Figure 4.6).

Finally, the main riff in "To Live Is to Die" grinds through a similar harmonic space as the other examples but does so with F# as the root (the others had all been based on Low E) (see Figure 4.7).

In all of these riffs the harmonic motion clearly visits more scale degrees than just the 1 and ♭2. While scale degrees 7 and 3 provide important identifying markers for the Phrygian mode, only in the example from "Creeping Death" does the Phrygian mode set the stage for lyrics broaching any kind of quasi-Eastern theme. Specifically, the apocalyptic imagery in "Creeping Death" revels in scenes of wrathful vengeance from the Old Testament, a setting distant from the modern West not only geographically but temporally as well. In every other case outlined above, though, the use of the Phrygian mode does not accompany exoticist themes. The bridge music in "Sanitarium," for example, is a pointed departure away from the E natural minor basis of the rest of the song and accompanies lyrics describing the state of mind of a patient in a mental hospital. "And Justice for All," like most of the songs on ...*And Justice for All*, deals with the topic of control and independence. In this case, the lyrics focus on the controlling power created through the ties between large corporations and government. Decrying the disappearance of justice, phrases such as "justice is gone" and "pulling your strings, justice is done" are given pronounced emphasis by the strong B–F–E motion described earlier. "To Live Is to Die," also from ...*And Justice for All* is an interesting example because it is a long instrumental song in the style of "Orion" (from *Master of Puppets*) and "Call of Ktulu" (from *Ride the Lightning*). As I pointed out in Chapter 3, this group of instrumental songs holds an important place in the discussion of the ideological implications of musical complexity in popular music and does not have anything to do with exoticist imagery.

Riffs from several other songs may appear to follow the same harmonic ambitus but nevertheless resist an uncomplicated Phrygian description and its implications for selfhood. While this group of riffs certainly features a prominent 1/♭2 relationship, describing them as straightforward instances of the Phrygian mode overlooks certain key elements of those riffs' construction and effect. Indeed, we must keep in mind the idea that, although the 1/♭2 relationship is crucial to the Phrygian mode, not all 1/♭2 relationships are the same in metal, and not all are "Phrygian." As I mentioned above, it is not at all uncommon for the ♭2 component of that relationship to serve primarily as a half-step-based rhetorical counterpoint to the 1 in much the same way a V chord relates to a I chord in standard tonal practice. In those cases the ♭2 does not merely decorate the 1, but by itself neither does it clearly proscribe a mode. The opening riff to "Damage, Inc." (from *Master of Puppets*), where four quarter-note hits on Low E are followed by a set of triplet-eighth-notes on Low F, makes this clear (see Figure 4.8). The triplets' rhythmic momentum pushes the riff to the next downbeat at the same time as the Low F pulls the harmonic motion ever so slightly away from the autonomy of the E and creates a desire for its return. While that kind of tension is certainly characteristic of the Phrygian mode, to describe this particular riff as Phrygian solely on the basis of the Low E–Low F pairing overlooks equally important factors as the stark percussive rhythms of the Low E.

Figure 4.8 "Damage, Inc.," opening riff, excerpt.

Figure 4.9 "Dyers Eve," opening riff.

Figure 4.10 "And Justice for All," verse riff excerpt.

The opening riff to "Dyers Eve" (from ...*And Justice for All*) features this same general idea, except in this instance the E and F share much of the same rhythmic emphasis, while the uneven metric scheme drives the entire riff forward (see Figure 4.9). The riff's movement up to G, the third scale degree, would seem to enable a fairly clear Phrygian label, but the G is far less important to the overall sound of the riff than the repeated Low E–Low F alternations. Much like the G that appeared as a last-second blip in the verse riff to "Whiplash," the G in "Dyers Eve" seems essentially to represent a harmonic move to "somewhere else." To be sure, were the riff to rise to F# instead of G, the rising chromaticism encompassing Low E, F, and F# would produce a very different overall effect. Nevertheless, the riff's repeated insistence on the Low E–Low F pair would still remain its most important element.

Finally, the verse riff to "And Justice for All" provides an important twist on the Low E–Low F relationship displayed in "Dyers Eve." As in that song, the single instance of Low F in the second measure of this riff colors the rhythmic actions of Low E to emphasize and reinforce the stability of the primary harmony (see Figure 4.10). Furthermore, the last measure of the riff also features a prominent B♭–A tag. While a Phrygian description is not very helpful because of those harmonies, should the presence of the B♭s, together with the presence of Low F, automatically mean we can describe this riff as Locrian?

I would argue, once again, that such a label would not be wholly appropriate and that there is another way of analyzing a riff like this one. In particular, the B♭–A tag in "And Justice for All" represents an instance of what might be called "The B♭ Question," a crucial complicating factor in the very application of modal labels to heavy metal riffs that feature a prominent E/F relationship. As in the other previous examples, where a Phrygian identification seemed questionable, the mere presence of B♭ and

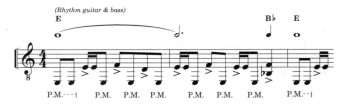

Figure 4.11 "Damage Inc.," bridge riff.

E in the same riff should not also lead directly to a Locrian conclusion. For instance, in the "And Justice for All" example I would argue that it is more important to hear the concluding B♭s primarily in connection with the E rather than as a diatonic fourth above the F in the Locrian mode. In other words, the harmonic structure of the riff fundamentally foregrounds the *tritone* between B♭ and E. Thus, although Low F functions as an important scalar component of the Locrian mode on E, the B♭ in this example is better described outside any Locrian label and instead should be heard more directly as a transgressive counterpoint to the Low E.[53] A similar situation occurs during the bridge of "Damage, Inc." (see Figure 4.11) where the guitar riff's character comes from the E–F–D–E–F–E single-note motion (always bouncing off Low E) while the B♭–E power-chord motion behind it returns the riff to its beginning.

Looking only at the single-note motion we might view this riff as a fairly clear example of the Phrygian mode. However, the B♭–E power chords at the tail end are heavily accented by the bass and drums, and these chords somewhat obscure the Phrygian "fit." In terms of scale construction and modal analysis, then, a Locrian label might at first seem warranted, but once again, the direct emphasis on the B♭–E motion itself points to a more significant relationship involving the tritone interval between those chords. Ultimately, therefore, The B♭ Question, that which involves riffs marked strongly by an E/F association but also features a specific relationship between B♭ and E, raises questions not really addressed in a strictly modal scheme. The danger of instantly labeling a riff as either Phrygian or Locrian is the same as for any kind of analytical tool: for everything that is revealed, something else is concealed. By greatly complicating any modal labeling, the B♭ Question also highlights the crucial affective dialectic between E and F as well as that between E and B♭. It highlights the specific intervals between the two pitches instead of describing them as two possible points along a scale.

Avoiding a Phrygian label in the examples above also forces us to move away from the analytical equality of pitch class and to realize that, in metal, not every E is the same. Moreover, the concept of octave equivalency also does not apply (and it is also a questionable approach to analyzing any kind of music) because the primary purpose of the abstract shorthand enabled by octave equivalency and pitch class is to reduce pitches (and chords) to a linear sequence that can then be easily labeled according to some kind of standard analytical schema. Simply put, pitches in different octaves are not equivalent in metal. For example, a distorted power chord on Low E resides in a particular affective space, one very much determined also by timbre and rhythm. As the lowest-pitched power chord possible on a six-string guitar, the Low E chord carries with it certain meanings that cannot simply be transposed to higher octaves.[54] When asked if "there could be a Metallica" if guitars did not have a sixth string, Metallica's lead guitarist Kirk Hammett chuckled and replied, "No, I don't think so. If there were no key of E, no key of F#, or no E–A# [sic] melodic configuration, I don't think we'd be around."[55] Additionally, as was illustrated with the riffs above, this lowest pitch is often the site for significant rhythmic action in which Low E serves as a means to an end: a percussive rhythm on a very low pitch.[56]

Range contributes an important analytical perspective because a power chord on the E an octave above Low E retains a different affect. The switch from the Low E register to what might be called the "seventh fret" octave (one octave higher than Low E), for example, frequently has a tension-building effect or serves as a point of rhetorical climax.[57] Moreover, as I have already mentioned, riffs based on Low E often have a significant rhythmic purpose. Following from this, the affective relationship between Low E and Low F must also be different from the same half-step pair in a higher octave. The difference can be heard, for instance, in the middle section of "Creeping Death" where the bright power chords of the seventh fret E and F offer a clear sense of melodic motion against the more rhythmically active Low E eighth-notes providing the transition between the melody points (refer to Figure 4.4).

The fundamental half-step basis of the guitar provides yet another way of thinking about the main theme in "Wherever I May Roam" and other riffs with a prominent E–F or 1/♭2 component. While the seventh fret 1/♭2 of "Wherever I May Roam" is easily heard as part of a larger melodic sequence, the song's verse music uses that pair in quite a different way. During the verses the music slides up one half-step from the stability of the opening Low E power chord to Low F before slipping back to Low E. The temporal space between these chords (each one held for two measures) creates a kind of self-contained world around each of them, and the change from one world to the next also foregrounds the essential half-step relationship between the two chords.[58] The stab up to B♭ following these movements retrospectively emphasizes the narrow half-step range of the E and F, creating a harmonic jolt not only through the sudden appearance of the tritone interval, but also from the relatively large leap of six half-steps.[59] Furthermore, the "slam" down to Low F at the start of the prechorus, following a short section of the main theme, demonstrates another instance where the octave location of a harmony plays a significant role in the interpretation of that harmony and its surrounding music. In that instance the Low F functions as something of rhythmic vamp under the vocals, followed shortly by a similar technique a half-step lower on Low E. Once again, the choice to land on an F is important for the articulation of the tension between F and E, but the choice to land on *Low* F determines much about the character of the specific chord sequence in the prechorus. Were the prechorus to begin on the seventh fret F, the F and E power chords would give the lyrics a strident, almost shrill feeling instead of the sense of confidence and self-assurance presented through the use of the lower octave.

So, how does the word "Phrygian" describe the main riff in "Wherever I May Roam?" More significantly, how is the linkage of the contour of the riff to notions of Orientalism, collective memory, and self/other identity construction effected by that musical-analytical label? I have discussed how the Phrygian sound has easily represented Others in Western music for hundreds of years, but my point, in the somewhat exhaustive discussion above, has been to investigate just how that bridge characterizes the sense of Self-ness in "Wherever I May Roam." While the exact label of Phrygian, at first glance a great equalizer, may not be the most useful way of linking the two, it is apparent that the characteristics of the main theme in "Wherever I May Roam" do nevertheless demonstrate a clear instance of the scalar identity that marks the Phrygian mode. The fact that the riff is comprised of a single-note melody operating above a Low E pedal rather than power chords also factors significantly in this determination. Indeed, the initial sitar timbre, with all of its cultural encodings, provides much of the impetus for hearing this theme as "Phrygian." Were the pitches of the main theme to reside in a lower octave, or be made up of power chords in the Low E octave, the relationship between E and F in the riff would sound closer to those of other riffs which use Low E as a rhythmic device, and the Phrygian label would be less sure (or at least less useful). Because of the way the theme is first presented, though, we carry the sitar/Phrygian association with us during subsequent appearances of the theme.

In order to consider a characteristic like Phrygian, the crucial dialectic in metal between the pitches E and F in any number of expressive registers must be considered. Those relationships often operate in ways not easily labeled according to traditional modal schema, and the theoretical concept of octave equivalence obscures this kind of registral specificity. Moreover, within the larger style of heavy metal (evidenced here in terms of Metallica) the musical details typically associated with the Phrygian mode carry with them several complicating caveats that are not typically found in other styles of popular music. Those caveats—expressive register, the significance of specific intervals, the rhythmic potential of repeated pitches—ultimately help to explain more than what might be revealed by a simple modal categorization.

Musical Tourism

As a piece of late twentieth-century culture, "Wherever I May Roam" functions as a way of seeing the world and operating within it from the particular vantage point of a modern Western self. The fundamental quality of "roaming" serves as the lens through which many other issues arise, and it is this notion of roaming that crystallizes many of the more directly political implications for meaning in this song. The ability of the song's narrator to roam, and Metallica's ability to insert themselves into a tradition of roaming by way of the American Road, is aligned here with the values of personal independence and free will, and resonates with the broader implications of tourism, specifically musical tourism. Even though images and sounds representative of the non-West have long been significant artistic tropes, in the postcolonial, postindustrial, and mass-mediated world of today nearly everyone has the cultural power to experience the adventure and identity-forming possibilities of tourism. In this world, almost anything can be manufactured (and therefore experienced), thus loosening the specificity that once guided interactions with the larger world. Moreover, cultural theorists Scott Lash and John Urry see this moment as specifically posttourist because "whether [people] are literally mobile or only experience simulated mobility through the incredible fluidity of multiple signs and electronic images," the distinction between tourism and "normal" life has largely disappeared.[60]

Posttourism has at its core the desire for the Journey, and the Journey encountered in "Wherever I May Roam" seems clearly to demonstrate the practice of Orientalist depiction. The song does not reflect a deep or sincere approach to any Eastern music, but instead constructs an Eastern soundscape through the technological tools of a posttourist society. The details of its opening musical atmosphere are not the product of studied interaction with Indian sitar music, nor does the song as a whole reflect any significant philosophical interest in a foreign culture. Indeed, the deafening silence of commentary (or even acknowledgment) on the creation of a specifically Eastern setting for the song's exploration of beliefs

crucial to American cultural history powerfully illustrates the very invisibility of much of the critical discourse on Orientalism to wider audiences.
In the journalistic coverage of the song, and in the fan discussions I have
come across, not once has the opening sitar been remarked upon, beyond
an occasional recognition of its existence. It would seem, therefore, that
the unremarkable presence of the sitar sound indicates that "Wherever
I May Roam" introduces nothing new (or at least nothing controversial)
in the history of musical depiction. One explanation for this possibility
might be that the song does not really colonize new territory insofar as
the territory, has, in effect, already been "colonized" by years of pop music
familiarity, even if the sitar in "Wherever I May Roam" stands alone in
Metallica's repertory. Indeed, Metallica occupies a well-established position of control over whatever "others" happen to be represented within.
Musical fragments representing non-Western locales and identities, such
as that heard in "Wherever I May Roam," may be somewhat troublesome,
but as Susan Fast asks, "would having longer, more developed examples
of music or more of the structural elements intact change the situation?"[61]
Should we read the development of George Harrison's long history with
Indian music or Robert Plant's knowledge of North African culture any
differently? In other words, what is the relationship between sincerity and
imitation? Fast's answer to the first of these questions is "no," for she recognizes the still-present filtering of those cultures through the various cultural and commercial mechanisms of the West. Furthermore, she notes,
"the emergence of a 'foreign' musical element in an otherwise Western
frame points very specifically to difference, to a separate identity, in a way
that cannot be mistaken" by Western audiences.[62] Moreover, ascribing to
the belief that some Western musicians have, through study and developed
references, "earned" their ability to work with non-Western musics con-
veniently removes the need to examine the intrinsic power relations that
enable those very interactions.

However, in debating the ways musicians interact with images and
sounds from outside the West, it is easy to structure arguments around the
assumption that those musicians uproot their material from some position
of cultural purity or unsullied "naturalness." To proceed in this fashion,
though, means ignoring the ways in which non-Western musicians themselves participate in a complex arrangement of cultural expression and
commercial action. Andrew Goodwin and Joe Gore have argued strenu-
ously that "[T]he 'purity' of third world music must always be questioned"
because of the "dangerous ideological assumptions about the 'authenticity'
of non-Western cultures" that can easily overwhelm questions of cultural
imperialism.[63] While the sounds available to the technological musical

tourist are often only representative of "traditional" instruments, those same sounds have become integral parts of popular music styles that are already the result of the increased globalization of the popular music industry. Furthermore, the kinds of interplay at work in genres like World Beat illustrate the ways supposedly pure ethnic musics obtain a significant part of their meaning through their combination with recognizably Western pop and rock styles. Yet, it remains crucial to remember how the modes of production and compensation can be (and usually are) heavily tilted toward Western musicians. Indeed, collaborations between musicians like Paul Simon and Lady Blacksmith Mambazo, as Goodwin and Gore point out, are "rooted in the privileged position of Western musicians vis-à-vis the recording and publishing industries," wherein third-world musicians can easily constitute the equivalent of cheap labor.[64]

Metallica's "Wherever I May Roam" may not be a collaboration with any real non-Western musicians, or borrow much from a non-Western musical sound beyond a timbre, but the above discussion remains relevant to the task of situating both the song and the band in the history of musical exoticism in popular music. The decision to couple the lyrical subject of the American Road with such a distinctly foreign musical representation means that Metallica engage with the broad issues of who gets to represent whom. To that end, "Wherever I May Roam" demonstrates one version of the embedded cultural practices and frameworks of Orientalism, distilling a wide range of cultural signs into a single guitar riff. The technological production of the sound of that riff illustrates Metallica's cultural ability to create the sound of the world as they wish, and to insert themselves into the powerful position of the musical tourist, one that rarely accepts responsibility for addressing any real political and economic situations that enable that position. By situating an experience of the Road into an experience of the East, moreover, Metallica roam through an important set of conventions that make up a powerful statement of musical identity.

CHAPTER 5

Shape Shift, Mutiny in the Air

The Sell-Out Question and Popular Music Histories

This record and what we're doing with it—that, to me, is what Metallica are all about: exploring different things. The minute you stop exploring, then just sit down and fucking die.

Lars Ulrich, discussing *Load*[1]

Excuse me while I tend to how I feel.

James Hetfield, "Hero of the Day"

Introduction

While setting up for an interview with rock critic Kurt Loder (taped as part of a *Rockumentary* episode for MTV) in 1996, James Hetfield made a startling off-hand comment:

Hetfield: " … yeah, we got interviews up the ass tomorrow—that's the big day."

Loder: [off-camera] "Well, something to look forward to …"

Hetfield: "Oh yeah ..." [chuckles]

Loder: " ... A few more interviews." [chuckles sarcastically]

Hetfield: [pauses, looks at Loder, smiling] "More lying!"[2]

Nervous laughter follows this last bit. Loder then asks the cameraman if everything is set up and ready before beginning the interview proper with a question asking Hetfield to discuss the band's state of mind immediately after Cliff Burton's death in 1986.[3] Hetfield, Ulrich, and Hammett had covered this topic dozens of times in other interviews, and Hetfield's particular answer is not of much historical interest here. But the situation itself—the retelling, once again, of that part of the band's history—illuminates how the apparent "truth" of interviews should also be understood in terms of performance. In the above dialogue, Hetfield's last response seems so outlandish it is taken as a joke by everyone present, but the nervous laughter quickly covers up the dialogue's revelation that the rock interview is not the transparent presentation of unfettered and sincere speech as we are accustomed to believing. Rather, both Hetfield and Loder understand that multiple agendas are being worked out in this situation and both know their roles in that process. Still, one can sense how the nervous laughter betrays a dirty little secret: if the rock media operates as the central means for constructing an ideology of authenticity and sincerity around artists, it can do so only if the artists perform in ways amenable to a sincere presentation.

By the mid-1990s, Metallica appeared to be part of mainstream rock music. That visibility resulted largely from the commercial success of the *Metallica* album (1991) and the lengthy world tours undertaken from 1991 through mid-1994. The increased cultural presence of the band during the 1990s also developed in concert with a wide range of commentary by critics and fans that encourages an investigation into the rhetoric of marketing and promotion and their effect on the reception of Metallica's 1990s music. This chapter therefore concentrates on the music Metallica released during the 1990s, a decade that witnessed a number of important changes in the band's cultural status and influence, changes that were linked quite explicitly to discrete stylistic developments in the band's sound, and accompanied most vocally by accusations of "selling out." These changes begin in 1991 with the release of *Metallica* and continued right through the release of *S & M* and the Napster lawsuit in 2000.[4] A nearly unending undercurrent of controversy accompanied the band's success as Metallica's audience swelled on the massive commercial accomplishment of *Metallica*. At the same time, the band's status as "thinking-man's metal" and its position as a subcultural and underground metal icon came into question from a number of perspectives.[5]

The most visible controversy, particularly following the release of the *Load* and *Reload* albums in 1996 and 1997, indicted Metallica for selling out, and I find Metallica's experience with the selling out accusation notable because of how it twists some of the long-standing elements of that idea. Celebrated for years for its intelligent detachment and an aesthetic that eschewed more traditional images of love and sex (of the sort widely understood as "authentic" expression), Metallica became the object of intense accusatory rhetoric the moment those ideas (in whatever form) began appearing in its music. While love and sex often become topics of authenticity in rock, they can also represent powerful challenges to a kind of authenticity built around personal independence. Moreover, as is typically the case with the selling out accusation, the amount of tangible evidence of particular claims is inversely proportional to the overall furor. Indeed, while individual claims can be found (and I will point them out where applicable), the accusation is the product of more than just documented discourse. Selling out tends to operate as an unspoken frame within the discourse of authenticity, and as such selling out is less a thing unto itself than it is part of a larger set of ideas. Selling out exists largely *through* the construction of authenticity and as a kind of inverted valuation made on its behalf.

Significant, too, is the question of how Metallica's music changed, for it is in the musical details that we find important clues to the various receptions of the band's 1990s music. I spent a good deal of time in the earlier chapters explicating Metallica's approach to musical form within the context of the thrash metal style, and I emphasized how structural complexity and song length represented ways of constructing difference (artistic, political, gendered, and so forth) for the band and its fans. How Metallica altered stylistic traits of their 1980s music or subsumed them under new developments deserves attention because the debates over the meaning and value of the band's 1990s music frequently recast that 1980s aesthetic in terms traditionally (and positively) reserved for "the music itself" as that concept might be used in academic musicology. In the second part of the chapter I explore how that idea, combined with deep-seated beliefs about the naturalness of personal interiority and artistic depth, folds into the rhetorical horizons of authenticity to form one element in the accusation of selling out.

Metallica's experience with selling out represents not only the latest significant instance of the topic in popular music, but the complexity of the issue also brings together a number of issues regarding the role and status of art in the postmodern era. That audiences, critics, radio DJs, and musicians continue to struggle against the anxieties produced by the fear of selling out testifies to the continuing power of modernist means of constructing personal identity. If the postmodern era has been celebrated as one in which signs can float free from their traditional signifiers and the possibilities for meaning can be greatly expanded, why do so many people remain so worried about the trampling of the truths and ideals of authenticity in rock music? Why does the rhetoric of authenticity, particularly the historically specific kind developed in rock from the late-1960s and 1970s, persist as the fundamental criteria by which art of many social spheres is evaluated?

A major aim of this chapter will be to analyze Metallica's defense of its music, particularly of the *Load* and *Reload* albums, and to uncover the various ways authenticity could be put forth as a defense against the selling out accusation. Obviously, the band's only realistic means for presenting themselves and their new music could come via the mediation of the rock press, but their statements must always be parsed with that mediation in mind. In exploring the interchanges between Metallica and the rock press, I have tried to avoid constructing a monolithic or totalizing sense of rock journalism, and at the same time avoid suggesting an image of fans as empty containers lining up to be filled with ideologies. Indeed, it is just as apparent that fans receive what they want, need, and can creatively use from various sources of information. If the ideologies central to the rock press factor into how fans structure debates over creativity and commerce, we should not claim to see past them in an elitist sort of way. In other words, simply to dismiss the tensions aroused by authenticity as the shortsighted constructs of misguided and duped fans severely overlooks how the rhetoric of authenticity always matters in the constructions of meaning. Furthermore, it crucially overlooks the historical basis for their appeal. What can seem like a cliché to an academic scholar also functions for music fans as an important means for making sense of the world; better to inquire as to what is at stake to make such ideas attractive and important than to dismiss them forthwith. From there we can begin to understand the cultural tensions informing the selling out argument: because it matters.

Selling Out

Though the term "selling out" frequently arises in the context of popular music, it is a deceptively simple shorthand signifier for evaluating actions taken by people outside of music. Generally, a common awareness provides understanding when that term is tossed around, regardless of context: politicians sell out to special interest groups and in the process they sell out democracy; bureaucrats sell out the children by not supporting "accountability" or school vouchers; musicians sell out by appearing too close to the music industry or by appearing to conform to a pop-friendly formula and make too much money. Nevertheless, the ideas surrounding selling out are historically situated. The *Oxford English Dictionary* (*OED*) defines "to sell out" as "to betray a person or cause for gain" and cites instances of the term as far back as 1857. It is perhaps not surprising that the *OED*'s references only go back to the mid-nineteenth century because in terms of aesthetics, selling out depends heavily upon a multifaceted relationship of creativity and commerce conceived in the early years of that century for its most basic meaning. This relationship results fundamentally from a particular notion of personal interiority developed most prominently by Romantic artists and thinkers beginning in the late eighteenth century as a response to the dramatic social changes then stirring in Europe. Specifically, the decline and large-scale disappearance of the aristocratic patronage system (which had been in place for centuries) and the concomitant rise of industrial capitalism necessitated that artists of all types operate according to some kind of marketplace economics. Historian Martha Woodmansee describes this general period as "a transitional phase between the limited patronage of an aristocratic age and the democratic patronage of the marketplace" and notes throughout the arts generally the increased importance of a marketplace in altering basic understandings of art and the artist's role in society.[6] As part of this transition, Art (with a capital A) came to require elitist defensive mechanisms on the part of artists and critics designed to insulate and elevate it above the morass of commercial culture; in other words, to preserve its status as the product of real human expression. Moreover, the Romantics theorized real Art as a freestanding, harmonious, and concrete whole whose value was intrinsic, and whose qualities must be approached and appreciated through the disinterested contemplation of the observer.

In moving away from a social position characterized by the centuries-old marriage of craftsmanship and inspiration as the defining marks of the writer, eighteenth- and nineteenth-century aesthetics favored the element of inspiration *over* craftsmanship, and, as I will discuss, that particular favoritism remains with us. Two further changes followed from the redistribution of emphasis though: first, inspiration emanated from within the autonomous writer himself and was discretely explicated in terms of "original genius." While music is certainly distinct from writing, as a culturally situated art form such distinctions do not wholly cover up the similarities. Indeed, both forms share many of the same concerns regarding creation and meaning, and understanding how issues of authorship and art developed in literature can inform our understanding of them in music.[7] The belief, transferred along the chain of cultural history, that people possess a self separate from the world around them fundamentally underpins the evaluation of artists, artistic expression and as a basis for the conception of genius. In many ways, psychological interiority (what we think of as the immutable "true" version of ourselves) is tightly entangled with the politics of identity and can be used in determining our interactions with other people. Important for the current study is the role played by personal interiority in framing the existence of artistic autonomy. As much as the Romantic thinkers tried to construct an idea of Art floating free of human signification, the modern sense of self they also created fundamentally relies on contemporary political concerns that reach beyond a limited application to art. The complex topics of interiority and ever-changing notions of autonomous selfhood may extend, in some form, back into the fifteenth century, but, as I have been discussing, the version of interior autonomy created during the nineteenth century is largely the one we live with today. It is also the one that plays a crucial role in any selling-out controversy.

The second development arising from the elevation of inspiration over craftsmanship came as a new ally in defense of the concept of Art: the legal concept of copyright.[8] Because of the shackles of the marketplace, wherein authors found themselves and their work in tension with the economics of publishing and piracy, the notion of intellectual property (that is, the property of a genius's intellect) became one way of thwarting the invidious aspects of that marketplace, and, consequently, isolating and preserving certain kinds of creativity from it. Copyright extends legal status to the idea that Art is the expression of an autonomous subject, and it tries to establish some kind of one-to-one relationship between expression and author. More than that though, copyright also carves out rights to govern and control the commercial interaction of expression, to reward creators with commercial protection and remuneration. Woodmansee's investigation of these interrelations between art and the marketplace provides important illumination into the stakes of their development, and her discussion powerfully describes the continued anxieties surrounding creativity and the marketplace. Still, it was the creation and solidification of copyright law, especially during the first half of the nineteenth century (and in a form still recognizable to us at the beginning of the twenty-first century), that became one of the most important elements in the debates over the proper function of the author/creator (as distinct from the writer/craftsman). Copyright accepted the notion that expression could exist for its own sake, self-contained and separate from its creator or physical representation. At the same time, these ideas remained very much based around the idea that an author conceives of the expression and maintains intellectual property rights to it regardless of published form. Thus, if Romantic aesthetic theory wrecked the marriage of craftsmanship and inspiration, it nevertheless supplanted that marriage with another tenuous union, that between original genius and legal copyright.

Selling out functions within various discourses of authenticity, but it has developed primarily as a way to *defend* notions of authenticity and autonomy, even while it is deployed to attack certain types of music or audiences. Crucially, the rhetoric of selling out is always also the manifestation of an anxiety about music's place in a commercial society. Yet, the *OED*'s attempt at definition notwithstanding, selling out seems nevertheless to lack definitive characteristics of its own. In many ways it is a negative concept, defined *against* something rather than possessing a clear definition. In the cases of the politician, bureaucrat, or musician, invoking the rhetoric of selling out necessarily invokes some umbrella of authenticity, and serves as a strategy of valuation: the cry of selling out signals the breaking of an unspoken social ideal. Because the concept of selling out relies so much on larger structures of idealized meaning, I would extend its purpose further: the charge of selling out is not simply an outright attack on an artist; rather it is deployed to shield *everything else* from a breach in the invisible wall separating the authentic from the assaults of the inauthentic. Indeed, the struggle for what counts as "real" in the first place often dictates the stakes guiding the charge of selling out. Thus, when we say that someone has "sold out," we generally know what we are saying, but mainly in that we know what the subject is *not*.

How do these concepts enter popular culture? Or do they arise there independently for similar reasons? Are they parallel developments, or does one directly feed the other? Understanding the concept of selling out in popular music involves juggling all the issues I have merely been able to touch on so far. Moreover, tracing the lines of aesthetic belief back to Europe at the beginning of the nineteenth century may seem to take us quite a ways from anything having to do with Metallica, but I have done so with a view toward denaturalizing those ideas and processes. Autonomy, interiority, the author, copyright: each by itself has been the topic of extensive treatment, and their interrelationships have an immense amount to say about the history of Western musical culture—to say nothing of their importance in understanding Metallica's situation throughout the 1990s— but to provide notions such as musical authenticity and copyright with a history means bringing them back *into* history and back into culture.

The Language of Authenticity

Much has been made in Metallica histories about Lars Ulrich's fascination with British metal of the late 1970s and early 1980s, known as the New Wave of British Heavy Metal, or NWOBHM. His pilgrimage from California to England as a teenager in the summer of 1981 to meet the bands he avidly read about each week in *Sounds* (a British music magazine that became the journalistic champion of the NWOBHM scene) has remained one of the more enduring symbols of the band's early years. While many commentators (including Ulrich) point to that pilgrimage as a fundamental education in how Metallica's *music* would sound, we should not overlook the additional rhetorical language Ulrich received each week from the pages of *Sounds*. The articles and reviews of bands such as Diamond Head, Iron Maiden, and Tygers of Pan Tang circulated in a discourse regarding the creation of a scene, but the specific language used to promote bands and shows drew liberally from the language of musical identity echoing that used in the 1960s. Indeed, British punk rock had also appropriated the general outline of such language only a few years before the consolidation of NWOBHM. At the same time that *Sounds* rechanneled certain aesthetic tenets of earlier years, it also borrowed celebrated concepts of authenticity now attributed to punk musicians such as shock value and the concept of Do It Yourself (DIY). The type of speech found in those *Sounds* articles therefore provided Ulrich with an education on the relationship between bands and the rock press. From the beginning of Metallica's own publicity efforts, Ulrich embraced the rhetorical style and the rules of "the game" gleaned from *Sounds* and other rock criticism and acted as the primary spokesperson for the band.[9] His personal history with the NWOBHM scene in turn served to pass on that knowledge to Metallica fans. Particularly in the 1990s, as NWOBHM sounds and structures faded as a direct influence for Metallica's music, the formative position claimed for it continued to act as something of a lifeline to the band's own early career. Ulrich's occasional mention of the NWOBHM in interviews, regardless of how brief or sentimental, continued to allow for the possibility that, beneath the exterior of fame, immense wealth, massive secluded mansion, as well as traditional family responsibilities, a real, streetwise Lars Ulrich of old, founder of the most important metal band in history, could still be glimpsed.[10]

If authenticity has resilience, therefore, it is one that is learned, and an important clue to this resilience can be found in the kind of ideologies propagated via rock journalism since the 1960s and 1970s. Ultimately, artists present themselves via rock journalism according to certain rules, and crucially, it is also where they learn the rhetorical strategies to defend themselves from the accusation of selling out. From the early 1960s, critics invested rock music with a transformative power and adapted much of the core of nineteenth-century thinking about Art to it. Accompanying their pronouncements about which musics were "good" were general criteria reaching beyond the music itself that told audiences *why* it was good. For example, critics such as Ralph Gleason cast rock in distinctly revolutionary terms, seeing it as part of a larger process that broke through entrenched social barriers like race.[11] John Sinclair's White Panther party, created in late 1968 as an outgrowth of his critical writing and activism, even put forth a much more explicitly militaristic linkage between rock music and racial politics to reconstruct white masculinity in terms of "rock 'n' roll guerillas."[12] As such, rock's political potential and its status as a product of a revolutionary social movement seemed to give it real meaning in the real world.

In early 1967, *The Oracle*, an underground publication based in San Francisco, took a clear stand on the status of rock music, stating unequivocally and quite polemically that rock deserved serious, thoughtful attention. In making this pronouncement, *The Oracle* also took the notion of seriousness to be evidence of rock's status as Art. Titled simply "Some Principles," the manifesto lists nine points, all designed to foreground the revolutionary nature of rock music and culture. It bluntly asserts that "rock is a legitimate avant-garde art form, with deep roots in the music of the past," and that "far from being degenerate or decadent, rock is a regenerative and revolutionary art, offering us our first real hope for the future since August 6, 1945."[13] The manifesto draws heavily on notions of forward-thinking youthfulness and intellectualism in its characterization of rock music, even as it claims for rock direct association with the power wielded by older and established cultural forms. Like many other firebrand statements about rock, *The Oracle*'s pronouncements include a conscious communal element characterizing rock culture, and theorize it as "group participation, total experience and complete involvement."[14]

In its argument that rock was specifically a form of revolutionary Art, *The Oracle* engaged directly with legitimating rock on the "high" end of a powerful high/low dichotomy, one which had, since the beginnings of rock 'n' roll, consistently positioned that music on the "low" end. Along these same lines, rock critic Robert Cristgau argued that "popular art … achieved a vitality of both integrity and outreach that high art had unfortunately abandoned."[15] It is important to note that Cristgau's statement does not reject the high/low dichotomy in order to judge popular art's vitality. In their efforts to legitimize rock as worthy of the terms of high culture, indeed by accepting the terms of the high/low split and acting accordingly, critics gained the ability to adopt other aspects characterizing the conception of Art. Significant among these was the notion of originality and its linkage to individual expression. For Lester Bangs, originality in rock music lay at the center of its authenticity, and it was the search for the "new" that gave the rock experience a sense of transcendence.[16] In its foregrounding of originality, moreover, rock criticism quickly absorbed the related topic of progress as a resistance to formula and as a way to judge music as "good."

By adopting the high/low dichotomy to elevate and legitimize rock, critics continued a powerful modernist tradition of writing about popular music. Brandishing concepts such as originality and seriousness as legitimating strategies, the critical writing on rock produced during the 1960s and 1970s tapped into the very language and ideology that had been used for over a hundred years to demean popular music. As Charles Hamm has shown, the power of modernist writing designed to differentiate, exclude, and legitimate stems from its status as a series of largely unquestioned meta-narratives such as "mass culture," "youth," and "autonomy." Each of these concepts not only privileges one set of characteristics over others according to arbitrary criteria, but the very arbitrariness of the criteria is covered up in the process by which the narrative is constructed. In other words, the celebration of youth as a fundamental component of rock's cultural power represents, according to Hamm, "assertions and assumptions in the nature of belief systems, and therefore not requiring explication or intellectual development."[17] Moreover, Hamm's exploration of modernist meta-narratives in writing about popular music also resonates with Lawrence Levine's exhaustive discussion of the boundaries of cultural hierarchy in America in the decades surrounding the turn of the twentieth century. Regarding the supposed permanence and naturalness of a "highbrow/lowbrow" split in American culture, Levine contends instead that such distinctions operate as patterns of historical contestation and negotiation. His argument that "the primary categories of culture have been the products of ideologies which were always subject to modifications and transformations …" also helps to explain how rock critics could defend the apparently low form of popular culture that was rock music by appropriating the terms and criteria used in the production of high culture.[18] The use of modernist assumptions about the way authenticity should sound in rock, indeed the very process of applying authenticity to rock music in the first place, illustrates how, in Levine's words, "the perimeters of our cultural divisions have been permeable and shifting rather than fixed and immutable."[19]

Building on the base created in the late 1960s by the rise of FM radio, counterculture-influenced publications such as *Crawdaddy* and magazines such as *Rolling Stone* and *Spin* have continued to expound on the relationship between creativity and authenticity in rock. As these sources have been influential conveyors of popular discourse on rock music, the ideologies expressed in them become further entrenched as the most important ones to matter. In short, their overwhelming visibility typically leaves them unchallenged. As such, the rock critic's role in the mass-mediated environment of popular music becomes, according to Simon Frith, ideological more than it is commercial. Though they are employees of the magazines they write for (and their opinions can have a direct impact on the commercial success of an artist), critics, as performers of ideology, function socially as experts who guide fans toward good music and away from bad music, and define "the ideal musical experience for listeners to measure themselves against."[20] Jon Stratton argues further that it is critics' "perceived independence of the companies which legitimates their position and which, correspondingly, gives a taken-for-granted credibility to what they write or say."[21] In projecting various components of the ideology of authenticity onto individual artists, the language of criticism, according to Stratton, "depends on the confusion of the subjective and the objective" in order to appear to resolve the contradictory tensions within authenticity.[22]

This is a significant postulation because throughout the selling-out controversy, the members of Metallica defended their new aesthetic in the rock press according to well-established rhetorical strategies developed over years of practice: assertions of artistic independence, the belief that successful art is the product of progress and experimentation, and so on. In an interview during the promotional activities before the release of *Load*, *Rolling Stone*'s David Fricke presents the band members as defiant independents who earned their fame and fortune after years of hard work. They had matured into solid artists and left the stifling confines of youthful thrash metal behind, such that *Load*, he writes, "gives those mid-1980s *Puppets*-era purists more to bitch about."[23] To launch the new album Metallica secured a headlining spot on the popular *Lollapalooza* tour that Summer (1996), a move that confirmed the band's "Alternica" status for some fans, while the presence on the tour of such a commercially successful group also angered supporters of *Lollapalooza*'s alternative, antimainstream philosophy (*Lollapalooza* cofounder Perry Farrell quit in protest). For their part, Metallica saw nothing wrong with joining the tour, and Fricke characterized the move as exemplifying "their typical disdain for the ordinary." In the interview, Hetfield takes pleasure at being the center of the controversy, claiming "[T]he part I like most is we're hated again," while guitarist Kirk Hammett downplays Metallica's huge financial and cultural influence and justifies the band's presence on the tour by noting

"[P]eople forget that Metallica started as an independent act." However, the term "independent" in this case appears to mean simply that the band's initial demo cassette (*No Life 'til Leather*, recorded in 1982) was given away to friends and other metal fans in the nascent thrash metal underground. Metallica's first record label, Megaforce Records, as well as their meager incomes and shoddy living situation (the band lived in a rehearsal hall in Queens for a few months after arriving in New York in the Spring of 1983), are all also mentioned in the interview to vouch for the band's "indie" roots.[24] Finally, in this interview the band views the *Load* album itself as a proving ground for Metallica's continued relevance, both to the industry at large and as part of their status as creative individuals. Progress and exper- imentation are defiantly central in this and other interviews which feature Hetfield and Hammett explaining in detail the multitude of guitars and effects employed in the recording of *Load*. In those interviews "experimen- tation" symbolizes both the mark of creativity and a privilege earned by the band through years of hard work. Fricke's article, moreover, reinforces the perception that notions of "experimentation" and "progress" necessar- ily (and positively) throw commercial concerns and genre identity in the face of those "*Puppets*-era purists" who would hold the band back.

These and other declarations on behalf of authenticity represent the resilience of cultural knowledge learned from much closer sources. We cannot really say that each of the above declarations misstates the "truth" or, more pointedly, that Metallica lies when they say they are glad to be controversial or that they are an indie band at heart. The statements are not intentionally designed to mislead, but they do need to be understood in the performative context of a rock interview. Metallica's pronounce- ments in the Fricke interview resound with extreme familiarity, and like all language, the terminology and grammar present above are products of social interaction, with implied and expected meanings actively presented and decoded by the participants (especially the audience). As such, we are supposed to smile at the thought of pissed-off and culturally backward *Puppets*-era fans and know *we* are not as lame as *they* are. Still, I want to underscore the idea of critically examining the rock interview and other interactions between artists and media in terms of communication *and* performance, and I am particularly interested in how we know to smile in self-satisfaction. Indeed, interviews, like all communication, are bound and guided by sets of social expectations and patterns of rhetoric largely specific to the situation at hand. Moreover, for the communications con- tained in something like the rock interview to have meaning they must interact and resonate with previous instances of communication. Speech has a history, and, as Mikhail Bahktin argued, is "filled with echoes and

reverberations of other [speech] to which it is related by the communal-
ity of the sphere of speech communication."[25] In other words, speech
communication is never wholly (or even partly) singular, and a speaker
is never the first to "disturb the eternal silence of the universe."[26] By this
Bahktin suggests that the history of speech and its meanings are always
the product and repositionings of previous interactions.

Bahktin argues that when listeners hear, they constantly and dynami-
cally perceive meaning in speech. While listening they also simultaneously
take an active response to it: they agree, disagree, augment it, apply it, and
so on. In any of these possibilities the listener remains an active participant. Importantly, listeners' responses are guided by loose "rules" of context that may not appear altogether obvious. We speak in diverse styles and
genres without suspecting that they exist, and it is this subconscious characteristic that gives speech its sense of naturalness, and therefore its self-
contained quality. Examining communication processes such as the rock
interview through the prism of active response enables us to understand
better the complex interaction taking place, even though much of it occurs
under the guise of natural, unhindered expression. Fricke's *Rolling Stone*
interview with Metallica does not just transmit the thoughts and ideas of
the band in some pure form. Nor is the "communication" simply between
Fricke and Metallica. Because the meaning of the speech contained in the
interview depends greatly on its place within a constantly developing continuum of the rock interview (a "speech genre" in Bahktin's terms[27]), it
therefore depends on the interpretations of that genre by the interview's
audience: the fans. And just as Ulrich became an active participant while
reading *Sounds*, Metallica fans respond and create meaning around the
interviews published about the band. Their reactions therefore need to be
understood as part of the process establishing rhetorical conventions that
comprise the speech genre of the rock interview, as well as ideologies of
identity and authenticity.

Our smiling at the journalistic skewering of *Puppets*-era purists can
also be explained in terms of "hip consumerism." Theorized by Thomas
Frank, hip consumerism is essentially a type of marketing strategy first
developed in the early 1960s that fosters the illusion of consumer independence and savvy as another way to sell goods and services. Frank identifies the development of hip consumerism as a crucial component in the
creation of 1960s countercultural style (itself an important site for the
development of rock journalism), but he contends that the relationship
between Haight/Ashbury and Madison Avenue was much more complex
than a mere appropriation of symbols. Indeed, ad agencies like Doyle Dane
Bernbach introduced new advertising methods centering on youth and

youthfulness some years before the Summer of Love infiltrated American homes as a reaction to established, decades-old ad techniques and corporate culture famously represented by Organization Man, dedicated participant in the system of hierarchy and conformity.[28] Essentially, not until 1967 and 1968—the same years that rock journalism began to make a name for itself—did advertising executives recognize the counterculture's potential as a well-spring of useful symbols that could embellish their already in-progress attempts to redefine consumerism. The changes in advertising content itself throughout the 1960s reflected the new methods of construction for the development of the hip consumerist model. Humor and irony, once seen as detractions from the very important and serious business of informing consumers about what was best for them (thanks to science and demographics), introduced, so the new thinking went, a more human element into advertising. Such advertising claimed to respect and support the consumer's knowledge, intelligence, and independence in the making of purchasing choices. The new ad strategy also worked by manufacturing and pitching a complicated disgust with mass consumer society and its symbols, a strategy Frank notes was its "aesthetic forte and its best product pitch, applicable to virtually anything: *Buy this to escape consumerism.*"[29]

But, as that last phrase clearly indicates, advertising designed to sell goods and services by appealing to the disdain for advertising and consumer culture is, nevertheless, still advertising in the most essential sense. As much as early 1960s advertising sought to escape consumerism and appeal to a type of consumer with intelligence and savvy, hip consumerism does nothing to remove the fundamental axis around which the advertising industry, and capitalist society as a whole, revolves. Hip consumerism, then, not only advertises products, it also advertises a compellingly different lifestyle grounded in the illusion of consumer independence. In so doing, it functions as yet another defense against ever-present temptations leading to selling out, and the lure of the hip consumerist aesthetic continues to offer a way for people to define themselves against some "mainstream," whether that mainstream is corporate rock radio or cellular phone service.[30] Moreover, those critiques (in whatever altered form they may appear today) maintain a powerful place in the public imagination because they are often the most visible ones offered.

The transference of the tenets of authenticity and independence, via the discourse of rock criticism and larger cultural processes like hip consumerism, to the debate about Metallica's selling-out controversy was largely played out in the disputes over the image of the "true fan." While such disputes played a significant role in fans' participation within the selling-out controversy, the definitions of a true fan seemed nearly as complex and contradictory as selling out itself. In Metallica's case, one type of true fan claimed a great appreciation for the band's musical aesthetic and, in rejecting the band's 1990s music, stood by the 1980s material as the definition of the true Metallica. Much of the band's popularity and critical success during the 1980s depended on an understanding that its music dealt with real issues taking place in the real world and offered thought-provoking questions quite unlike mainstream pop music or the hedonism of bands such as Poison or Mötley Crüe. Anything that moved Metallica away from that sense of realism was grounds for the selling-out accusation. Conversely, another type of true fan also professed a great appreciation for the music, but, in accordance with the belief that Art can only be the product of progress, supported the band's right to develop artistically without considering specific musical direction (or image) too heavily. In negotiating the tensions between these two archetypes, fans argued passionately for a particular set of meanings over others.

Through the late 1990s, the sell-out question continued to receive a great deal of attention in various forums. On Internet discussion boards, such as those hosted by About.com, long and intensely argued threads about Metallica's new music and selling out run for pages with fairly evenly balanced numbers of adherents for either side. However, in the letters section of each issue of Metallica's fan club magazine, *So What!*—the direct accusation of selling out plays less of a direct role than does the topic of the "true" fan. *So What!* is, after all, concerned with many aspects of Metallica fandom, and so it prints letters on a wide array of topics, ranging from fans' reviews of Metallica concerts, letters praising the band (without mentioning selling out in any way), and fans' experiences with events and goings-on of the fan club itself. Still, most of the letters engaging with the selling-out controversy defended the band according to the contested criteria of the true fan. As such, some letters respond vociferously to specific detractors, with usually no printed rebuttal:

> … I would like to say something to Sasa T. (Yugoslavia): "You suck!" I've been a fan since "One" was released as a single. I like the new stuff a lot, I'm a real fan and I'm not leaving (I'm a real fan 'CAUSE I'm not leaving)." — Bob B., The Netherlands (5 no. 2 1998, p. 4)

More frequent are the hyperbolic responses to a whole category of fans labeled "whiners" and "complainers," as in the following:

> Ahhhh! Enough already!!! Me and about a hundred thousand other people are tired of hearing your complaining. You know

who you are. The real fans would never say things like "Speed up your music" or "what happened to your hair?" Their hair doesn't matter—the music does! — Annie S., Bradenton, Florida (p. 6)

As I mentioned above, the recognition of progress as fundamental to the development of any band plays a significant role in some responses to Metallica's new music and other fans:

"Fight for my own, to live my own way." I think in many ways, Metallica still lives by that code. Like it or not, they still do what they want, and do it their own way, and don't really care what anyone thinks of their actions. Why should they? I would not want to be bound by a bunch of fickle, and demanding fans who can't deal with the fact I cut my hair, or stopped wearing jeans that are three sizes to [sic] small. — ZXZXZXZ[31]

These letters also engage with one of the most notable and controversial aesthetic changes accompanying the *Load* and *Reload* albums: the visual image put forth by Metallica in the album art. Both album covers display a new version of the Metallica logo, one featuring a far more uniformly block-like reinterpretation of the long lines and sharp angles of the 1980s version. More significant was the actual album cover artwork itself. For both albums, the band chose pieces from the collection *Blood and Semen* by New York avant-garde artist Andres Serrano, who, using his own bodily fluids, created nine abstract smears in response to the AIDS epidemic. Metallica, however, seem not to have been drawn to the images out of any explicit desire to align themselves with Serrano's political goals in creating them. Indeed, Hetfield and Newsted accepted Ulrich's and Hammett's idea to use the *Blood and Semen* images only after overcoming reservations they had regarding the implications of sexuality in the imagery. Newsted in particular noted, "I argued [against] it from day one … that I did not want semen on the cover, that does not represent Metallica. We're not homosexuals, that's not something that I am into."[32] At the same time, Hammett claimed his attraction to the images came from their quality of abstractness, and the way they challenged the aesthetics of the band's previous album covers. In his view, the amorphous character and materiel of the *Blood and Semen* images seemed open to broad symbolism and interpretation in contrast to the more concrete, direct imagery from previous covers (see Figure 5.1).[33] The hammer-in-a-pool-of-blood image on *Kill 'Em All*, the battlefield crosses connected to the heavens by strings on *Master of Puppets*, or even the almost-completely black cover of *Metallica* had all functioned as relatively lush and obvious visual references of

Figure 5.1 Metallica, *Load* (1996).

the lyrical themes found in those albums while also operating within the visual palette of metal albums generally (see Figure 5.2).

Additionally, the inside group photographs of the *Load* and *Reload* albums presented a very different visual representation of Metallica. Previous photographs, such as those on the back cover of *Master of Puppets*, were designed to convey a sense of streetwise toughness, and of the members as survivors in a cold, harsh social landscape (see Figure 5.3). As illustrated in the *Master of Puppets* photo, the group stares directly back at the viewer, serious and unsmiling. With arms crossed or bent outward slightly and feet spread, their stares become part of an overall statement of defiance. Yet, Hetfield's ripped jeans and Burton's fingerless gloves, which largely frame the image, are in this instance also symbols of decay and of a kind of destitution. Also on the back cover, individual photos of the members performing on stage partially surround the group shot, framing it with a sense of translation without transformation. In other words, the on-stage action tries to emphasize simply a different instance of the identities in the group shot, rather than a fantastic escape to a completely different set of identities altogether.

Load and *Reload* dispense with the leather-jacket-and-jeans look of earlier albums and instead feature the band members in a number of different poses and costumes. In many of the photos Hammett and Ulrich wear

Figure 5.2 Metallica, *Master of Puppets* (1986).

Figure 5.3 Group photo on back cover of *Master of Puppets*.

Figure 5.4 Back cover photo of the *Load* CD booklet.

extreme amounts of black eye liner, and indeed the sense of these photos explicitly engages with fantastic visual identity. The photos in the *Load* CD booklet, particularly the back cover, contain the most surprising imagery (see Figure 5.4). A far cry from the representation of industrial desperation on *Master of Puppets*, here the band sits at a massive table, glasses of wine half-finished, as though they had just finished a fine (and perhaps expensive) meal. Hetfield and Hammett work through what must be expensive cigars. Each member wears dark sunglasses and seems occupied with his own space and thoughts in stark contrast to the more obvious group presentation of earlier photos. All four wear black dinner-style jackets, with Ulrich and Hammett standing out via their funky-collared shirts. Only Ulrich seems to notice the camera this time, and it is almost as if in passing. In a gesture reminiscent of glam metal musicians such as Poison's Bret Michaels, his mouth purses slightly, almost as a statement of self-important vanity.[34]

The *Load* photo might seem to be an attempt to capture the increased financial situation enjoyed by Metallica since the early 1990s, but the band consistently emphasized the element of aesthetic experimentation underlying these images. The construction of a visual image had always been fundamental to Metallica's success as commercial musicians—especially because the resulting image seemed not to be constructed—and in breaking away from the aesthetic found in earlier album imagery the band experimented with a visual identity that coincided with their ongoing experiments with musical identity. Experimentation or not, however, in both the online forums and the fan club letters the new results were extremely controversial. Most accusers pointed to the more stylized visual image that accompanied *Load* and *Reload* and the embrace of mainstream media—centering on MTV—as evidence of a general softening in what Metallica should represent, both in terms of musical style and masculinity. For example:

> Metallica went from being the harshest, meanest fucking metal band, to some Alteri-metal [sic] happy MTV shit. They've totally lost all their thrash roots, and sold out. They said they'd never do a video, that MTV sucked. Look at them now. I just want to know what in god's name happened to them. I can see change too, but they didn't just change, they did a 180 in the wrong direction ... Man, I'd kill myself if I ever changed. — ROSS94321 (About.com msg. 1523.6, 2000)

Other fans reinforce their accusation of selling out by pointing the finger squarely at Bob Rock, who produced the *Metallica, Load,* and *Reload* albums. Rock had a successful career in the late 1980s producing albums for mainstream bands such as Aerosmith and Mötley Crüe, and Metallica's decision to work with Rock was controversial by itself even in 1991. As such, he is credited either with helping to develop Metallica's musical aesthetic or blamed for destroying it:

> What the fuck happened to you guys? What did Bob Rock do to you in the last six years? You guys were just kickin' mad ass until *Load* and *Reload* came out ... You guys lost the speed, the crunch, and the aggressiveness that were in your previous albums. You let the media get to you, and you all sold out ... I just hope that one day you guys will tell the media to fuck off and start writing like yourselves again. — Blue P., Lawrenceville, Georgia (*So What!* 5 no. 2, 1998 p. 5)

In addition to direct concerns about the band's musical and visual aesthetic, the critique made by ROSS94321 includes perhaps the most common element found in the critiques of Metallica in this period: the invocation of Lars Ulrich's denunciation of MTV in the mid-1980s. Apparently, when asked about the possibility of seeing a Metallica video sometime in the near future, Ulrich made a statement to the effect of, "Fuck MTV! We'll never do a video!" The exact wording differs from account to account, and some instances contain more detail (such as a specific year, 1986), but the verbal tone of Ulrich's alleged statement reinforces a tough, defiant image cultivated at a time when the band and the thrash metal style in general existed very much outside the purview of mainstream visibility. For older fans in the late 1990s, though, the statement assumes the quality of a severe litmus test, a test that Metallica has evidently failed: by copiously producing videos since the release of *Metallica*—after denouncing the medium—the band had actually *lied* to its fans. That Metallica could be accused, however implicitly, of actually lying to fans demonstrates the deep personal marker of identity constructed around Ulrich's initial statement, and the presence, for some fans, of a powerful but unspoken bond between the band and its fans.[35] Making videos, indeed *trafficking in the very symbols of the mainstream music business*, therefore, not only broke the bond of outsiderness in the mind of fans such as ROSS94321, but it exemplified the broader disingenuousness of Metallica in the 1990s. As such, that sense of disingenuousness, for those fans who formulated the band's actions in that way, most fundamentally characterized Metallica's selling-out controversy.

It is important, though, to note that Ulrich never seems to have made the statement that has been the symbol of so much uproar. Fan web sites stamp the two-sentence statement with an evidentiary date and citation, usually the *Cliff 'Em All* home video from 1987, as damning proof that the band did sell out, but even when a source is given no corroboration can be found. It is certainly reasonable to find Ulrich's infamous statement more of a condemnation of MTV than of music video as a medium, but it is also clear that the statement is rarely parsed so delicately in critiques like those of ROSS94321. Perhaps the biggest issue in dealing with the continuous recycling of the antivideos statement is that, in that in their zeal to condemn, fans ignore other discussions by Metallica about the video topic that present the band's views as more thoughtful and nuanced than a straight up-or-down opinion of the medium. Even before 1987 Metallica had plans (and footage apparently) for a video for the song "For Whom the Bell Tolls," from the *Ride the Lightning* album, and many other interviews that broach the topic relate the band's potential interest in the possibilities of music video.[36] What held them back seemed to be ensuring the right kind of video was made, one that would challenge the accepted video styles of the time. Metallica's first video, for the song "One" (from *...And Justice for All*), was not, given its momentous position as the first Metallica video, a video for the sake of having a video. Once it aired on MTV though, it quickly functioned like most any other promotional video, and it is this complex relationship between wanting to control the creation of content (in this case, a video) and presenting it to the world that has, for better or for worse, characterized Metallica's image and aesthetic across its career.

Napster of Puppets

> I sort of have this quiet peace with the fact that anybody who doesn't really get it, or is vehemently opposed to what we're saying, doesn't know the information or doesn't really understand the issue ... [Y]ou cannot really oppose the fact that whoever creates something should have the right to decide what happens to it. It's not an argument.

Lars Ulrich defending Metallica's actions against Napster, 2000[37]

The pain of Metallica's "lies" was only exacerbated throughout the Spring and Summer of 2000 when the band filed a lawsuit against the Internet company Napster, and in the course of those proceedings urged related action against 370,000 specific individuals "caught" using Napster's popular file-sharing service to obtain Metallica studio recordings. While the band was writing the song "I Disappear" for the *Mission Impossible II* soundtrack, demo versions of the song were leaked by studio personnel and made accessible through Napster. Prior to that notification, Metallica had apparently never heard of Napster and had generally maintained only a basic presence on the Web. Napster had already been defending itself against an earlier suit filed by the Recording Industry Association of America (RIAA), a lobbying group representing the interests of about 90% of the American recording industry, yet that suit had only received the attention of the hi-tech world. When Metallica filed their own suit in April 2000 the issue became much more newsworthy. While both lawsuits essentially sought the same legal end—to close down Napster—the direct participation of an artist with the stature of Metallica quickly put the previously arcane topic of digital rights management (DRM) into the forefront of American society.

Firmly grounding both the RIAA and Metallica lawsuits was the issue of control.[38] Faced with the challenge of a stunningly simple distribution method that threatened to make traditional record industry practices obsolete, the RIAA elected to use the legal system to sue the competition out of existence and reconfirm its authority. As Reebee Garofalo notes, legislation and lawsuits comprised the industry's primary strategy for dealing with file sharing, and the effect of this strategy would also be the "demonization of the users of [file-sharing] services as pirates and thieves."[39]

Following on the heels of its successful efforts in 1998 to secure the passage of the Digital Millennium Copyright Act (DMCA), which created a heavily skewed playing field upon which future threats to control can be contested, the recording industry had very little incentive to rise to the challenge of online distribution and adapt its business practices.[40]

If the efforts by the RIAA to control digital content were ostensibly meant to benefit thousands of faceless artists, Metallica's lawsuit against Napster was primarily personal. Ulrich's first statement about the lawsuit drew liberally from the idea that Metallica's music was the result of concerted artistic efforts, and its circulation through the computers of millions of their fans and other Napster users represented a kind of cheapening of that Art. For instance, in the band's press release announcing the lawsuit, he claimed that "[I]t is therefore sickening to know that our art is being traded like a commodity rather than the art that it is." Ulrich quickly backed away from such an obviously elitist stance, but from that point on he struggled instead against the strong view that Metallica's legal efforts were primarily about recouping financial loses caused by the free trade of the band's music. The overall backlash was severe, as Ulrich's arguments about control, authorship, and the freedom of artistic choice got lost in a maelstrom of anti-Metallica Web sites and parodistic cartoons decrying the band's greed.[41] No matter how often Ulrich attempted to make clear that Metallica's legal expenses dwarfed whatever they might have lost in album sales through Napster, the perception remained of a wealthy group of technophobic rock stars greedily screwing the kids. Furthermore, that Metallica would expend so much capital and energy in the pursuit of such a detailed level of control seemed too incredible to be possible. Yet, after having successfully wrested control of all their master recordings away from Elektra in 1994 (and in the process increased their share of royalties to 50%),[42] Metallica's emphasis on controlling the ownership and distribution of their music—to the point of spending large amounts of money to enforce that claim—was thus not entirely out of character. Indeed for many Metallica fans who were opposed to the legal actions, the Napster case represented a stringent application of the band's highly touted independent aesthetic: if you claim to find inspiration in Metallica's no-compromises rhetoric of personal choice and independence from the pop music mainstream, how do you react when the band turns around and apparently applies that rhetoric directly against many of its fans, including, perhaps, you?

By concentrating his argument on the topic of authorial control, Ulrich's statements consistently ignored the possibilities of Fair Use, a section in the U.S. copyright code that allows for certain royalty-free use of copyrighted materials, particularly when the users are not making any money on that use.[43] I raise this issue because Metallica's lawsuit also named three universities as codefendants alongside Napster. The universities were named because they had failed to block Napster-related file-sharing, which, as the *de facto* ISP under the DMCA, they were required to do according to the band. Nevertheless, Ulrich argued that Napster was not some grassroots organization that built its system for humanitarian ends, but was an extremely well-funded corporation with millions of dollars in investment capital in the bank. By removing any notion that Napster represented the efforts of harmless geekdom, and inserting the idea that Napster was itself a greedy corporation, Ulrich could present the band as victims of that corporation. While he was careful never to rely on the word "victim" or to give off any kind of woe-is-me attitude, the ability to remove Napster's grassroots image focused the band's complaints more precisely. As such, Metallica's concerns over control could be divided into two related concerns: freedom for artists to opt-in or opt-out of Napster, and a deep conviction that with authorship comes total control.

Attacking Napster as a corporation allowed Metallica to claim it had never assented to the availability of its music in the service and the company was therefore generating income using music it had no right to.[44] Ulrich maintained that the band did not oppose the file-sharing technology *per se* (though he did not seem to understand it, as I discuss below), but noted that artists always had the freedom to choose how their works interacted with such technology. In other words, artists were perfectly able to allow music to be distributed via Napster, but they should be just as able to restrict access in any way necessary. Instead of thoughtfully considering how digital file sharing affected long-held beliefs about the concept of copyright, Metallica adopted the sue-first-ask-questions-later path taken by the RIAA, and the particular *hostility* of that approach formed one of the central points of contention in this segment of the selling-out controversy. It did not matter in the least to Ulrich that he had no significant experience with the Web or Napster. Rather, the Web was perhaps just another means of doing what you do in your everyday life. Of course, we cannot assume that if the members of Metallica had been more experienced with the Web generally, they would have automatically taken a different, less hostile stance regarding Napster. But their inexperience did shape the way they thought about how it was used. Ultimately, according to Ulrich, the issue was consent, and Fair Use only served to hinder an artist's freedom of choice.

It can only be about consent, however, if there is a strong belief that artists, due to their status as authors, have the right to withhold that consent.

As I outlined at the beginning of this chapter, the system of creating works by a single author depends most visibly on the union between the creative expression of an original genius (here understood as the long, hard work expended by Metallica in writing music) and legal copyright for its legitimacy. Furthermore, the function of copyright is tied fundamentally to the workings of commerce, and Ulrich's defense starkly revealed how business-like and corporate the Metallica behemoth had become over the course of the 1990s. To be sure, Metallica had always been a business and if at first it was not a very profitable business, in earlier years the band could at least conceal business dealings from its public image and emphasize the more traditional artistic and fan-based elements of the band. During the 1990s, though, Metallica's ever-increasing participation in mainstream pop music business practices (and as their lawyers issued more and more restraining orders defending the word "Metallica" from unauthorized use in things like lipstick, wheel rims, furniture, and sunglasses) forced a shift in their multivalent public relationship between art, commerce, and the fan. Ulrich always appeared calm and confident with regard to the commerce portion of that relationship. His responses to the Napster controversy presented an image of someone deeply engaged in running the Metallica corporation, and mentions of the NWOBHM aside, he rarely cast himself as a man of the fans, particularly where the corporate interests of Metallica might be at stake. Speaking in one interview in 1999 about surviving in the often antagonistic atmosphere between artists and record companies, Ulrich revealed a very ambivalent attitude toward the massive fan base for Metallica. For him, his attitude revolved around a question of scale and "status": he had very little personally in common with fans and the job of maintaining the multimillion-dollar Metallica business required much of his attention and energy. In his view, that attitude was also a matter of practicality: Metallica was simply too large for any of the members to consider seriously any type of unsupervised or unscripted contact with fans.

In an episode of the PBS talk show *The Charlie Rose Show*, taped soon after the band filed its lawsuit, Ulrich discussed the Napster issue with rapper Chuck D and outlined Metallica's view as a matter of respecting the band's desire to disallow its music to be part of Napster.[45] Chuck D, on the other hand, felt there was little choice for artists but to accept the new paradigms presented by Napster-like technologies. Likening the new file-sharing technology to a spilled bag of M&Ms, he asserted that once the M&Ms have spilled it becomes impossible simply to force people to stop picking up the candy. Moreover, he saw much positive potential in the shift in control of access to popular music away from the tightly ordered practices of the corporate recording industry. Obviously envisioned by Charlie Rose and his producers as a pro-vs.-anti-Napster "debate," Ulrich and Chuck D actually spend more time arguing past each other in the segment. Ulrich attempted to make clear that he is not simply "anti-Napster" or antitechnology in principle, and even tended to agree with much of what Chuck D said regarding the need for new business models and access available through technologies like those used by Napster. Still, Ulrich wanted to use his considerable influence to put a timeout in place so the effects of the technology could be properly studied and that some level of artistic control could remain.[46] He saw his cause as combating a larger notion that free and unrestricted access to content gathered from the Internet necessarily came without financial responsibility on the part of the user. Where he and Chuck D disagreed was in the valuation of Napster's potential to upend the entire intellectual property/capitalist basis of the entertainment industry as a whole. Chuck D generally found the possibilities liberating, while, in this interview and others, Ulrich clearly worried about the effect such an upheaval would have on the idea of intellectual property and the author, as well as the consequences for compensating artists for their efforts.

How Napster users themselves theorized the impact their actions have on the intellectual property system is only beginning to be determined in any studied detail, but it generally varied according to the multiple uses of the technology. Challenged with the question of whether "free" entitles one to access, Napster defenders were generally less than convincing, and during the height of its use access to Napster clearly contained a class-based component in that many users were college students with modern computers living in dorms or others able to afford both leisure time and high-speed connections. The notion of "sharing" among fan communities (the initial application of the technology) also quickly became difficult to defend once the music being shared left the realm of the obscure, old, or out-of-print. The simple access to the complete catalogs of major artists, coupled significantly with the fact that users could download music without offering anything in return, masked such ideals and sharing became a means to a simple end: free music on demand.

Ulrich particularly objected to the sharing conception (in more heated moments he simply equated "sharing" and "stealing"), but his objections seem to have been based on a revealing misunderstanding of the file-sharing concept itself: "Sharing means we each get something. Like, if I share my sandwich with you, you get half and I get half."[47] Importantly, Ulrich objected because he could not see what Napster users were sharing *with him*. Not understanding that the act of sharing digital music files exists outside the commercial transaction system of which he is part, his misunderstanding underscores the litigious priority of Metallica's overall response at the expense of technical experience: the will to take on Napster required that they become informed about the technology only in ways that would support their claim. In other words, Ulrich only knew what his consultants told him, and it was based on that information that he pursued his rhetorical stance. In existing beyond such a commercial transaction system, though, file sharing acts to separate the identity of a song from an artist (or record company) in ways always previously secured by a maze of copyright and licensing restrictions, and in missing this point, Ulrich's priorities became very clear.

The proximity of the *Charlie Rose* interview to the heady drama of Ulrich's statement before the U.S. Senate Judiciary Committee in June 2000 requires that we consider the rhetoric and imagery used to convey the band's argument as a significant component of the argument process itself.[48] Indeed, when asked by Rose about the impact of lawsuit on the band's relationship with fans, Ulrich relied on boilerplate language about securing an end to the lawsuit that would be beneficial to Metallica, the Napster company, and the fans. Later when Rose asked a similar question Ulrich seemed to forget about his earlier statement, and went so far as to dismiss with a wave of good-bye those unnamed fans who did not at least respect Metallica's choice. At first glance such a move marks a profoundly antisocial gesture of personal independence taken to an extreme. On a deeper lever, however, Ulrich's wave reinforces the hidden but defensively isolationist stance inherent at some level to the concept of intellectual property and authorship, one which artificially divides cultural work into "art" and "commodities." Moreover, Ulrich makes a point of briefly looking into the camera and smirking as he finishes the gesture, thus consciously broadcasting his contempt for those who dared disagree with him.

The Sound of Selling Out

If an accusation of selling out comprised the most visible reaction to Metallica's 1990s music, what exactly is it about the music that became so contested? It is significant that for all the elevated rhetoric regarding hair length, music videos, and copyright, much of the impact of the selling-out controversy resides at the level of musical detail. Indeed it is unlikely that the intensity of the selling-out controversy would have been lessened had the band members kept their long hair, for fans would still be confronted with the very different musical aesthetic of *Load* and *Reload*.[49] As I will discuss, these albums introduced guitar techniques and performance styles quickly heard as a general "bluesy-ness," and getting at what made Metallica's music sound "bluesy" means understanding how seemingly minor details of performance articulation can balloon into major anxieties about style and identity. While mode may form an important component for theorizing popular styles along terms of traditional notation-based analysis, it is also clear that articulation (particularly the role played by palm-muting) and timbre maintain at least the level of importance in heavy metal generally reserved for pitches and harmony. Articulation and timbre are two aspects of analysis that traditionally receive less attention and even fall outside of standard notational abilities, but their marginalization only reinforces the importance of studying the details of popular music: from the perspective of traditional analysis, a detail of articulation does not carry with it the weight of other details related to pitches and harmony. However, analysis of styles such as heavy metal must recognize different sets of priorities.

I begin, though, by examining the song "Mama Said," from *Load*, a Metallica song that seems neither to sound like a typical Metallica song or like one from the style of heavy metal. In terms of structure it could very well be a typical 1980s rock power ballad, featuring a strummed acoustic guitar, muted drums, and an expressive, distortion-filled section two-thirds of the way through. "Mama Said" also continues the balladic style laid out in "Nothing Else Matters," itself a development of the paradigm initiated with "Fade to Black." While each of these three songs shares the presentation of personal and emotion-laden lyrics, important aural markers distinguish "Mama Said" according to familiar and widely recognized patterns of musical interiority. Moreover, "Mama Said" marks a significant change in the way James Hetfield presented the idea of subjectivity in his lyrics, and the content of this song offers an important perspective on his general self-fashioning after the huge commercial success of the *Metallica* album.

Hetfield's rich baritone and steel-stringed acoustic guitar are the only instruments in the first verse, with everything close-miked and kept relatively dry in order that each syllable, breath, and nuance be as direct as possible. Along with the strummed minor chords of the guitar and the subtleties of phrasing in the vocal melody, the immediacy of the vocal production presents the lyrics in ways we are immediately accustomed to read as honest or sincere:

> Mama, she has taught me well,
>
> Told me when I was young.
>
> ....
>
> A son's heart's owed to mother,
>
> But I must find my way.

Presented via the aural codes of the singer/songwriter, these lyrics convey a quiet appreciation for a mother from a grown son, and a sense not only of a kind of sentimentality-through-loss (it is evident that the son is remembering his mother), but also of unresolved (and irresolvable) issues such as childhood neglect, even hints of abuse. Yet, the first word in the title and in the lyrics—"Mama"—instantly signals a very particular socio-cultural subjectivity, and in so doing recognizes the realization of a private emotionality hidden underneath an outwardly more aggressive front as the true essence of the individual.[50] Typically a term used by small children, the word "mama" in adult popular culture represents a way of looking up to a mother-figure in an endearing, respectful manner. It appeared in many "advice" songs by both black and white artists over the course of the twentieth century, and each time it generally maintains that sense of respect even if the advisor and advisee are not consistent across all examples. Hetfield's use of this specific form of address, though, places him into a kind of sentimental and nostalgic world typically derived from images of rural white family life. Importantly, "mama" functions here, and in other examples, more as a marker of social class than race and indicates an identification (or at least the desire for identification) with a working class background. In this context, the word Mama perhaps recalls lyric imagery familiar from country music, a genre that has, particularly since Hank Williams in the early 1950s, developed specific rhetorical techniques for the exploration of male interiority as expressive of the true self. At the same time, we should also consider how the specific subjective position evident in "Mama Said" resonates with the kinds of white masculinity popularized by musicians in the Southern Rock movement during the 1970s.

Already from the first word of the song, then, we have a significant set of verbal cues quite unlike the nonspecific emotionalism and reflection found in "Fade to Black" and "Nothing Else Matters." Moreover, at the first chorus of "Mama Said," the full band is prominently joined by what at first listen sounds distinctly like a pedal steel guitar. A most remarkable instrument in the context of a Metallica song given its nearly singular association in the rock imagination with country music, its melodic swoops and perfect resolutions convey desire but also stability, matching a sentimental accompaniment to the son's quiet but firm need for emotional closure. In call-and-response fashion, the steel guitar answers each lyrical statement by the singer, affirming his wish to "Let my heart go" and to "Let your son grow." Though the harmonic activity of the verse and chorus are very similar (both are based on a Dm–C–Am movement), the chorus compresses that progression from two bars of 4/4 into one bar of 3/4, before continuing past the Am to a long residence on an open G chord. It is in this harmonic "holding space" where the steel guitar and its sentimental character reside. The open-faced G chord comes from a set of standard chords not generally part of the heavy metal harmonic language, and especially when strummed, the chord's perfect, six-string diatonicism acts a marker of interiority across many styles of popular music. Indeed, merely *strumming* diatonic open-faced chords evokes certain styles of interiority.[51]

Similar kinds of call-and-response activity occur throughout the second verse, but the timbre of the answering instrument is subtly different. While it displays a comparable flexibility of pitch and floats above the texture, the instrument here sounds closer to an electric guitar played with a metal slide, with the sound wrapped in the further ambiguity of a wah-wah effect. No steel player is credited on this track and Hetfield offers only that he "played slide on 'Mama Said' " without referring to specific parts of the song.[52] He may have played the important chorus parts with a slide, but the actual timbre on the recording nevertheless closely resembles pedal steel. Arguably, this timbral closeness provides much of the reason some critics have heard this song as a "bona fide country song" or "a fully successful stab at country-blues."[53] The very presence of these two timbres also goes a long way in fans' valuation of the *Load* and *Reload* songs. However, as was the case with the sitar sound in "Wherever I May Roam," organological authenticity is only one component of how a specific timbre encodes meaning. What I am calling the steel guitar sound may have been played on a regular guitar, but by mimicking the timbre of a steel guitar, with all of its generic and ideological associations, the character of the entire song changes. From the standpoint of genre, moreover, the speech genre from which these instruments come, coupled with the word "mama," challenges how we might hear this song as a Metallica song.

Hetfield describes writing "Mama Said" in a hotel room at a time when he was "real big into country music."[54] He says he wrote it for himself and did not intend for it to be released by Metallica. The lyrics' reflection on a maternal relationship and the lost opportunity for reconciliation were outside his usual style and he even thought briefly about selling it. Like *Metallica*'s "Nothing Else Matters," also written by Hetfield outside the orbit of Metallica, recording "Mama Said," with its direct display of vulnerability, on *Load* was a risk. In addition to the ideological likenesses mentioned above, the sentiment of male vulnerability in this song also resonates with the music of George Jones, Johnny Cash, Waylon Jennings, and Merle Haggard in songs like "Mama, Don't Let Your Babies Grow Up to Be Cowboys" and "Mama Tried." Though the musical details differ significantly, Haggard's "Mama Tried" (1968) presents a very similar set of lyrical images between mother (deceased) and son (reflecting). There, the son looks back on his relationship with his mother, whom he credits with trying (unsuccessfully) to keep him on the straight and narrow. Haggard's song is not filled with the same kind of brooding angst found in Hetfield's song, but the centrality of the mother figure to the personal history of her male child, and the sentiment toward her, clearly provides some sort of commonality between the songs. "Mama Said" distinctly looks back over the narrator's life in philosophical and metaphorical terms, providing an often-tortured reassessment from the vantage point of many years in the future. Although the songs on the earlier Metallica albums may have explored interiority and the extremes of the human psyche, they did so in a more general, exploratory way. In the past, it was less obvious that any occurrence of the personal pronoun "I" should have been taken to represent Hetfield's own experience. Here, though, the aural codes indicate we are intended to identify the "I" as indicative of Hetfield. The specific move to explore his own past was a significant choice for the notoriously private Hetfield, and the reception of Metallica's new music largely hinged on this particular aesthetic development. Most critics and other writers generally praised this new approach in familiar terms of songwriterly craft and maturity, but, as I pointed out in Chapter 2, such a valuation often also includes a significant repositioning of the band's earlier music as overindulgent or immature.

Hetfield points to the death of his father, Virgil, in early 1996 as a major catalyst for the changed approach to song lyrics. Virgil died after a two-year illness with cancer and, according to James, never wavered from his strict Christian Science beliefs, an act of faith James ultimately found admirable. While he had spent years lambasting the strict religious doctrines that dominated his childhood, Hetfield's new-found admiration for his father as the elder Hetfield's health deteriorated grants an air of authenticity to the explorations of his own feelings. At the same time, his reconciliation with his father, the tying of loose ends in their relationship after years of separation, also plays out as a particular kind of masculinity. Hetfield's view of his father as a hero, as "Pops Hetfield," in the years since his death also represents part of a distinctly conservative turn toward the very values he spent so long rebelling against. It also strengthens the sociocultural worldview articulated in a song like "Mama Said." Indeed, according to Hetfield an important aspect of the renewed bond between he and his father came through a shared interest in the music of country singer Waylon Jennings.[55] Additionally, the increased importance of hunting and self-sufficiency, drag racing and the working-class white masculinity of its attendant "gear head" mind set, as well as the mythology of Harley Davidson, offer ways of experiencing the world seemingly disconnected from the huge capitalist success (and accompanying pressures) he experienced in the first half of the 1990s, even if that very success has allowed him to explore and develop those interests in the first place. Those activities also have a decidedly "macho" component to their character, one that carves its masculinity in the stock of a rifle or patches it onto the sleeve of a leather biker jacket.

The decision to use stylistic elements drawn from country music in "Mama Said" ensures that it will resonate along the lines of "the expression of the real feelings of a real person," and the emphasis on the band members' individual personalities in commentary during the *Load* and *Reload* years provides important context for that reading. Understanding "Mama Said" in this way also allows it to be positioned along familiar lines of authorship. Metallica certainly assisted in the presentation of these new identities, as many interviews foreground and detail how the members spent time away from the Metallica collective in 1994–1995 in pursuit of personal activities. Most interviews given during the publicity campaign for *Load* also stressed the new approach taken toward writing and recording the songs for that album and its companion *Reload* once they had returned: specifically the greater emphasis on musical input from bassist Jason Newsted and guitarist Kirk Hammett; a looser and more improvisatory way of recording; and a greater willingness to experiment with new types of expression in a number of different forms.[56] Indeed, Metallica's press kit for the *Reload* album explicitly directs interviewers to these kinds of observations by providing a short list of suggested (as well as off-limits) interview topics, such as "What's it like being free of previously self imposed [sic] inhibitions?" and "What's happened to the 'metal' in your name?"[57]

The belief that for Art to be original it must progress from the concerns of the past provides a crucial underpinning to the critical understanding of the *Load* and *Reload* albums. Hetfield remarked in the press kit "I remember walking into the studio, hearing Kirk playing rhythm guitar during the *Load* sessions and thinking, 'hmm, things are gonna change and why fight this?'"[58] In Metallica's situation, therefore, an important pathway toward progress lay in the breaking down of the Hetfield/Ulrich songwriting and recording monopoly. Whereas in the past Hetfield wrote the riffs and recorded all of the guitars (except the virtuosic solos—the only things Hammett recorded on the first five albums) as well as dictated the bass guitar part to Newsted, several interviews contain some mention of the liberating effects of allowing Hammett to contribute both riffs and recorded rhythm guitar parts to the new songs.[59] Newsted's specific contributions are less clear though he constantly affirmed the general feeling of openness by noting how he felt much less frustration with his musical role during the writing and recording.[60]

Another apparent pathway to progress lay in the writing and arrangement of the songs themselves. If the modular approach to musical form had been a musical hallmark of Metallica before 1991, by the late 1990s that technique had all but disappeared from the band's music. The combination of structural complexity, vigorous ensemble virtuosity, and an insistent lyrical detachment characterizing albums such as *Master of Puppets* and *...And Justice for All* was replaced by simpler song forms with far fewer riffs per song on *Load* and *Reload*. In their praise for these newer albums, critics consequently repositioned the earlier 1980s aesthetic as immature and even incomprehensible: what once was celebrated as a sign of musical intelligence became revised, according to *Rolling Stone*'s David Sprague in his review of *Load* for example, as "the carpal-tunnel riffing they once reflexively fell back on."[61] Looking back from the late 1990s, the implication in the word "reflexively" is significant: it implies that Hetfield and Ulrich, having no mature sense of songwriting during the 1980s, simply added more riffs to each song to cover for their lack of artistic depth. The band's music from the 1990s, so the theory goes, jettisons all that structural baggage in favor of more welcome moments of immediacy and human feeling. While the notion of masking insecurity with structure resonates with other areas of Western musical practice and suggests a tantalizing point of inquiry regarding that particular period in Metallica's career, it does not mesh with the fact that contemporary descriptions of the band's 1980s music rarely described it in terms of overindulgence. It also strikes odd with Metallica's own efforts in the early 1980s to distinguish themselves based on formal structure, arguments critics accepted and supported almost wholesale. Still, most journalists who wrote about the new music sang its praises in the terms of progress and according to some innate value of the new. What interests me, then, is the nearly complete critical reversal necessary in order to present *Load* and *Reload* as the products of musical evolution.

Generally the new songs feature more improvisatory playing across all instruments with greater possibility for ad-lib variations on riffs and more commingling between typically segregated lead and rhythm guitar parts. The attention to rhythmic precision is noticeably less important aesthetically while not lessened technically on *Load* and *Reload* (the music is still very precise). In large part this has to do with the generally slower tempi of the songs, which in turn foreground larger groupings of the beat. The slower feel of the larger metric groupings also allow the guitar parts more rhythmic subtlety and melodic variation, particularly at the ends of riffs. The drumming patterns are also much less intense and rely on a straightforward kick/snare pattern with little variation over the course of a song.

Again, this less-busy approach shapes the rhythmic characteristics of the guitar riffs in ways quite different than before. The absence of physically concentrated drum patterns also compounds the scarcity of physically intense downstroked power chords on the guitar. Moreover, in many of the *Load* and *Reload* songs single-note "box" pentatonicism replaces the power chord as the basis for riffs.

Nevertheless, stylistic elements from the band's 1980s music can still be heard on these albums even as the songs feature less complex structures. To be sure, at first listen the aesthetic changes seem more pronounced than any aspects of continuity, a situation that perhaps offers an initial explanation for the negative reactions of many fans to the new music. Still, on *Load* and *Reload* we hear snippets of the earlier metal language at the moments of downstroked and palm-muted Low E power chords in the song "Attitude"; the chromaticism and Phrygian accents in the main riff from "Thorn Within"; the accented tritones and particular syncopation of the Low Es under the verses in "The House Jack Built" and "Devil's Dance"; the rolling double bass drums in the choruses of "Fuel" and "Bad Seed"; and the tight palm-muting in the verse music of "Carpe Diem Baby." Most of the songs listed here are slower-paced (~80 to ~100 bpm) and illustrate the continuation of a particular kind of heaviness first explored in the song "The Thing That Should Not Be" on *Master of Puppets*, but better known from "Sad But True" from *Metallica*. Aside from a similar tempo, the firm four-on-the-floor drum pattern and harmonic range of "Sad But True" allows the Low E-based riffs to plod along, reveling in the weight provided by finely tuned distortion and reverb. Additionally, the Low Es in "Sad But True" and "The Thing That Should Not Be" actually sound as Low Ds, part of a strategy of *scordatura* designed to increase the sense of heaviness further. The detuning of all six of the strings by a whole tone in this song is itself a special effect, and distinguishes "Sad But True" from other songs on the *Metallica* album. *Load* and *Reload* adopt this strategy across the board: the "default" tuning is shifted down a half step, from Low E to Low E♭, thereby contributing that particular kind of heaviness to most of the songs listed above.[62]

Two songs, "Cure" and "2X4" (both from *Load*), offer illustrative glimpses into how elements of Metallica's earlier harmonic language combine with newer methods of articulation. Here I find it useful not only to examine individual riffs in detail, but also to explore how those riffs may have hypothetically sounded had they been written by Metallica in the 1980s. Part of what contributes to fans' worries over Metallica's musical changes in the 1990s is the belief that the new riffs maintain very little in common with the band's 1980s style. While most of the basic building blocks are still there, relatively small changes to the manner of their presentation so strongly evoke other styles of popular music (or at least seem so distant from metal) that, in reception, any similarities are easily suppressed in favor of the differences. My discussion, therefore, does not try either to upend or confirm those worries; rather I am interested in this as an example of the subtlety of genre and the implications such subtlety has for identity. The general absence of palm-muting in most of the riffs on *Load* and *Reload* is particularly crucial in this regard. As I noted in earlier chapters, the sonic modification palm-muting makes to the distortion timbre is a key component in the creation of musical tension in metal and provides a sense of goal direction in a single riff or from one riff to another. Essentially, palm-muted notes and power chords point toward other places in a riff and typically provide a sense of resolution at the end. Additionally, palm-muted notes contribute greatly to a riff's rhythmic characteristics, usually through some form of alternation between palm-muted and non-palm-muted notes and are thus an important rhetorical tool for conveying meaning. The absence of palm-muting is therefore enough to shift recognition of these riffs and blur boundaries of genre.

For example, the verse riff in "Cure" begins with a solid E–G–E motion followed by a repeated A–B♭–D tag, and Ulrich's straight four-on-the-floor drums give the riff a slight swagger. The repeated tag is played as three single notes that slide one note into the next, thus minimizing the individual articulation of each. In particular, sliding to the B♭ makes that pitch sound much the way the flat-5 scale degree might sound in typical "bluesier" styles: as a modification or embellishment to scale degree 4. This kind of specifically slurred articulation between the A and B♭ is a product of the 1990s; on previous albums those two notes would likely have been palm-muted, allowing a nonpalm-muted *power chord* on D to sound accented and thus act as a melodic goal point from the springboard of the A–B♭ motion (see Figure 5.5). In "Cure," however, the B♭ is swept along with the rest of the phrasing and sounds much less like a marked jumping-off point. My hypothesis tries to reintroduce the B♭'s function as a tritone to the E, in much the way it would have acted in the 1980s. Furthermore, both the A and B♭ could also have been played as palm-muted power chords on previous albums, as is indicated in the example.

The song's chorus riff features a similar kind of technique. Though the main portion starts on B♭ and skips up to E before two chromatic descents, the phrase is once again built with single notes without palm-muting. In the 1980s the B♭, E, and E♭ would have been palm-muted and the mid-measure arrival point on D would most likely have been accented by a power chord (see Figure 5.6). Additionally, all three notes in the second

Figure 5.5 "Cure" main riff; original version and 1980s version; palm-muted sections indicated using "P.M."

Figure 5.6 "Cure" chorus riff; original version and 1980s version.

chromatic descent would have been palm-muted in a classic example of the goal-direction possibilities of the palm-muting technique (though probably not played as power chords), as the palm-muting would point the riff back to its beginning. In my hypothesis, though, a different sense of arrival would have taken place in the middle of the riff, at the power-chord D, while the descending chromaticism functions completely differently when it is played with palm-muting, building affective tension for the return of the riff's beginning.

Finally, the absence of palm-muting also has a rhetorical effect on the verse riff for the song "2X4." In particular, I am focusing here on the role of repeated Low Es in riffs and how differences in articulation alter the relationship between Low E and B♭, as well as ultimately altering how we hear the riff in terms of genre. The two initial Es of Figure 5.7 may be

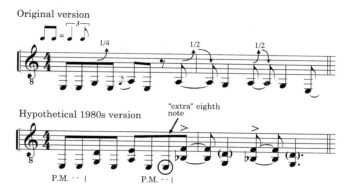

Figure 5.7 "2X4" verse riff; original version and 1980s version.

familiar from the 1980s, as Metallica's riffs frequently utilized Low E as a pitch off of which to launch other parts of the riff, but the lack of palm-muting changes how we hear the rest of the pitches in the riff. As in "Cure," though, the notes to this riff are played as single notes without palm-muting. Centered once again on motions around E, G, and A, the original verse riff also hints at B♭ in places through the use of a slight bend on A. Notated as a half-step bend in the official transcription book, the bend is actually more fluid than a solid half step. Indeed, the bend accompanies the articulation of the A and destabilizes the firmness of that A without necessarily hitting B♭ solidly. This is an important performance technique because it is, among other things, a characteristic articulation found in the blues scale, an issue I will return to below. Played in the 1980s, I hypothesize that two things would have been different about "2X4": (1) the Low Es would definitely have been palm-muted, to the extent that *another* Low E would have replaced the eighth-note rest at the end of the first measure in the original; and (2) the riff would have passed right through A to emphasize the (nonpalm-muted) B♭ to G motion, such that the difference in timbral quality would have effected a more distinct presence for the B♭ power chords. Furthermore, the G and A could also have been played as power chords.

But the lilting rhythmic presentation in the original and Hetfield's vocal timbre also introduce significant components to the riff's (and the song's) effect. Instead of straight eighth-notes, the rhythms in "2X4" are predominantly *swung*. This rhythmic feature, understood usually as a characteristic of jazz and blues-based rock 'n' roll, gives the aggressive and semiviolent imagery in the lyrics a much more unstable feel than straight eighths could provide, and links the ritualized violence of a mosh pit with an understanding of the blues as a site of instability, disruption, and bodily abandon. Most moments in the lyrics, however, present those things as distinctly pleasurable: "The joy of violent movement pulls you under." Above all, the "death swing" style presents a problem for exactly how to move to this music, and how the song is to be understood in terms of genre.

Which Blues? Whose Blues? I

It's so corny when you use the word "bluesier." I like the word *"greasy."*

Lars Ulrich[63]

Greasy? If articulation can effect such an important shift in affect, it also provides a window into understanding the reception of these riffs, and the overall sound of *Load* and *Reload*, as "bluesy." Yet, why might Ulrich object to a blues label as "corny"? Long held to be a central foundation for all of rock, the blues' benchmark-like quality has played a major role in evaluating the authenticity of rock musics for decades, and one of the most frequent ways of describing Metallica's post-1996 music has been via that very association. Generally, such imagery positively links Metallica's music to an understanding of the blues as somehow natural, relaxed, or expressive, and for most critics Metallica's bluesier music represent true artistic development without the loss of some essential Metallica sound. But, while incorporating elements of the blues may be a good way for the band to expand musically, it also serves as a means of generic experimentation. Indeed, the positive aspects of experimentation and artistic progress served as a key component of the band's defense and ultimately underlie much of the critical praise.

What kind of understanding of the blues is put forth by descriptions of Metallica's music as "bluesy?" What characteristics lead to the notion that Metallica's music is bluesy? Moreover, we need also to ask: Which blues? and Whose blues? Here I am visiting some of the issues probed by jazz scholars such as David Ake and Robert Walser.[64] Their work situates understandings of jazz as first and foremost the products of a discourse of subjectivity, and much like the study of how jazz is continually remade and understood, the reception of Metallica's music according to some criteria of the blues underscores the continual remaking of that genre. Like the cultural form called "jazz," the blues does not represent a monolithic extrahistorical "thing." Similarly, as an array of cultural practices, the blues is the product of people and their interaction with various understandings of the past through the mediations of contemporary situations and desires. It is more productive, following Ake, to take a view of the blues "that necessarily entails contestation, contradiction, and plurality" than to try to argue for one style of blues or era of blues history as the definitive example.[65] In short, to associate a particular kind of expression as the "real" blues goes against the importance of people in the development of culture. Various moments in the history of the blues mean different things for audiences and performers at the turn of the twenty-first century because history is always only remembered and, as such, it is always subject to some amount of interpretation. My purpose at this point, then, is to pry open some of the understandings of Metallica's bluesy-ness in order to examine how the blues mean in the context of their production in the 1990s by the most successful heavy metal band in the industry. It should be fairly clear that the label "bluesier" is not meant in this instance to invoke direct images of solo blues minstrels of the 1920s and 1930s like Robert Johnson or Leadbelly, or to have much to do with the harmonic leanings of early country blues, black or white. Furthermore, the reverence for the specific kind of individual authenticity typically associated with those figures, so important to white rock musicians of the mid-1960s, is absent from bluesy understandings of Metallica's music. Among other things, Metallica's music relies heavily on guitar distortion technologies and, as such, specific elements that make the music bluesy find their historical antecedents in the guitar styles of later decades.

In addition to the importance of nonpalm-muted riffs and bent notes on the third and fourth scale degrees, *Load* and *Reload* feature prominent use of double-stopped pentatonic thirds and fourths in the medium register. While these dyads have been a staple of rock guitar solos since the 1960s, and can readily be heard in Metallica solos from before the 1990s, the presence of thirds and fourths within the *rhythm* guitar riffs quickly points the ear toward the bluesy label, regardless of what may be happening around those double-stops. For instance, like the timbral coding in "Wherever I May Roam" or "Mama Said," the element of difference created by the double-stopped fourths in the main riff of "Carpe Diem" (from *Reload*) overshadows the more traditional components of that riff, such as the descent over a Low E pedal tone. In a few songs, though, the double-stop idea reigns supreme. Played in a halting rhythmic style, the double-stopped components in much of the music to "Poor Twisted Me" (from *Load*) convey a sense of short bursts of intense emotion followed by pauses seemingly designed to let the protagonist catch his breath (see Figure 5.8). "Poor Twisted Me" contains no large-scale musical ideas (and little on a small scale either) to contrast with the double-stop riff, and as

Figure 5.8 "Poor Twisted Me," main riff.

such stands as one of the most obvious of the new sound styles interpreted as "bluesy."[66]

Probably the most visible precedent for this sound in the popular history of rock can be found in the guitar techniques of Chuck Berry in the late 1950s, heard explicitly in the openings of songs like "Johnny B. Goode," "Roll Over Beethoven," and many others. Yet, Berry's use of the dyad fourth derives in many ways from the slide guitar techniques of guitarists like Muddy Waters. Further, the interaction between pianists and guitarists beginning even in the 1930s when boogie woogie piano techniques began to be transferred to the guitar also plays a key part in the history of double-stops on the guitar. Pianist Johnny Johnson worked for years with Berry and others in the 1950s and dyadic fourths in the context of boogie woogie piano (for example) appear frequently in his playing, in addition to the boogie woogie bass patterns Berry employs during verse music.[67] We should also not forget the flashy blues guitar of Sister Rosetta Tharpe in the 1930s as an early instance of the kinds of guitar-centric transformations later popularized by Berry.

If double-stopped thirds and fourths function as a significant aural identifier for blues influence in popular music, the context within which those techniques appear ultimately gives them their meaning. For that context (as it informs the current study) it is necessary to jump forward to the 1960s and early 1970s, when the notion of a virtuoso *rock* guitarist was being created. The kinds of song structures and instrumentation of the rock era transform the meaning of these particular musical details once again as part of that era's interpretation of the blues and blues guitar music. Establishing, among other things, the hegemony of the electric guitar as the instrument for expression, rock guitarists also solidified blues-based guitar techniques as a significant language of that expression in the popular mind. The effects of that transformation surround us still as cultural images of the guitarist (whether alone or in a band, playing solos or strumming open-faced chords) stand as prominent symbols of "real" expression throughout popular music. What do the sounds of blues-based rock guitar, with all their larger symbolism, mean when they appear in a song by Metallica, and what does it really mean to call those appearances "bluesy?" In other words, how might the appearance of those sounds within the context of other prominent soloistic approaches to the guitar be explained? As I mentioned above, blues-based double-stops and pentatonicism have frequented rock and metal guitar solos for decades, but during the 1980s, aided by the new emphasis on metal guitar pedagogy, minor scales and single-string chromaticism (combined with astounding speed) became the focus of critical attention. Moreover, such a scalar diatonic approach became fairly conventional as the normative sound of the metal guitar solo, and continues to play a defining role in the identification of metal guitar solos. Providing contrast to his personal history as a top virtuosic metal guitarist, Kirk Hammett's solos on *Load* and *Reload* rely almost exclusively on slower-paced dyadic and pentatonic materials. Indeed, anything resembling a fast scalar run or flashy virtuosity is almost entirely absent from these albums. Beginning with his work on *Metallica*, Hammett's solos are also usually bathed in a thick wah-wah sound, and the importance of the wah pedal to his playing evokes the sounds of another important musician in the transformation of the notion of bluesier: Jimi Hendrix.

The meaning and transformation of the blues in the 1960s counterculture has been well discussed from a number of different aspects, but it is worth reiterating that in many respects the concept of the blues functions as an ideal, hovering over and framing the whole of rock music at the time. The complex racial component of playing blues-based sounds during the 1960s also complicated Hendrix's own position in contemporary musical circles. Even while he made an effort to downplay his race as any essential element of his musical ability (preferring instead to speak of the blues as part of a more general spirito-psychedelic "electric church"), the image of a black man playing blues-based music within the context of rock nevertheless forced white blues-rock musicians to evaluate their own role as blues-based guitarists. Studying Hendrix reception as part of the history of black male sexuality, Steve Waksman writes that for white guitarists like Eric Clapton, John Paul Hammond, and Pete Townshend, all of whom steeped in the expressive power of the blues, Hendrix's very blackness represented a way into the blues ultimately beyond their own reach, regardless of their chops or studied knowledge. Indeed, Hendrix's decision to channel his blues-based background specifically into rock music was also understood on some level as his *reappropriating* ownership of "the symbols from which [white] rock performers drew their power."[68]

Important to my discussion here, then, is the particular version of the blues demonstrated in Hendrix's blues-inflected rock songs. The transformations found in the music for "Voodoo Child (Slight Return)," for example, emphasize difference-marking techniques and sounds developed in 1960s guitar rock while also positioning those sounds in an overall atmosphere

Figure 5.9 Jimi Hendrix, "Voodoo Child (Slight Return)," intro riff.

Figure 5.10 Metallica, "Prince Charming" intro riff excerpt.

guided by a larger cultural significance of the blues. The distorted Low E pedal (a single pitch, not a power chord) combined with pentatonic improvisations based around the E one octave higher may have been around in older blues eras, but the *sound* of this riff in the late 1960s (accompanied by the loud drums and doubled on bass guitar) places it in a specific historical moment in the development of the blues genre (see Figure 5.9). Moreover, it is eminently possible to imagine this riff and this sound (or perhaps even the general outlines of the whole song) appearing on either *Load* or *Reload*. Indeed, the main riff to Metallica's "Prince Charming" (from *Reload*, Figure 5.10) is one of several Metallica riffs from the 1990s to display striking sonic similarities to that heard in "Voodoo Child."

Of course, obvious differences abound in these two riffs: the Low E pedals emphasize different rhythmic moments ("Voodoo Child" is consistently on the downbeat whereas "Prince Charming" always anticipates the downbeat); the Low E in "Voodoo Child" is allowed to ring out whereas in "Prince Charming" this pitch sits inside a more active motive and serves as a rhythmic and melodic jumping-off point; and while the tessitura of the pentatonicism is similar in both riffs, Metallica's consistent figuration contrasts with Hendrix's bursts of improvisation. Yet, the two riffs share a common overall style, harmonic range, and sonic character, and it is instructive to examine the Metallica riff with an ear toward how this particular sound represents a crucial aesthetic shift for the band. It is a shift that, unlike the riffs examined in previous chapters, moves away from anything resembling their sound on previous albums.

The observation of possible sonic connections between Hendrix and Metallica is not to postulate some definitive and direct influence passing from one to the other, or to argue that Metallica's 1990s music attempts to capture some universal essence of Hendrix. Rather, I am trying to highlight one particular historical moment—the late 1960s—that perhaps drives the appearance of the term "bluesy" as it is applied to Metallica. Certainly, the element of psychedelic sexuality so important to Hendrix's aesthetic occupies no observable place in any of Metallica's music under consideration here. At the same time, however, the fact that such imagery is stripped from Hendrix's original should also remind us that the choices made by later artists are heavily influenced by their mediated understanding of earlier aesthetics. That is to say, an important piece of my investigation rests with the observation that Metallica made the choices it did nearly thirty years after Hendrix died. Furthermore, while the music of both artists has been understood on some level as bluesy, Metallica's participation in that historical conversation helps to reshape that label through their appropriation of specific components of prior statements. Thus, we can hear Metallica's riff with an ear toward how its particular sound represents a significant aesthetic shift for the band, but we should also listen to those changes in the context of larger cultural understandings of the blues.

Throughout the 1990s, Hammett repeatedly asserted an affinity for the music of that 1960s icon of guitar rock, finding a compelling image of artistic creativity and freedom in Hendrix's work.[69] Unlike Lars Ulrich, Hammett had no objection to the descriptor bluesy. Indeed, throughout Metallica's career many of the traditional rhetorical-performative mannerisms of rock authenticity and stardom have appealed to him, and in interviews he often espouses the most simplistic rhetoric of any member of the group, usually couched in painful cliché and transparency. Ulrich's apparent thoughtfulness and honesty prevents him from sounding as transparent as Hammett, but as we have seen, Ulrich still performs according to many of the same well-established rhetorical rules of authenticity followed by Hammett.

Still, a major component in labeling Metallica's music as bluesy resides in Ulrich's basic unease with the label bluesier. His apprehension reveals a particular cultural understanding of how the idea of bluesier means in popular music, and how it is not limited necessarily to musical specifics. In particular, Ulrich's notion of bluesier seems to draw on a broader set of socially received meanings having very much to do with the issues of race I have been discussing throughout this book. Moreover, I would argue that Ulrich's use of the word "corny" to negatively judge the word "bluesier" reveals the same kinds of anxieties about the blues that were expressed by rock critics in the 1980s in their appreciation for Metallica's particular style of heavy metal. Like those critics, the specter of what critic

Erik Davis called the "white-blues whipping post,"[70] with its contested and complicated political implications, evidently haunts Ulrich's conception of bluesier. Yet, he obviously recognizes some usefulness to that descriptive term through his preference for another word that is not completely unrelated. His overall response, however, downplays the idea of some kind of blues-based style on *Load* and *Reload*—he draws attention away from "the blues" as a crucial signifier—and deflects interpretations away from the appearance of a sudden attraction to a style of music with which, as a wealthy white rock musician, he doesn't feel comfortable forming a public identification. Clearly, "corny" functions in this instance as another shorthand semantic defense against the concomitant loss of a white subjective interiority to the trappings of black forms of expression through an identification with "bluesier." "Greasy," on the other hand, retains a certain flexibility and ambiguity. Above all, Ulrich uses "greasy" to maintain a distinction (albeit a slight one) between appropriating aspects of black music and the appropriation of cultural images of black sexuality and identity. As such, the term "greasy" props up the rhetoric of authentic aesthetic experimentation as one explanation for Metallica's generic wanderings, and it defends against the charge of selling out, without the need to delve into the messy issues of race and popular music.

Which Blues? Whose Blues? II

Metallica's predilection for the rambling, multi-part epic, almost charming when their music passed for stoner Stravinsky, seems pretty dumb applied to the sort of side-long boogie jams that went out of fashion before Gregg married Cher.

Critic Jonathan Gold, panning *Load*[71]

But the messy issues of race and popular music are always present. To note that Ulrich rhetorically releases himself from a potentially controversial identification with blackness does not insulate him from the topic of race. The common equivalence in popular culture of the word race with black lures us into the false belief that if we are not dealing with black we are therefore absolved of dealing with race. However, when we look deeper into the racial conceptions of bluesy put forth by Metallica on *Load* and *Reload*, we can find helpful explanation in the exceedingly complex racial strata attached to the 1970s Southern Rock style. In his exasperated embarrassment, critic Jonathan Gold's comment above hints at the very tension of racial identity surrounding Metallica's forays into bluesier material, a move Gold not only characterizes as a significant artistic step backward for the band (made clear by his reference to the extremely short-lived marriage of Allman Brothers Band guitarist Gregg Allman and pop-culture icon Cher in 1975), but one which also would seem to place them into some blandly amorphous category of "blues rock." Most important for my discussion of Metallica's selling-out controversy is the specific kind of working class white masculinity contributed by the country music components of Southern Rock, which constituted, for some Metallica fans, yet another disastrous break from the band's past. Furthermore, the shift into Southern Rock also entails a shift in how we talk about Metallica by raising the issue of authorship: I must make clear that I am returning primarily to the image of white masculinity demonstrated specifically by James Hetfield. In the same way that I have focused on Ulrich's unease with the label bluesier and his response to the Napster controversy, we should see the development of Hetfield's quasi-Southern Rock image as representative of the expression of a single individual presented through the larger collective aesthetic of Metallica. Indeed, the Southern Rock image fits poorly when applied to Kirk Hammett (and Lars Ulrich, for that matter), and Hetfield borrowed elements found in Southern Rock and reconstituted that image with much greater consistency than the other members of the band. Finally, as the main songwriter for the band, Hetfield also carried it over into Metallica's music.

The 1992 documentary video *A Year and a Half in the Life of Metallica*, filmed during the recording of *Metallica* and the initial tour for the album, presents Hetfield constructing this image on quite a few occasions. In one segment, he stands outside the studio in a red flannel shirt and brown leather cowboy boots picking on a Fender Telecaster (perhaps *the* guitar symbolizing blues or country affiliation). Later, we follow him into a blues bar where he walks onto the tiny stage, puts on the Telecaster, and tentatively picks out a solo over a slow blues progression. The sound engineer even introduces Hetfield over the P.A. as a special guest "who's got the blues tonight." Remember that at this time Hetfield was also at work creating one of the most successful heavy metal albums ever, and examples such as these hint at developments in musical identity by Metallica's main songwriter throughout the 1990s. That the nonmetal portion of that life would become dominant on *Load* and *Reload* is only reinforced by the numerous publicity pictures of Hetfield in a kind of rockabilly version of blues-rock garb: white t-shirt with rolled sleeves and tucked into Levis jeans, slicked back hair, looking away from the camera and wearing either a Telecaster or a Gibson Les Paul guitar (another guitar model typically associated with blues-rock or country music).[72]

Southern Rock stands as the most obvious form of identity for explaining Hetfield's image, even if it is not the only one. As I mentioned during my discussion of "Mama Said," the element of "outlaw" country music permeates the affect of that song, and, as a general atmosphere, has significance beyond that song as part of a Southern Rock identity. Jonathan Gold is not wrong to evoke Gregg Allman, even if Metallica's music only vaguely suggests Southern Rock in any sonic detail.[73] He does so primarily as an off-the-cuff sarcastic jab, but a Southern Rock identity provides a more realistic descriptor for Hetfield's 1990s identity than a strictly outlaw country image because of the way Southern Rock encompassed elements of hard country and country blues aesthetically. Particularly important for Hetfield's appropriation, Southern Rock also accompanied those musical styles with elements of masculinity drawn both from rock and country, particularly the themes of independence, ramblin', and male bonding. In forming its version of white masculinity, Southern Rock also merged the figure of the cowboy, heroic and fearless, with what Ted Ownby has discussed as the "helluvafella" tradition, reworking it all into the particular outlaw image found throughout Southern Rock.[74] The components of this merger draw heavily on tensions between the ideals of Home and Road that were particularly developed in postwar country music (discussed in Chapter 4), yet in the context of 1970s Southern Rock, the hard-living helluvafella generally lacked the balance provided by an evangelical culture and the ideals of a stable home life.

I am interested in the way Metallica's effacement of the race issue in their bluesier/greasier sound resembles a similar smoothing away of those same issues in the reception of Southern Rock. I point to reception because, while some of the musicians clearly understood the issues of race and at least attempted to come to terms with them (in particular the Allman Brothers Band), the success of "southern-male-ness" and the helluvafella tradition that made the style so commercially distinctive obscured much of any reconciliatory effort. Paul Wells, moreover, argues that "southern rock distances itself from the politics of race by essentially ignoring it," in the sense that Southern Rock bands were (and continue to be) more concerned with defending and celebrating the notions of simplicity and honesty of some mythical Southern ways of life.[75] On the other hand, Mike Butler argues that songs like "Luther King Was a Good Ole Boy" (by Black Oak Arkansas) and the cradling of a young black child in the arms of white musicians on the cover of Wet Willie's album *Wet Willie II* demonstrate the willingness of Southern Rock bands to reach some sort of rapprochement regarding the blues and race in the post-Civil Rights American South. But this image of reconciliation cannot be squared with the strategies eventually used to market these bands to the rest of the country.[76] Instead, the Wet Willie album cover example only furthers the centuries-old stereotype of simple-minded purity that imagines African-American musical styles as unencumbered (and thus child-like) by the strains of modernity.[77] 1970s Southern Rock was never overtly racist, yet its strategy of refusal with regard to race functions as a key characteristic for defining a specific form of whiteness. Moreover, it is this general sense of resistance to ideological revisionism and a refusal to signal an engagement with anything having to do with an outside set of beliefs called "political correctness" that I find at the core of Hetfield's personal aesthetic. In other words, Hetfield's image has less to do with a sense of regional identity (he has never lived anywhere near the South, though his father moved to Arkansas several years before he died) than with a class-based identity. As I noted earlier, the embrace of a working-class image also serves as something of a foil against whatever pressures he experiences in his "other" life as a multimillionaire heavy metal star.

Finally, Gold's mention of the marriage between Gregg Allman and Cher, an event that severely damaged the credibility of the Southern Rock style, indicates that perhaps we are removed in time sufficiently for the identity politics of Southern Rock to have become blurred with and folded into the understanding, in later decades, of the identity politics found in mainstream country music. Located and identified with a very specific cultural moment—the South in the early 1970s, redefining itself in the post-Civil Rights era, the continuing malaise of the Vietnam War, and the broad cultural gaps created by the ideological challenges of the counter-culture—Southern Rock's commercial appeal did not last into the 1980s, and its existence in recent years only as part of recurring "reunion" tours has, in effect, tightly fused its image to the early 1970s. The perception of Southern Rock as a form of country music would be a significant development useful toward understanding both the positive critical reaction to a song like "Mama Said" as well as the negative fan reaction to the bluesy elements of the *Load* and *Reload* albums. Even as it became the most commercially successful genre of popular music in the 1990s, country music's mass media significance became secondary to the worldwide developments in mainstream pop, rendering it a repository for self-consciously old-fashioned ideals and values.[78] While one journalist praised *Reload* as "heartland-friendly," other reactions to the perception of a country tinge in Metallica's bluesier style were not nearly so amicable. That this might be the case is interestingly evidenced in one fan's reaction to the kind of company Metallica chose to keep in the late 1990s. In a 1998 issue of *So What!* Hetfield and Jason Newsted are pictured with country music icon

Garth Brooks. The editors of *So What!* captioned the picture with the faux-incredulous: "Jason, James and ... Garth?!" and the image spurned one fan club member to write in and announce he'd had enough:

> Let's see ... we had a 'cunt'ry singer who wouldn't know country music if it bit him on the ass. Then their [sic] was James and Jason. Yo! Jason, what's new in hip hop? James ... I wish you nothin' but the best, but I've got to tune out ... I like the new stuff alright, but half the fun of being a Metallica fan was being on the fringe, sort of a loose cannon. If you guys think rubbing elbows with Garth is cool I've got to say adios. — Gregory H., Texas (*So What!* 5, no. 1, p. 7)

Gregory takes issue not with Metallica simply hanging out with country musicians (or hip-hop musicians), but with the fact that their success has so turned them into mainstream celebrities on the order of Garth Brooks. At the same time, his distaste for Brooks is more violent than any feelings he may have for country music, and it is the mere fact of Hetfield and Newsted in the same picture with Brooks that drives Gregory *que se vaya*. Still, his nasty spelling of "country," coupled with other fan reactions equally as derisive of an influx of country's aesthetic characteristics, points to an important flattening in the contemporary understanding of Southern Rock. While it is harder to pin down any specific musical comparison between a song or riff from *Load* and *Reload* and something directly from a Southern Rock song, Metallica's presentation of a bluesier aesthetic operates from the possibilities engendered by this flattening. Songs such as "2X4" and "Mama Said" therefore slip into the creases of genre that have been created by the continual reevaluation of the borders marking earlier moments of generic identity. In its broadest conceptions, then, Metallica's selling-out controversy (indeed any such controversy) lies somewhere at the intersection of commerce—perhaps signaled by Hetfield and Newsted hanging out with Garth Brooks—and the folds of musical genre that represent microcosms of unwelcome instability and ambiguity.

Metallica's experience with selling out broaches a broad array of topics. It crosses paths with long-established values of authorship and control, it intersects with more recent understandings of tensions between creativity and commerce, and it unfolds against a backdrop of deep-seated ideas about the linkage between musical genre and personal identity (of both artists and audiences). Moreover, each of those aspects relies on the specificity of historical circumstance for their creation and the continued transference across history for their interpretation in the 1990s. Selling out may defend a complex combination of absolute music, musical authenticity, and personal interiority for its existence, but such defenses have never fully been able to combat the ever-present connection between art and commerce in Western culture. In the sphere of the authentic the ties between the two are so close that art is always already commercial. At times, we experience brief but intense moments where "real" music becomes real because it lends itself to careful consideration, conscious appreciation, and an identification with an independent subjectivity unfettered by any commercial concerns. In other words, playing real music really matters sometimes. But we are still left with the idea that we *allow* ourselves to experience such moments, for they are not some objective truth or reality, and in a sense we do more than just passively experience them: we actively create them as the desire arises while at other times the need for that kind of authenticity is not there. The very accusation of selling out signals foremost the uncomfortable realization that the mask enforcing some "real" has fallen away. The anxiety over that disintegration is thus the recognition that the mask itself was always just a mask, and that its removal only exposes what has been there all along.

Epilogue

Somewhere in the Bay Area, 2003—A day's jamming and rehearsal ends. The musicians put down guitars and come out from behind drums, in high spirits and energized after hours of loud and powerful heavy metal. The singer, looking like a skatepunk in a grey knit cap pulled over his ears, walks over to the drummer emerging from behind his kit (and who sports a bleach-blonde buzzcut that makes no effort to hide his receding hairline) and gives him a hug. Turning toward the lead guitarist, who has just finished packing some equipment, the singer gives him a hug as well. Finally, he meets the band's bass player (and newest member) and at that point I think to myself, "Is he going to hug him too?" The bass player does indeed get a hug from the singer, accompanied by much backslapping. In all, the hugs are quick, but they are also deliberate, almost methodical and ritualized as the singer and his bandmates conclude their musical activities for the day.

In mid-2001 James Hetfield checked into a rehabilitation facility to begin treatment for what was officially announced as problems with "alcoholism and other addictions." His treatment effectively put Metallica on creative hiatus for six months and capped a tumultuous year in which longtime bass player Jason Newsted quit and the band played not a single show. Details of Hetfield's "other addictions" remained sketchy at the time of course, but it was clear that he came out of rehab in early 2002 a more thoughtful and, in some ways, a more spiritual person. After resuming production on the album *St. Anger* his contributions to the band members section of the fan club magazine were personal in a distinctly confessional way. For instance, as part of "James' Gratitude List" penned in November 2002, Hetfield was grateful "For those who have helped me look inside," "For the gift of creativity," and he concluded with "For the awareness to want to write such a list ... and share it."[1] The band's decision to allow fans to see the end of the rehearsal described above and its expressions of brotherly camaraderie stands as an outgrowth of this sense of confessionality.

In subsequent interviews about his time away from the band Hetfield described his having been gradually swallowed up by what he called the "Metallica machine," that confluence of music, business, and celebrity whose complexity increased dramatically for the members of Metallica in the mid-1990s. As I discussed in the last chapter, the largely negative responses to Metallica's actions against Napster were so heated because the band had chosen to reveal the latent business venture that had always been complementary to fans' emotional experience of the music. Thus, Hetfield's very desire to escape the Metallica machine was also an attempt to reclaim (or perhaps assert for the first time) a latent personal venture that had been subsumed by the constant presence of Metallica since his teenage years. The musical and economic success of the band, as well as his own celebrity status, had never allowed Hetfield to present himself as anything other than "James Hetfield."

Hetfield's need for treatment also reveals something important about the thematic history of power and powerlessness in Metallica's career. After working so hard to construct a musical identity built around maintaining personal control in the face of threats like addiction, the fact that Hetfield himself succumbed to the power of an addiction has the potential to dramatically reconfigure how songs like "Master of Puppets" or "Eye of the Beholder" are heard by contemporary listeners. Even as songs such as "Fade to Black" (and others from the Fade to Black Paradigm) represented excursions into various levels of vulnerability, and "Eye of the Beholder" and "Master of Puppets" avoided unambiguous and celebratory empowerment over the forces of oppression, the fundamental power of those songs rested on the implicit separation of Hetfield's personal life from the themes present in the music and lyrics. What might those songs mean when played and sung by a recovering Hetfield? Indeed, on a more general level Hetfield's submission to temporary powerlessness through rehab radically demonstrates the historically contingent nature of reception, and illustrates how it is influenced through the mediations of so many other social forces. The construction of confident detachment that shadowed so much of that music's composition and reception does not, however, suddenly turn out to be false or fake. Rather, we get a stronger sense of the constructed nature of detachment itself and its contribution to the production of meaning within, for instance, the discourses of genre and musical style.

At the same time, it must be remembered that Hetfield's experience of powerlessness and, significantly, his recuperation within the band were also at times accompanied by video cameras and press releases. The intense sincerity expressed in his notes to fans and the video clips showing him goofing off with the other members were also part of a mammoth autobiographical effort to document the production of the band's music. The video clip described earlier actually begins with footage of the band blazing through mid-1980s classics like "Battery" and "Master of Puppets," as well as a ten-second teaser of new material from St. Anger. Placed on an official "Jump in the Studio" Web site dedicated to daily updates on the recording process, the clips (as well as photographs) formed a repository of many types of "performances," at once open to fans but also carefully controlled by the band.[2] For instance, photos of Metallica working in the studio control room showed the band in various activities, but any writing on the whiteboards that hung on the back wall was always carefully censored in the final images, as were shots containing anything sitting on music stands in the large rehearsal room. Moreover, most of the video clips were taped in the kitchen area of the studio building or in the parking lot where it was easier to avoid accidentally capturing unauthorized details related to the album. Indeed, such self-censorship represents the seams in the fabric of the band-to-fan-to-band relationship created by the documentation project. While these instances of control do not necessarily negate whatever sincerity is depicted in such things as Hetfield's list or Ulrich's rambling video monologues, they nevertheless form a discrete barrier, subtly reinforcing the experience of the Web site and its purpose of band/fan interaction as one of representation. Our recognition of the authenticity of the Web site content occurs precisely because of this process of representation.

Concurrent with the fan-oriented video clips was the filming of a professional documentary about Metallica and the making of St. Anger, its footage creating still another kind of representation, and engaging with another layer of control. Bruce Sinovsky and Joe Berlinger's film Some Kind of Monster, released in early 2004, was originally planned as a long-form infomercial and was initially financed by Elektra Records. The film captures many moments wholly unsuitable for posting on the fan Web site, particularly the intense and lengthy group therapy sessions with therapist Phil Towle, but in doing so it marks an important moment in the development of the band's stance toward the prospect of being read by others. To that end, Metallica even purchased the filmmakers' contract from Elektra in early 2003 in order to transfer significant artistic control from the record label to the filmmakers and enable them to put together a feature film that would not shy away from unflattering topics.[3] Like Hetfield's willingness to share his Gratitude List, the band's willingness to share potentially embarrassing footage of themselves marked an assertion of both the members' own self-confidence and a reevaluation of the structures of personal control that had guided their earlier aesthetic.

The subject of Phil Towle deserves further attention because the steadfastly communal approach to creating *St. Anger* (including those postrehearsal hugs) was intimately connected to Towle's therapeutic strategies.[4] Hired at the end of 2000 by Metallica's management company to help the band during the departure of Newsted, Towle's presence was controversial, not least because he preferred the less clinical title "performance coach" to "therapist."[5] Some fans in the message forums at the "Jump in the Studio" Web site expressed encouragement for Towle's presence, believing the decision to work with him represented a solution to whatever problems required his assistance, and that the band would surely be stronger afterward. Objections to Towle came largely in the form of derisive comments about the larger concept of psychological counseling for individuals: the very notion of turning to someone else, especially someone outside the band's inner circle of members and close associates, to help deal with personal issues seemed to symbolize the acceptance of powerlessness and a touchy-feely weakness obviously antithetical to both metal and Metallica's role within metal. Indeed, Slayer guitarist Kerry King dismissed Metallica's relationship with Towle in these general terms, saying, "No way would you catch [Slayer] talking to someone about things that aren't working right. If you can't handle your own (expletive) problems, then too bad."[6] The relatively public presence of Towle certainly did not lessen those concerns, as the band made no special effort to conceal its dealings with him (but neither did it parade him in front of fans). As with the earlier concerns over Bob Rock's role in shaping Metallica's music beginning with *Metallica*, the concerns regarding Towle also represented anxieties about a supposedly pure aesthetic endeavor threatened by individuals who lacked legitimate cultural credentials to justify their influence. Because the scale of Towle's involvement was in many respects far greater than Rock's—Rock participated equally in the group discussions led by Towle—Towle represented, in the view of some fans, a much higher level of uncertainty and therefore a much broader threat. At some point in the Spring of 2003 Hetfield and Ulrich also began to perceive Towle as an intrusion, if not exactly a threat, and their final resistance to him (as depicted in *Some Kind of Monster*) presents a fascinating reassertion of the long-dormant masculinity implicitly sought after in fans' opposition to Towle and therapy. Like something out of the Gong Show, the film cuts off Towle's explanation of a quasimeditative "zone" midsentence with a loopy jazz-sounding studio outtake. The "cheesy" musical underscore directs us to a similar interpretation of Towle at this point. In this way the film positions him along the lines of previous feminine "meddlers" such as Yoko Ono or even David St. Hubbins's astrologically minded wife-*cum*-manager, Jeanine Pettibone, in *Spinal Tap*. Finally, with Hetfield and Ulrich standing together once again, Towle is deposed.[7]

In actuality Towle accompanied Metallica for the first few weeks of the band's lengthy 2003–2004 world tour following the release of *St. Anger*.[8] That tour also enabled the members to revisit their musical past in ways more self-conscious than before, beyond the traditional importance of performing expected greatest hits material. As such, most of the concerts opened with "Blackened," not performed since the *...And Justice for All* tour of 1988–1989. Beginning in March 2004, moreover, "Dyers Eve" (one of the band's fastest and most virtuosic thrash metal songs from *...And Justice for All*) made several appearances on the set list. Like the performances of the full version of "Master of Puppets" in 1997–1998, the premiere of "Dyers Eve" on this tour marked the clearest indication of how Metallica's psychological reexaminations of the recent past became accompanied by the reexamination of their musical past.

Prior to 2004, it could be argued that with all the success the band had had with singles from *Metallica* and the *Load/Reload* albums, it had apparently decided to leave the performance of obscure songs from the 1980s, such as "Dyers Eve," to fans themselves. And, indeed, fan-based tribute bands in the years between *Load/Reload* and *St. Anger* were where performances of those songs took place. The regular performance of "Dyers Eve" by Metallica tribute bands such as the Southern California-based Creeping Death, for example, functioned as a special entertainment element for Creeping Death's shows at the same time that it served to "remember" powerful and complex music Metallica had apparently decided to forget. In this way, the performances of "Dyers Eve" by tribute bands can be seen as a complementary engagement with musical identity alongside the band's own. Populated by musicians in their thirties playing music first experienced in their teenage years, metal tribute bands perform for audiences nostalgic for their own youth and who are also perhaps alienated by the latest releases of the ever-changing commercial soundscape. While further examination of Metallica's engagement with its older material would be useful, it seems to me that such issues as they relate to the musical identities of tribute bands and their audiences may be even more valuable.[9]

I relate these observations less as a biographical update and more from a speculative standpoint having to do with the writing of history. My response to the activities described above can only be mediated through the experience of the previous pages of discussion. Indeed, it is exactly this sort of process that makes a large project on a still-active single artist difficult to contain. On one hand it is easy to block off the years addressed in this project as a distinct whole and to see the attitudes described above as "new," as the beginning of another whole yet to be written. On the other hand, I quickly return to many of the questions explored throughout the preceding chapters as the continuation of Metallica's career plays out in video clips like the one discussed above. For example, how does the addition of bass player Robert Trujillo, who comes from a Spanish-American and Hispanic background, fit in the context of the constructions of whiteness so important to Metallica's reception history? While most metal musicians have been white, metal fans have always represented many different ethnicities, and most are also quick to reject the notion that one's racial or ethnic background has anything at all to do with the quality of good metal. In fact, until Trujillo's arrival Lars Ulrich's Danish heritage had been the most visible example of some foreign "otherness" within Metallica. Still, fans' flattening of racial and ethnic identity also contributes to a sculpting of normalcy where, at least in metal, understanding the music usually requires organizing the experience according to different kinds of concerns such as power and powerlessness.

Such an idea should not be surprising, however, as this is how culture operates: meanings, whether found in a quirky video clip, a knit cap, or a stream of palm-muted sixteenth-notes, are always shared, "kept afloat only because communities of people invest in them."[10] However, it is only through careful attention to the taxonomic data of representation—the video clip, the cap, sixteenth-notes, as well as set lists—that we can arrive at an understanding of the cultural power of musical knowledge.

Notes

Chapter 1

1. VH1, "Tape A13: Johnny and Marsha Zazula," collected raw materials for *Metallica: Behind the Music*. No date. During my research I was granted access to almost all of the raw footage used in the making of the episode on Metallica for VH1's "Behind the Music" series in 1998. My thanks to Professor Steven Baur for gathering that material for me.

2. Elektra re-issued *Ride the Lightning* under its own imprint in November 1984, and commissioned two recordings of NWOBHM covers as part of a 12" EP release of the song "Creeping Death." The two cover songs (Diamond Head's "Am I Evil?" and Blitzkrieg's "Blitzkrieg") were also later appended to Elektra's reissue of *Kill 'Em All*.

3. Megaforce's finances were in such bad shape that it could not fund the recording of *Ride the Lightning* in early 1984. Instead, Megaforce's primary European partner, Music for Nations, financed the album.

4. Though not as large as other labels, Metallica decided to sign with Elektra because that label had fewer metal acts on its roster and had a reputation for being willing to support more challenging acts. See Pushead, *Thrasher* 6 no. 8 (August 1986). An interview with Kirk Hammett and James Hetfield. No title or pagination available.

5. This kind of arrangement can be seen as something of a stylistic marker within the heavy metal market during the 1980s. Thrash metal bands on major labels (for instance, Metallica or Megadeth) were engaged in a different kind of marketing plan, one that did not push songs to radio or participate in the same style of spectacular masculinity so important to glam or pop metal bands. Metallica's ability to continue working with Danish engineer

189

Flemming Rasmussen (with whom they had recorded *Ride the Lightning*) and be considered coproducers of their albums therefore differed significantly from the way pop metal bands would frequently be molded via the musical "finishing school" of a well-respected producer such as Beau Hill, Michael Wagener, or Tom Werman. Such a process was certainly apparent at the end of the 1980s and into the early 1990s as the marketing strategies for managing new pop metal acts solidified. Beau Hill achieved great success with four albums by Los Angeles-based Ratt from 1983–1988, and that success led to similar roles with "second-wave" pop metal acts Winger and Warrant a few years later. Michael Wagener worked with Dokken and then White Lion, while Tom Werman produced the mid-1980s breakthrough albums of Mötley Crüe, Twisted Sister, and Poison.

6. Robert Walser, *Running with the Devil: Power, Gender, and Madness in Heavy Metal Music* (Hanover: Wesleyan University Press, 1993), 33.

7. M.M Bahktin, "Discourse in the Novel" in *The Dialogic Imagination: Four Essays by M.M. Bahktin*, Ed. Michael Holquist (Austin: University of Texas Press, 1981, 291). Much of what Bahktin writes about in regard to the Russian novel can be applied to discussion about music simply by inserting the words "music" or "musical" for words such as "words" or "literary." Indeed, many the ideas in this chapter are informed, if not always cited, by Bahktin's perspectives.

8. The New Wave of British Heavy Metal (NWOBHM) represents a large number of metal bands that all emerged in the period 1979–1982 in and around northern British cities.

9. Specifically, Metallica's *Kill 'Em All*, Anthrax's *Fistful of Metal*, and Slayer's *Show No Mercy*. Megadeth's first album, *Killing Is My Business…And Business Is Good*, appeared in early 1985, but Mustaine's prior association with Metallica played an important role in the early association of Megadeth with the other three groups.

10. Joel McIver's generally celebratory survey of metal musicians' memories of both the term "thrash metal" and the music provides the basis for this statement. See his *Justice for All: The Truth about Metallica* (London: Omnibus Press, 2004, chap. 5).

11. "DIY" is an acronym for "Do It Yourself." The most comprehensive account of the hardcore scene in the U.S. is Steven Blush, *American Hardcore: A Tribal History* (Los Angeles: Feral House, 2001).

12. As used in "California Über Alles," and in the context of Dead Kennedys's position within American hardcore, it's important to note that the E–F emphasis is better understood as an ironic move pointing back to early 1960s surf and rockabilly music.

13. Steve Waksman analyzes Motörhead's representation of masculinity as a kind of "born-to-lose" ordinariness. See his "Metal, Punk, and Motörhead: Generic Crossover in the Heart of the Punk Explosion," *ECHO: a music-centered journal* 6 no. 2 (Fall 2004), http://www.echo.ucla.edu/volume6-issue2/waksman/waksman1.html.

14. See Waksman, "Rock Brigade: The New Wave of British Heavy Metal." Unpublished manuscript. My thanks to Professor Waksman for allowing me access to this work.

15. Certainly Rob Halford's studded leather stage costume informed thrash fans' and musicians' sense of visual style, though the S&M context from which he drew his inspiration was largely invisible or unrecognized by later audiences.

16. A fundamental redirection did occur, however, beginning with the album *Painkiller* (1990), Halford's last with Judas Priest until 2005. The music on *Painkiller* is illuminating for how it so radically embraces the harmonic language and virtuosity of speed metal.

17. The history of "Hit the Lights" and the *Metal Massacre* compilation is intimately connected to the formation of Metallica. Lars Ulrich was a friend of the album's producer, Brian Slagel, and landed the slot on the *Metal Massacre* compilation before Metallica even existed and had any original music. Ulrich apparently chose the name "Metallica" after being asked by his friend Ron Quintana whether Quintana's new metal fanzine should be named "Metal Mania" or "Metallica." According to legend, Ulrich told Quintana that "Metal Mania" was a far better name for the fanzine in order to keep "Metallica" for the *Metal Massacre* recording. James Hetfield had written "Hit the Lights" in the months before Ulrich contacted him in October 1981 about forming a group to contribute a song for the compilation. Hetfield and Ulrich had jammed once previously earlier that year without anything coming of it, and it was this second meeting that led to the creation of the band. For the *Metal Massacre* compilation Hetfield recorded the rhythm guitars, bass, and vocals, and Dave Mustaine (who had just joined the group) contributed the many lead guitar breaks in the song. As part of the line-up developments in early 1982, Lloyd Grant then rerecorded one of the lead spots just in time for the initial release of the album. Making matters more complicated, after the initial release of *Metal Massacre*, Metallica, by this time having played a few shows, completely rerecorded "Hit the Lights" (without Lloyd Grant and with bass player Ron McGovney) for subsequent pressings of the album.

18. In Chapter 3, I discuss specific ways in which musical contrast contributed to the reception of Metallica's music in the later 1980s.

19. Hetfield uses a similar shriek in "Metal Militia," another song from *Kill 'Em All* whose lyrics celebrate a distinct heavy metal subculture. In "Metal Militia" Hetfield shrieks twice, first at the initial statement of the verse riff and again at the return of that riff in preparation for the song's third verse.

20. In 1999, Hetfield attributed being made to sing during childhood piano lessons with helping reduce his discomfort about singing in public. Lorraine Ali, "Metallica: Symphony of Destruction" *VirginMega Magazine* (November 23, 1999). http://www.virginmegamagazine.com/default.asp?aid=19D (accessed on December 14, 2004).

21. From the beginning of the band Hetfield served as the lead vocalist, but he and the other members vacillated as to whether he should also play rhythm

guitar on stage. Though Hetfield had played guitar in a couple of earlier groups and had recorded the rhythm guitars on the *Metal Massacre* version of "Hit the Lights," for Metallica's first two shows in the Spring of 1982 Metallica performed with Hetfield solely on vocals and Dave Mustaine on guitar. The band's third show was its only performance as a five-piece group, featuring a second guitarist (a mysterious figure named Brad Parker, a.k.a. "Damien Phillips") in addition to Dave Mustaine. Parker left after that show and Hetfield then agreed to play both rhythm guitar and sing. His role as vocalist was again up for discussion for a very short period prior to recording *Kill 'Em All* in 1983 when the band offered the role to John Bush, then the singer for Armored Saint. Bush declined and the whole matter was never raised again. In 1986 and then in 1992 Metallica performed as five-piece band after Hetfield first broke his wrist while skateboarding and then was severely burned in an on-stage pyrotechnics accident. In both situations John Marshall (then Kirk Hammett's guitar tech) substituted on rhythm guitar while Hetfield remained on vocals.

22. Hetfield did receive vocal training and vocal conservation techniques in preparation for the lengthy tours supporting the *Metallica* album (1991). This vocal "image" of Hetfield is also the one satirized by Michael Tierney (a.k.a. Jaymz Lennfield), vocalist for the satire band Beatallica, which mashes Beatles songs into a quasi-Metallica thrash metal style. Recordings of this material are available from Beatallica's Web site: http://www.beatallica.com.

23. The case for the significance of the body as a site of musical meaning has been cogently argued by Susan McClary in her "Music, the Pythagoreans, and the Body" in *Choreographing History*, Susan Leigh Foster, ed. (Bloomington: Indiana University Press, 1995, 82–104) and most of her other work. Likewise, Elisabeth Le Guin's work on the intersection of the body and performance in the music of eighteenth-century cellist Luigi Boccherini is fundamental. Important theoretical background for the content that follows can be found in her " 'One Says That One Weeps, but One Does Not Weep': Sensible, Grotesque, and Mechanical Embodiments in Boccherini's Chamber Music," *Journal of the American Musicological Society* 55 no. 2 (Summer 2002): 207–254. David Ake's work on posture and embodiment in the music of jazz pianist Keith Jarrett bears importantly on my own work here and is found in chapter 5 of his *Jazz Cultures* (Berkeley: University of California Press, 2002). I will explore further areas of Metallica's bodily representation, specifically as they relate to their representations of masculinity, in Chapter 3.

24. "Low E" simply refers to the lowest open string on the guitar. Because pitches in different octaves have different meanings in metal, I use "Low E" as shorthand to specify the E in the lowest octave on the guitar. Low E is of fundamental significance to heavy metal.

25. Though a blip on either F or B♭ would introduce an additional layer of meaning, I would argue that the rhythmic interruption would still be more important to the affect of the riff than the harmonic change.

26. The footage is included on the compilation video *Cliff 'Em All: The $19.98 Home Vid* (Elektra Entertainment, 40106-2, 1999), compiled following the death of bassist Cliff Burton in 1986. The "Whiplash" footage was shot at The Stone in San Francisco during Burton's second show with Metallica in early March 1983. All references to video footage in the following discussions refer to this compilation.

27. Hetfield and Mustaine provide a similar sequence of statuesque nonmotion followed by dramatic headbanging accents during the chromatically descending triplet quarter notes of the song's primary riff. The primary riff occurs at the beginning of the song and after each of the verse/chorus cycles. Like the verse riff, this riff is two measures long, beginning with a 24-note stream of Low Es before the triplets.

28. As I will discuss in the final chapter, the simple lack of palm muting can also transform the character and reception of a riff with important consequences for broader cultural issues, such as "selling out."

29. Hypermeter is the organization of musical units, such as a two-measure riff, into larger structural patterns. In rock, complete riffs or chord sequences are typically repeated four times (or some multiple of four). In such cases, the complete repetition scheme is hypermetric.

30. Note that the three iterations of the two-measure riff followed by one more measure of drum fill represent an unusual instance of hypermeter.

31. *Master of Puppets* was released on March 3, 1986.

32. David Lidov, "Mind and body in music," *Semiotica* 66 (1987): 82.

33. For examples of this particular change see Slayer's "The Antichrist" and "Die By the Sword" from the album *Show No Mercy* (1983), and "Anthrax" from Anthrax's album *Fistful of Metal* (1983).

34. Harris Berger, *Metal, Rock, and Jazz* (Hanover: Wesleyan University Press, 1999, 195).

35. Richard Middleton, "Form" in *Key Terms in Popular Music and Culture*, Bruce Horner and Thomas Swiss, eds. (Malden, Massachusetts: Blackwell Publishers, 1999, 142).

36. The classic discussion of sonata form remains Charles Rosen, *The Classical Style* (New York: W.W. Norton & Co., 1997). Medieval music is also understood as a parade of forms that signal primary historical developments. Indeed, the overwhelming reliance on tracing the development of the three medieval *forme fixes* (rondeau, ballade, virelai) has served as a kind of insulation from the difficult task of interpretation of the lived content of this music.

37. Allen Forte's work on early twentieth-century popular song, though it is heavily concerned with details of pitch and harmony (and deploys highly theoretical tools to analyze them), is paradigmatic of this approach. See Allen Forte, *The American Popular Ballad of the Golden Era 1924–1950* (Princeton: Princeton University Press, 1995), and *Listening to Classic American Popular Songs* (London: Yale University Press, 2001).

38. This argument is an outgrowth of previous statements by Middleton about the relationship of musicology to popular music studies filled out in his

Studying Popular Music (Milton Keynes & Philadelphia: Open University Press, 1990). For example, he writes that "it will be better to *look both ways, living out the tension* [between formalist musicology and sociological studies of popular music] ... [S]tanding in the margin, two-sided as it is, it offers a golden opportunity to develop a *critical* musicology which could provide a vastly increased analytical power." (p. 123, original emphases.)

39. Charles C. Keil, "Motion and Feeling through Music," *Journal of Aesthetics and Art Criticism* 24 no. 3 (Spring 1966): 337–349. See also Andrew Chester, "Second Thoughts on a Rock Criticism," *New Left Review* 62 (July/August 1970): 75–82. Middleton also discusses both Keil's and Chester's arguments in *Studying Popular Music*, pp. 115–116.

40. Within heavy metal the use of large-scale modular development is found most often in the work of progressive metal groups such as Dream Theater. An example of this practice occurs in the song "Beyond This Life" from that band's album *Scenes from a Memory* (2000). In that song the main 5/4 riff is transformed and presented in 12/8 (beginning at 6:10) as the beginning of a lengthy series of solos. More extended examples involve quotations and variations of riffs and chord progressions between different songs on a single album or between songs on different albums.

41. A filled-out texture is one containing all the instruments playing "normally." The creation of this texture itself can be the result of a process akin to accretion, wherein the addition of instruments gradually fills out a texture.

42. Early in its life, "The Four Horsemen" had a somewhat different form and was titled "Mechanix." Sometime between late April and June 1983, following Mustaine's firing from Metallica, the Bridge B and Chorus' groups were added and the song's lyrics changed to the dramatization of the four horsemen of the apocalypse. Mustaine later reclaimed the original title, form, and lyrics (a sort of car-as-female sex fantasy) for Megadeth's first album, *Killing is My Business...And Business is Good* (1985). However, Mustaine is credited as cowriter of "The Four Horsemen" on *Kill 'Em All*. He is also credited as cowriter on three other songs from that album, as well as two songs on Metallica's second album, *Ride the Lightning* (1984).

43. Quoted in David Fricke, liner notes for Metallica, *Garage Inc.*, Elektra Entertainment Group 62299-2, 1998.

44. Jeff Kitts, "Metallica plays the heavy hits & kills 'em all," *Guitar World* 18 no. 12 (December 1998): 60.

45. Although it may have been unintentional, Hetfield's exclamation of "Whiplash!" over Ulrich's tom fill, discussed previously, also bears a striking similarity to the exclamation of "Witching Hour!" and its drum fill texture in Venom's "Witching Hour" (1981).

46. In the version of "Hit the Lights" recorded for *Kill 'Em All*, the flourish gradually fades in and effectively hides the distinctive drum fill that starts it. The fill is untouched on the *Metal Massacre* recording.

47. This particular detail is related in the *Garage Inc.* liner notes, and if it is true (there is anecdotal evidence to suggest it is not), my guess is that this policy probably had something to do with the licensing issues of public perfor-

mance of copyrighted songs. Furthermore, a "no covers" policy certainly disappeared by the late 1980s.

48. Lars Ulrich, May 1986. Quoted in Mark Putterford, ed. *Metallica in Their Own Words*. (London: Omnibus Press, 1994, 76). A collection of quotations from band members, mostly Lars Ulrich, arranged into larger topics and spanning much of their career. Putterford provides no primary source information.

49. For discussion of the relationship between American classical music and American cultural identity, see Charles Hamm, *Music in the New World* (New York: W.W. Norton and Co., 1983, 410–459) and Richard Crawford, *America's Musical Life: A History* (New York: W.W. Norton and Co., 2001), 372–386.

50. Lars Ulrich, December 1984. Quoted in Putterford, 75.

51. Though it is but a short step from claims of compositional prestige to the claim of classical music, I doubt Ulrich was really making that leap. Rather, I believe he was tapping more into the general status of intellectualism in American culture, specifically the status of intellectualism and individuality as "good." In any case, the strategy of highlighting learned musical skill to secure greater social acceptance has also become central to the writings of pop theorists of metal such as Wolf Marshall and Andy Aledort. I will return to much of this in more detail in the next two chapters.

52. Slayer's first album is the only debut album of the major thrash bands not to contain an obvious genre song.

53. I discuss this phenomenon in more detail in Chapter 3. The eventual devaluing of Metallica's late 1980s music during the mid-1990s is discussed in Chapter 5.

54. John Fiske, *Understanding Popular Culture* (London: Routledge, 1989, 134–137).

55. The kind of compressed lyrical intensity combined with music representing the chaotic that is heard in "Necrophobic" is not a new invention. Indeed, there are striking similarities of affect between Slayer's music and the vivid imagery and wild chromaticism used by Carlo Gesualdo in the late sixteenth century for madrigals such as "Moro, lasso, al mio duolo." Cultivating an image of dark brooding and violence, Gesualdo murdered his wife and her lover and left their bodies to rot as a warning to others.

56. The first album contains such gems as "The Ballad of Jimi Hendrix" (:04), "Diamonds and Rust (Extended Version)" (:02), and "Anti-Procrastination Song" (:03).

57. I will have more to say about the role of race in the reception of thrash metal, and the particular kind of whiteness put forth by Metallica during the 1980s, in Chapter 3.

58. The element of frustrated rage in S.O.D., aside from its parodist presentation, shares many things in common with the representation of white male frustration found in the film *Falling Down* (1993). While the main character of that film, D-FENS, does not explicitly represent hate, he nevertheless lashes out at various other groups who seem to him to simply make his

tortured existence all the more troubled. Fred Pfeil provides a detailed look at this film in the context of its presentation of the crisis of white straight masculinity in "Chips off the Old Block" in *White Guys: Studies in Postmodern Domination and Difference* (New York: Verso, 1995, 238–243). See also Richard Dyer *White* (New York: Routledge, 1997, 212–222).

59. Quoted in Daniel Hinds, "Stormtroopers of Death." http://www.the-plague.com/sod.html (accessed on September 23, 2002).

Chapter 2

1. Quoted in John Gore, "Metallica: Hell of Energy, No Posing," *Guitar Player* 23 no. 4 (April 1989): 26.
2. Metallica and its fans refer to "Welcome Home (Sanitarium)" simply as "Sanitarium."
3. In much the same way that a modular approach can be read as "compositional," the horror aesthetic of a writer such as H.P. Lovecraft ("The Call of Ktulu") can be elevated and understood as literature with a capital L.
4. Deborah Frost, "Metallica: Not Confused," *Village Voice* 32 no. 37 (September 15, 1987): 83.
5. Wolf Marshall, "Introduction," *Ride the Lightning*. (Cherry Lane Music Co., Inc., 1990), 2. Emphasis added.
6. Ibid., 2–3.
7. Chris Crocker. *Metallica: The Frayed Ends of Metal* (New York: St. Martin's Press, 1993, 75). Original emphasis.
8. In those instances, *guitar harmonies* refers to single-note lines harmonized diatonically in thirds.
9. In his liner notes to the 2002 rerelease of *Killing Is My Business...* Mustaine writes that the guitar part of this prelude was inspired by "a Beethoven piece." It is actually a near-copy of the opening of the fugue section to the well-known *Toccata and Fugue in D Minor*, BWV 565, by Johann Sebastian Bach.
10. On the topic of soloistic virtuosity in metal, see Walser, *Running with the Devil*, chap. 3.
11. The instrumental prelude concept also operates as an element in the cultural significance of musical complexity. I will return to that topic, particularly as it relates to issues of race and gender, in Chapter 3.
12. Allan Moore, *Rock: The Primary Text* (Buckingham: Open University Press, 1993, 170–171). Original emphasis.
13. See Mikhail Bahktin, *Speech Genres and Other Late Essays*. Ed. Caryl Emerson and Michael Holquist (Austin: University of Texas Press, 1986).
14. Quoted in Putterford, *Metallica in Their Words*, 52.
15. The members of Metallica have given an explanation for the motive behind these lyrics, but it is strangely undramatic. Essentially, the depressed imagery in "Fade to Black" stemmed from the theft of the band's instruments after a show in early 1984. While it may in fact be the case that that incident was traumatic and very upsetting, I find it very difficult to reconcile the

relatively pedestrian nature of property loss with the wrenching suicidal depression in these lyrics.

16. One of the most significant developments in Metallica's music in the 1990s would be Hetfield's use of a more personalized "I."

17. The controversies over metal lyrics and teen suicide (discussed by Walser in *Running with the Devil*, 145–151) have also embroiled "Fade to Black." In their defense against claims of "irresponsibility," the members of Metallica have consistently pointed to these sorts of fan statements.

18. Similar "expressive" solos can also be found in the middle of longer songs such as "Master of Puppets." In those songs, though, expressive solos contribute an element of artistic breadth to an over-arching performance of musical complexity. I address this topic at length in Chapter 3.

19. "Open-faced" chords are the most basic of strummed chord shapes on the guitar, and are sometimes referred to as "campfire chords." They use open strings, are diatonically triadic, and rarely (if ever) contain chromatic pitches.

20. Basically, the power chord shape comprises three notes: root-fifth-octave. However, it may omit the octave portion, often in very fast passages and very low, palm-muted passages. For a discussion of the sonic-rhetorical mechanics of the power chord, see Walser, *Running with the Devil*, 43.

21. Malcolm Dome and Mick Wall, *The Complete Guide to the Music of Metallica* (London: Omnibus Press, 1995, p. 26).

22. For the most part I have omitted the individual chord qualities (major or minor) in the rest of the discussion because, although the sequence of harmonies does work within a framework of a key center, each power chord is largely a root with a fifth-octave embellishment.

23. Above the twelfth fret or so, the space between frets makes playing power chords more difficult as the hand shape must conform to a smaller area and making precision harder to attain. I will return in more detail to the idea of expressive register as an analytical component in metal in Chapter 4.

24. In live performance Hetfield always echoes the words "good bye" so that the image of leaving becomes closer to "disappear." For years this vocal addition seemed only to be done during live performance, but it is nevertheless present on the *Ride the Lightning* studio recording, albeit at an extremely low volume. On the remastered version of the album, released in 1992 and out of print shortly thereafter, the echoed "good bye" is much easier to hear.

25. Chapter 1 and Chapter 5 further explore the idea of repeated Low Es as a generic identifier in metal.

26. See Warren Kirkendale, "Circulatio-Tradition, Maria Lactans, and Josquin as Musical Orator," *Acta Musicologica* 56 (1984): 69–92.

27. John Blacking, ed. *How Musical Is Man?* (London: Faber and Faber, 1976), 51. In her discussion of these concepts, Susan Fast describes the jarring ring of the telephone during pauses in music as one realization of the split between virtual time and everyday time. See *In the Houses of the Holy: Led Zeppelin and the Power of Rock Music* (Oxford: Oxford University Press, 2001, 123–138).

28. Fast, 137–138. Mark Johnson, *The Body in the Mind: The Bodily Basis of Meaning, Imagination, and Reason* (Chicago: University of Chicago Press, 1987, 119).

29. Donna Gaines, *Teenage Wasteland: Suburbia's Dead End Kids* (New York: Harper Perennial, 1992, 204).

30. Ibid. Emphasis mine.

31. Hammett employs much of the same grammar and organization at the conclusion of his solo to "Creeping Death" (also from *Ride the Lightning*) though that song deals with imagery from the Old Testament. As in "Fade to Black" the final section of the "Creeping Death" solo is an orderly (though accelerating) ascent of arpeggios leading to a repeated half-note high E.

32. Walser, *Running with the Devil*, 151.

33. Jeff Kitts, "Metal Reflectors: Kirk Hammett and James Hetfield Look Back on Some of Metallica's Brightest Moments." *Guitar World* (October 1991). Reprinted in *Guitar World Presents Metallica* (Wayne, New Jersey: Music Content Developers, Inc., 1997, 15).

34. The sense of aggression in the final section is certainly heightened during live performance when Hetfield shouts "Leave me the *fuck* alone!" instead.

35. The very presence of lyrics in the final section of "One" (and in "Sanitarium") is itself worth noting in the context of the Fade to Black Paradigm.

36. See Walser, "Forging Masculinity" in *Running with the Devil*, 108–136.

37. This last point was made fascinatingly apparent in Limp Bizkit's 2003 performance of "Sanitarium" at the MTV Icon award show honoring Metallica. In addition to other musical updates the band made to the song (particularly Fred Durst's monorhythmic rap-like vocal delivery), Limp Bizkit used a breakdown and build-up on the initial Low E of the section as a powerful springboard into a return of the chorus before ending the song with a single statement of the clean-timbred opening chord arpeggio. Returning to the chorus in this way essentially cast "Sanitarium" into a recognizable "pop song" form.

Chapter 3

1. Quoted in Mark Putterford, ed. *Metallica in Their Own Words* (London: Omnibus Press, 1994, 53).

2. For a discussion of this characterization, see John Fiske, "Commodities and Culture" in *Understanding Popular Culture* (New York: Routledge, 1989, 23–48).

3. The complex political status of these events is usefully surveyed in Reebee Garofalo, *Rocking Out: Popular Music in the USA* (Boston: Allyn and Bacon, 1997, 375–389).

4. Robert Walser, *Running with the Devil: Power, Gender, and Madness in Heavy Metal Music* (Hanover: Wesleyan University Press, 1993), 104. See also his "Highbrow, Lowbrow, Voodoo Aesthetics," in *Microphone Fiends: Youth Music, Youth Culture*, Ed. Andrew Ross and Tricia Rose (New York: Routledge, 1994, 235–249).

5. Interestingly, Ulrich and Hammett were emphatic in singling out Hetfield as the exception in the area of drug use. Their comments were originally published as separate interviews in the fan club magazine *So What!* in 1996, but are compiled in Stephan Chirazi, ed., "A Load O' Lolla and Beyond" in *So What!: The Good, The Mad, The Ugly* (New York: Broadway Books, 2004, 62, 68).

6. Other bands have done similar nostalgic performances, outside of the generalized reunion and greatest hits tours that became so successful in the 1990s. For instance, on their 1996–1997 tour the progressive hard rock band Rush featured a full-length performance of the 20-minute suite "2112," (1976) music arguably as central to the Rush canon as "Master of Puppets" is to the Metallica canon. In a slightly different vein, the metal band Queensrÿche performed an entire *album* of material, *Operation: Mindcrime*, as the main focus of its 1990–1991 tour supporting the band's follow-up album, *Empire*. Moreover, in a fascinating and surreal twist on the nostalgic performance of "Master of Puppets," the progressive metal group Dream Theater performed the entire *Master of Puppets* album at a few shows in 2002.

7. I introduced the concept of "modular composition" in Chapter 1 as a way of explaining the specific structural relationships in metal and hard rock. Briefly, a module is an organizing component that is repeated enough to establish it as an independent component within the form of a song. Modules can either be individual riffs or combinations of riffs into structural elements such as a verse-chorus cycle. Because metal harmonic language depends on riffs, the modular idea is also very dependent on riffs for content instead of standard chord sequences or progressions.

8. As discussed in Chapter 1, palm muting is a technique of dampening the guitar strings slightly with the outside of the picking hand. Palm muting is not simply a detail of performance but a rhetorical device used to sculpt and shape the rhythmic and harmonic character of individual riffs.

9. The transcription almost makes it seem more complicated than it is. It is highly unlikely that Metallica specifically intended to write a riff that included a bar of 5/8. However, the transcription parses the flow of time into a discrete visual representation, and the very appearance of a bar of 5/8 in a pop song is typically taken as a visual cue that signals "complexity." For a discussion of the effect of complex meters and their relationship to the body see Theo Cateforis, "How Alternate Turned Progressive: The Strange Case of Math Rock" in *Progressive Rock Reconsidered* Edited by Kevin Holm-Hudson (New York: Routledge, 2002, 243–260).

10. For instance, Anthrax's comic rap song "I'm the Man" (1987) specifically samples one exclamation of "Master!" as *the* representation of Metallica (occurring at 1:55). In this context the phrase positions Metallica as a "serious" band.

11. Notably, during the second half of the lengthy interlude the same exclamation of "Master!" appears, but this time it functions as a direct address by the Addict to the Addiction (labeled as module 7 in Figure 3.1). Over the rumbling half-step alternation of F# and G power chords, the subject position of

the lyrics has again shifted, this time to accusatory and desperate statements by the Addict: Master, Master, where's the dreams that I've been after? / Master, Master, you promised only lies …

12. A version of "Master of Puppets" had always been performed during the 1990s, but the band always stopped after the second chorus.

13. This solo was one of only three that Hetfield recorded in the 1980s. Notably, the other two also appear in quieter interludes like the one in "Master of Puppets."

14. The most detailed memorial biography is Greg Mainer's piece "Smashing Through the Boundaries: The Late Cliff Burton," published in Metallica's fan club magazine, So What! 5 no. 1 (1998, 30–33). There are also dozens of memorial websites and sections of Web sites dedicated to Burton's life and his impact on Metallica's early music.

15. "Anesthesia (Pulling Teeth)," Burton's composition for solo bass (recorded on Kill 'Em All), is an excellent example of the "lead bass" concept. Driven by a distorted tone, "Anesthesia" features such learned elements as harmony and counterpoint surrounded by moments of flashy expression typically heard in guitar solos of the time. Indeed, the impact of "Anesthesia" remained so strong after Burton's death that Guitar for the Practicing Musician even published a transcription of the solo in 1989, an extremely rare occurrence for a magazine dedicated to metal guitar.

16. "Radio Address to the Nation of Federal Drug Policy October 2, 1982." The Public Papers of President Ronald W. Reagan. Ronald Reagan Presidential Library. http://www.reagan.utexas.edu/archives/speeches/1982/100282a. htm.

17. Mitchell Morris, "Kansas and the Prophetic Tone," American Music 18, no. 1 (Spring 2000, 1–38).

18. Mike A. Males, The Scapegoat Generation: America's War on Adolescents (Monroe, Maine: Common Courage Press, 1996).

19. Dan Baum, Smoke and Mirrors: The War on Drugs and the Politics of Failure (Boston: Back Bay Books, 1997, 200).

20. Baum, Smoke and Mirrors, 118–121.

21. Walser, 138.

22. Patrick Goldstein, "Pop Eye: The PMRC is Back on the Attack," Los Angeles Times, Sunday, December 7, 1986, Calendar section, 88.

23. Baum, 33.

24. In some journalistic commentary, the album has even been positioned as a "concept album," an understanding that taps into larger cultural tensions regarding musical complexity, intelligence, and art. As an idea, "concept album" carries with it one of the more revered historical lineages in rock, reaching back to the fabled power of such 1960s albums as Pet Sounds (1966) and Sgt. Pepper's Lonely Hearts Club Band (1967). However, so much of Metallica's music from the 1980s is about control and manipulation that the songs on Master of Puppets hardly form a self-contained statement on those topics. Moreover, there is no evidence that Metallica embarked on the creation of a concept album during the Master of Puppets sessions.

25. To be sure, the Swaggart and Bakker scandals occurred after "Leper Messiah" (and "Jesus Saves" for that matter) were released, and my argument is not to claim that those songs were a direct reaction to the scandals. However, the political strength of the evangelical movement was at its peak in the years 1984–1986, and televangelism in particular had created a great deal of wealth for the movement's leaders. The literature on televangelism and the Christian Right is, of course, vast. For a useful introduction to the historical and social context of American evangelicalism, see Steve Bruce, *The Rise and Fall of the New Christian Right: Conservative Protestant Politics in America 1978–1988* (Oxford: Clarendon Press, 1988). See also Michael Lienesch's *Redeeming America: Piety and Politics in the New Christian Right* (Chapel Hill: University of North Carolina Press, 1993).

26. Hetfield returned to the subject of his religious upbringing in "The God That Failed," on *Metallica* (1991). Written about his mother's death from cancer, the lyrics in that song engage less with a derisive attack against blind followers than with a distinct sense of angry bitterness at his mother's trusting of the healing power of prayer (according to her Christian Scientist beliefs) at the expense of modern medicine.

27. Even though two conservative Catholics helped found Moral Majority in 1979, Steve Bruce argues that the powerful influence of the Catholic Church hierarchy played a significant role in limiting the participation of Catholics in movements like Moral Majority, unlike the much looser "federal" structure of Protestant denominations. Catholics of course remained staunch supporters of the moral issues raised by Protestants. See Bruce, *The Rise and Fall*, 85–90.

28. Lars Ulrich has described the lyrics to the first song on *...And Justice for All*, "Blackened," as something of an environmental statement, addressing "how the whole environment that we're living in is slowly deteriorating into a shithole." Quoted in Malcolm Done and Mick Wall, *The Complete Guide to the Music of Metallica* (London: Omnibus Press, 1995, 50). Many others also see this song as taking a decidedly environmentalist stance. Yet, as a whole the lyrics read much less like a detached statement about environmental degradation and instead seem more obviously concerned with the apocalyptic threat of nuclear winter. Certainly nuclear winter is an extreme form of environmental degradation, but the lyrics to "Blackened" do not engage with that topic in terms of a *process* of degradation alluded to in Ulrich's comment: there is no sense in the lyrics of things in the process of deteriorating. Rather, the lyrics frame the devastation as having already happened. In particular, the specific mention of "Callous frigid chill" and "Millions of our years in minutes disappear" is much closer to the way nuclear winter might be described, and does not really mesh with an awareness of long-term degradation processes claimed by Ulrich.

29. Simon Reynolds, "*...And Justice for All*," *Melody Maker* 64 no. 37 (September 10, 1988, 36).

30. The fact that the bass guitar is simply mixed too quietly on this album certainly did not help this situation. Indeed, the most intriguing explanation

for the low levels assigned to the bass guitar involve bassist Jason Newsted's absence from the mixing sessions as well as Hetfield and Ulrich's continuing unease with Newsted's "newness" in the group. This explanation is summarized in McIver, *Justice for All*, 193–195.

31. A gate is a studio device that alters the envelope of a sound, comprised of attack, sustain, decay, and release. Cutting off the decay can be visualized as slicing off the curve of the sound wave to produce a sharp and dramatic angle from sustain to release (in other words, from sound to silence).

32. Hetfield noted in interviews that the lyrics to "Eye of the Beholder" were inspired by a First Amendment legal case involving hardcore singer Jello Biafra and the Dead Kennedys's 1985 album *Frankenchrist*. Biafra was sued over the explicit imagery on the album cover, and though no legal outcome was ever decided, the court battle bankrupted him and his record company. See Joe Gore, "Hell of Energy, No Posing," *Guitar Player* 23 (April, 1989): 26, and Chris Crocker, *Metallica: The Frayed Ends of Metal* (New York: St. Martin's Press, 1993, 126–127).

33. Tightly palm-muted rhythmic ostinati are also heard in other Metallica songs, ranging from the straightforward gallop in "Motorbreath" from *Kill 'Em All* to the faster, more complex figures used in the verses of "Disposable Heroes" and "Damage, Inc." from *Master of Puppets*.

34. Quoted in Jon Pareles, "Heavy Metal, Weighty Words," *The New York Times*, Sunday, July 10, 1988, section 6, 26.

35. Phil Nicholls, "The Terminator Race," *Melody Maker* 64 no. 35 (July 27, 1988), 36. Emphasis in the original.

36. Richard Harrington, "Metallica's Platinum Overdrive: The Band and Its High-Decibel Departure from the Heavy Metal Mind-Set," *The Washington Post*, Thursday, March 9, 1989, Style section, C1.

37. The role of explicit politics as a metaphorical dividing line between punk and (thrash) metal is discussed in Chapter 1.

38. Keith Kahn-Harris, "The 'failure' of youth culture: Reflexivity, music and politics in the black metal scene," *European Journal of Cultural Studies* 7 no. 1 (2004), 106.

39. Black metal is a style of extreme metal popular beginning in the mid-1980s. Black metal lyrics are unabashedly occultist, with frequent paganized references to the mystical power of the northern European natural environment, and often explicitly anti-Christian. Sonically, black metal differs from thrash in its frequent use of a "blastbeat" drumming technique (where snare hits are exceedingly fast to the point of losing completely their traditional back-beat function), single-note tremolo-picked guitar figures, as well as choir-like synthesizer textures. The most notable black metal bands, such as Darkthrone, Mayhem, Bathory, and Emperor, were also Norwegian in origin, though the style became more internationalized in the late 1990s as it became more commercially visible. The style derives its name from the album *Black Metal* (1982) by the British group Venom, discussed in Chapter 1.

40. Only since the early 2000s has the Right been able to close that gap, largely due to the increased mainstreaming of country music across the U.S.

41. As mentioned previously, the video for "One" was Metallica's first music video aimed at the MTV market. As such, it had the dual purpose of presenting a visual companion to the song as well as visually introducing Metallica to the pop audience. Rather than constructing a narrative that followed the lyrics or story of "One," the video, like many other heavy metal videos of the era, focuses on the stylized performance of the song by the band. However, unlike the fantastic performances created in videos like Poison's "Nothing But a Good Time" (which are as much about displaying the performers as they are about performing the song), "One" relies on medium-distance group shots of the band gathered around Ulrich's drums as well as close-ups of hands playing guitars and drums to present Metallica as less-concerned with visual image and instead representative of a specifically "musical" version of heavy metal.

42. Many Revolutionary-era flags used the rattlesnake (sometimes coiled, sometimes not) or the "Don't Tread on Me" phrase. However, the flag of the Culpeper militia in Virginia is the most well-known flag to use both of those elements as well as the phrase "Liberty or Death."

43. Quoted in Jonathan Gold, "Metallica and the Poetry of the Power Chord: The New Metal is Soul Music for Suburban White Boys," *The Los Angeles Times*, Sunday, October 23, 1988, Calendar section, 69.

44. The concert, recorded in Seattle, Washington, was released as part of an extensive video and audio box set called *Live Shit: Binge and Purge* (Elektra Video 61594-3, 1993).

45. Large metal concerts in the 1980s relied heavily upon this general kind of audience participation. Besides the simple call-and-response pattern, some groups also pitted one half of the crowd against the other in a yelling "contest" that culminated in a massive roar by the entire crowd. Iron Maiden's singer Bruce Dickenson even took to "conducting" the crowd through various stages of volume, again culminating in an ear-shattering roar from the crowd that could easily drown out the P.A. system.

46. The crowd, somewhat to its credit, does not actually answer Hetfield's calls once he moves beyond "shit" and "fuck." Their response, though, is not stunned silence, but a general yelling in approval of the transgression of the entire exercise.

47. Teresa de Lauretis, "The Technology of Gender," in *Technologies of Gender*, (Bloomington: Indiana University Press), 5.

48. Susan McClary, *Feminine Endings: Music, Gender, and Sexuality* (London: University of Minnesota Press, 1991, 7). Emphasis mine.

49. Pareles, 26.

50. When asked "how women presently fit into the Metallica scheme of things," Ulrich was careful to emphasize that the band has grown beyond the apparent immaturity of sex, drugs, and rock 'n' roll: "We all live fairly normal lives at home, each with our female companionship." Quoted in Toombs.

51. Walser, *Running with the Devil*, p. 136. For a useful summary of the development of masculinity studies in the academy, see Rachel Adams and

David Savran, eds., *The Masculinity Studies Reader* (New York: Blackwell Publishers, 2001, 1–8).

52. Of course, the same tension exists in the representation of femininity.

53. Patrick D. Hopkins, "Gender Treachery," 123.

54. It is also, obviously, about homosociality, a set of relationships between men explored most prominently by Eve Kosofsky Sedgwick in *Between Men: English Literature and Male Homosocial Desire* (New York: Columbia University Press, 1985).

55. Walser, 132.

56. Denim jeans have a deep history in American culture, and the multiple meanings associated with them make identifying a jeans wearer by race, economic status, or gender an almost impossible task. Among other things, the foci of meanings for jeans, John Fiske writes, function "as centers of meaning rather than as social categories." See Fiske, "The Jeaning of America" in *Understanding Popular Culture* (New York: Routledge, 1990), 1. Thus, people wearing jeans may not directly identify themselves as young or working class, but are engaging with what those categories signify: vigor or the mythic dignity of labor. In rock music, moreover, denim jeans evoke a specific version of organic working class masculinity. Bruce Springsteen's use of jeans in the representation of the "ordinariness" of his mid-1980s image stands as only the most recognizable instance of this particular construction of masculinity in popular music. Fred Pfeil discusses Springsteen's construction of this version of white masculinity from about 1984–1986 as representative of a type of "authenticity" precisely because the working class component of it did not exist during the Reagan era. See his "Rock Incorporated: Plugging in to Axl and Bruce" in *White Guys: Studies in Postmodern Domination and Difference* (New York: Verso, 1995, 79–88). On Springsteen's "ordinariness" see Gareth Palmer, "Bruce Springsteen and Masculinity" in *Sexing the Groove: Popular Music and Gender*, Ed. Sheila Whiteley (London: Routledge, 1997, 100–117). Importantly for my discussion, the adjectives "free" and "natural" provide the widest understanding of the meaning of jeans. Within existing forms of cultural organization, jeans grant the wearer the power to be "free" and to "be oneself," but they also have the power to erase personal display behind the guise of the "natural," an action that greatly contributes to their normalizing potential.

57. Lenny Stoute, "Metallica ponders the inevitability of death, taxes," *The Toronto Star*, Friday, April 7, 1989, Entertainment section, D10.

58. James Hetfield, quoted in Pareles, "Heavy Metal, Weighty Words."

59. Stoute, ibid.

60. Phil Nicholls, "The Terminator Race" 36. Original emphasis.

61. In Metallica's case, such characteristics broadly intersect with other images and other values that might be broadly labeled as "American." Indeed, sociologist Michael Kimmel's concept of the "Self Made Man" in American history provides a useful framework for positioning the type of masculinity centering on independence, freedom of choice, and control that was so

important for the band's reception in the 1980s. Michael Kimmel, *Manhood in America: A Cultural History* (New York: Free Press, 1996).

62. Reaction to Metallica's second album, *Ride the Lightning*, employed similar images drawing superficial parallels with classical music and the composer mystique. Terms such as "learned" had been applied to J.S. Bach while Johannes Brahms wore the title "academic." It is significant that these hierarchical positions continue to exist in American society regardless of attempts by musicians, particularly in the 1990s to do away with rigid distinctions. Indeed, it is often the perception that musicologists are still viewed as the keepers of what is "correct" in music and, crucially, what is "good."

63. Steve Hochman, "Metallica does itself justice with 'New Metal'," *The Los Angeles Times*, Friday, December 9, 1988, Calendar section, Part 6, 1. Hochman is most likely referring to the lineup of King Crimson recording in the first half of the 1970s, a version that employed distorted guitar timbres, pointed chromaticism, and a more general rock feel.

64. Jonathan Gold, "Metallica: *Load*," *Spin* 12 no. 5 (August, 1996): 97.

65. One reviewer of *…And Justice for All* described Metallica's performance in less derogatory terms, but still along racial lines. "The band's breakneck tempos and staggering chops would impress even the most elitist jazz-fusion aficionado." See Michael Azerrad, "*…And Justice for All*," *Rolling Stone* no. 538 (November 3, 1988): 112. Azerrad is perhaps referring to performers such as Weather Report, Chick Corea, and the Mahavishnu Orchestra, all featuring racially mixed ensembles.

66. Simon Reynolds, "*…And Justice for All*," *Melody Maker* 64 no. 37 (September 10, 1988): 36.

67. Erik Davis, "Freedom of Screech: *…And Justice for All*," *The Village Voice* 36 no. 37 (September 10, 1991): 77.

68. George Lipsitz, *The Possessive Investment in Whiteness: How White People Benefit from Identity Politics* (Philadelphia: Temple University Press, 1998, 121).

69. For discussion of the sociopolitical implications of Clapton's relationship to Robert Johnson, see Lipsitz, 121–123.

70. Susan McClary, *Conventional Wisdom: The Content of Musical Form* (Los Angeles: University of California Press, 2000, 59–60).

71. Jonathan Gold, "Metallica and the poetry of the power chord," 69.

72. Metallica's musical relationship to the blues became significantly more complicated in the second half of the 1990s. As I discuss in detail in Chapter 5, the separation of Metallica from the blues-rock aesthetic is completely overturned as all traces of the aesthetic of complexity disappeared from the band's music. Most critics embraced those changes. However, as I will argue, Metallica's apparent aesthetic reversal raises important questions that have an impact on the historiography on the blues in rock music.

73. Toni Morrison, *Playing in the Dark: Literature and the White Imagination* (New York: Vintage Books, 1992); see also bell hooks, "Representations of Whiteness in the Black Imagination," in *Killing Rage: Ending Racism* (New York: Holt, 1995, 31–50).

74. See David Roediger, *The Wages of Whiteness* (London: Verso, 1991); Theodore V. Allen, *The Invention of the White Race*, 2 vols. (London: Verso, 1994, 1997); Eric Lott, *Love and Theft: Blackface Minstrelsy and the American Working Class* (Oxford: Oxford University Press, 1993); Lipsitz, *The Possessive Investment in Whiteness*.

75. Lipsitz, *The Possessive Investment in Whiteness*, 3–5.

76. On "The Cosby Show" see Sut Jhally and Justin Lewis, *Enlightened Racism: "The Cosby Show," Audiences and the Myth of the American Dream* (Boulder, CO: Westview Press, 1992).

77. Mike Hill, "Introduction: Vipers in Shangri-la: Whiteness, Writing, and Other Ordinary Terrors" in *Whiteness: A Critical Reader*, Ed. Mike Hill (New York: New York University Press, 1997, 7).

78. Richard Dyer, *White* (London: Routledge, 1997, 28).

79. Ibid, 38.

80. Walser, *Running with the Devil*, 17. Rock critics in the 1960s had, of course, reveled in the particular fusions of Led Zeppelin and Cream, and later used the apparent *lack* of such musical-cultural fusions as a potent weapon for attacking mid-1970s progressive rock. For a discussion of the value systems behind such attacks, see Durrell Bowman, "Permanent Change: Ambiguities of Ideology and Genre in the Music of Rush" Ph.D. dissertation, University of California, Los Angeles, (2003) and Edward Macan, *Rockin' the Classics: English Progressive Rock and the Counterculture* (New York: Oxford University Press, 1997, 167–178).

81. Ian Chambers, *Urban Rhythms: Pop Music and Popular Culture* (New York: St. Martin's Press, 1985, 67). Quoted in McClary, 55.

Chapter 4

1. The title *Garage Days Re-Revisited* was itself a play on the name given to the B-side material on the "Creeping Death" single, released in Europe in 1984. Titled "Garage Days Revisited," the package included the band's first recordings of cover songs: Diamond Head's "Am I Evil?" and Blitzkrieg's "Blitzkrieg."

2. Malcolm Dome and Mick Wall, *The Complete Guide to the Music of Metallica* (London: Omnibus Press, 1995, 62).

3. At the same time, Said was careful to argue that Orientalism is not merely "a structure of lies or myths which, were the truth about them to be told, would simply blow away." The continued persistence of Orientalist discourse and imagery over the last 150 years or so demonstrates "considerable material investment" in the practices that are called Orientalism. See Edward Said, *Orientalism* (New York: Vintage Books, 1979, 6).

4. See Susan McClary, *Georges Bizet: Carmen* (Cambridge: Cambridge University Press, 1992, 29–61).

5. This beat is considered to be "half time" because its accents occur at half the speed of the accents characterizing the standard "four-on-the-floor" beat. In

that pattern the kick and snare drum accent alternate beats of the four-beat measure.

6. Since the 1990s, these drums have also played an important role in various versions of the "men's" movement. See John Mowitt, *Percussion: Drumming, Beating, Striking* (Durham: Duke University Press, 2002, 166–207).
7. For a discussion of the two kinds of Mother Nature see Jacques le Goff. "The Wilderness in the Medieval West" in *The Medieval Imagination*, trans. Arthur Goldhammer, (Chicago: University of Chicago Press, 1988).
8. I will have more to say about the relationship between Low E and Low F in metal later in the chapter.
9. Bass guitarist Jason Newsted points out this specific instrumentation during the segment on "Wherever I May Roam" that is included in the *Classic Albums* episode about the *Metallica* album (Eagle Eye Media, EE19001, 2001).
10. Kirk Hammett's main guitar solo in this song also relies heavily on the Phrygian dominant scale. Basically, this scale is characterized by half steps between both the first and second scale degrees and between the third and fourth degrees. Melodically, the relatively large "space" between the second and third scale degrees provides a phenomenological intensification of the smaller movement between the second degree and the first. As will be discussed below, the Phrygian dominant scale most often appears as a special effect in Western pop and rock music.
11. The Road rarely has an explicitly masculine gender, most likely because of how such a label would come uncomfortably close to homoeroticism. Perhaps an explanation lies in the way the Road is experienced: people go "on" the Road, they "use" the Road for personal experiences, and so forth. All sorts of social red flags are raised if the Road is also imagined to be male in those instances. Furthermore, movies like *Thelma and Louise* raise interesting questions about whether this same situation is present when women go "on" the Road.
12. See Cecilia Tichi, *High Lonesome: The American Culture of Country Music* (Chapel Hill: The University of North Carolina Press, 1994, 59–63).
13. Greil Marcus, *Mystery Train: Images of America in Rock 'n' Roll Music* (New York: Obelisk/Dutton, 1990, 14).
14. Ibid., 15.
15. Tichi, *High Lonesome*, 66.
16. Marcus, *Mystery Train*, 25.
17. Ibid., 31.
18. Hazel V. Carby, " 'It Jus Be's Dat Way Sometime': The Sexual Politics of Women's Blues," *Radical America* 20, no. 4 (1986): 238–249.
19. Robert Palmer, "Metallica: *Metallica*," *Rolling Stone*, no. 612 (1991).
20. George Lipsitz discusses these same issues with respect to Eric Clapton's self-professed relationship to Robert Johnson. See George Lipsitz, "White Desire: Remembering Robert Johnson," in *The Possessive Investment in Whiteness: How White People Profit from Identity Politics* (Philadelphia: Temple University Press, 1998, 118–138).

21. The Quest, as it is understood in the second half of the twentieth century by middle class whites, is also represented by a book, Jack Kerouac's *On the Road* (1955), a novel of white ramblin' that became a crucial ideological tool for advocates of American countercultural bohemianism in the 1960s and 1970s (and has remained important in the decades since).

22. David Laderman, "What a Trip: The Road Film and American Culture." *Journal of Film and Video* 48 no. 1–2 (1996): 41.

23. Ibid., 43.

24. J. Gerald Kennedy, *Imagining Paris: Exile, Writing, and American Identity* (New Haven: Yale University Press, 1993, 6).

25. George Lipsitz, "Kalfou Danjere" in *Dangerous Crossroads: Popular Music, Postmodernism, and the Poetics of Place* (London: Verso, 1994), 4.

26. Ibid., 5, 12.

27. Timothy Taylor, "World Music in Television Ads," *American Music* 18 no. 2 (Summer 2000): 163–192.

28. For a discussion of the ways in which corporate America constructs itself musically, particularly its use of specific styles of classical music, see Robert Fink, "Orchestral Corporate," *ECHO: a music-centered journal* 2 no. 1 (Spring 2000), http://www.echo.ucla.edu. An interesting offshoot of the strategies used to sell a successful lifestyle are the DeBeers diamond ads which, at first hearing, use classical music. Closer examination reveals that this "classical" music is as faked as the world music accompanying the business ads I am discussing. My thanks to Professor Fink for pointing out this example to me.

29. Kennedy, ibid., 12

30. Fredric Jameson, "Reification and Utopia in Mass Culture," *Social Text* 1:1 (Winter, 1979): 132.

31. "The very definition of the real becomes: *that of which it is possible to give an equivalent reproduction.* This is contemporaneous with a science that postulates that a process can be perfectly reproduced in a set of given conditions, and also with the industrial rationality that postulates a universal system of equivalency ... At the limit of this process of reproductibility, the real is not only what can be reproduced, but *that which is always already reproduced.* The hyperreal." Jean Baudrillard, *Simulations*, Paul Foss, et al.; trans. (New York: Semiotext(e), 1983): 146. Original emphases.

32. Paul Théberge, *Any Sound You Can Imagine: Making Music/Consuming Technology* (Hanover: Wesleyan University Press, 1997), 203. See also Tony Mitchell, "World Music and the Popular Music Industry: An Australian View," *Ethnomusicology* 37/3 (Summer 1993): 309–338.

33. Jonathan Bellman, "Indian Resonances in the British Invasion" in *The Exotic in Western Music*, Jonathan Bellman, ed. (Boston: Northeastern University Press, 1998, 292).

34. Bellman, ibid., 300.

35. Ibid., 301ff.

36. The functioning of Indian sitar music as cliché at the close of the counter-culture years was brilliantly illustrated during Ravi Shankar's performance

at the Concert for Bangladesh in 1971 (organized by George Harrison). Philip Hayward summarizes the most revealing moment of cross-cultural interaction and miscue as "the exchange between Shankar and the audience ... when after minutes of twanging, unstructured musical meandering, the audience bursts into applause. Shankar politely thanks them for having enjoyed listening to the musicians tuning-up and begins his concert." Quoted from Philip Hayward, "The Cocktail Shift: Aligning Musical Exotica" in *Widening the Horizon: Exoticism in Post-War Popular Music* Philip Hayward, ed. (London: Perfect Beat Publications, 1999), 11. For Hayward, the audience's inopportune applause does not simply represent ignorance of the complexities of "real" Indian music, but demonstrates how "exotic *sounds* [i.e., timbre] are key to the exotic imaginary and the satisfactions such products offer." Ibid. Original emphasis.

37. Bellman, ibid., 305. Original emphasis.
38. See Middleton, *Studying Popular Music*, 103–115.
39. David Brackett, *Interpreting Popular Music* (Cambridge: Cambridge University Press, 1995, 19).
40. For an example of this kind of analysis, see Walser, *Running with the Devil*, 47.
41. We should of course also consider what it means to have a musical selfhood, and how that particular construction informs any assignment of musical details to specific forms of identity. I will return to the issue of selfhood and its implications for understanding Metallica's "selling-out" controversy in Chapter 5.
42. Quoted in Joe Gore, "Metallica: Escape from Blues-Box City," *Guitar Player* 23 (April 1989): 29.
43. Heinrich Glarean, *Dodecachordon* (Basel, 1547). Quoted and translated in Steven Krantz, "Rhetorical and structural functions of mode in selected motets of Josquin des Prez," (Ph.D. dissertation, University of Minnesota, 1989, 361).
44. This not to argue that images of the exotic did not appear at all during the Renaissance. What has come down to us, however, are largely descriptions of dances and theatre pieces. For an overview of early exoticism see Miriam K. Whaples, "Early Exoticism Revisited," in *The Exotic in Western Music*, 3–25.
45. Peter Manuel's study of Andalusian (that is, Moorish) music shows how a similar kind of "Phrygian tonality" developed alongside (with some commingling) the Northern European Gregorian modal practice, and persisting into the present. See Peter Manuel, "From Scarlatti to 'Guantanamera': Dual Tonicity in Spanish and Latin American Musics," *Journal of the American Musicological Society* 55 no. 2 (Summer 2002): 311–336.
46. See Ralph P. Locke, "Cutthroats and Casbah Dancers, Muezzins and Timeless Sands: Musical Images of the Middle East," in *The Exotic in Western Music*, 104–136.
47. See Ellie Hisama, "From *L'Étranger* to 'Killing an Arab': Representing the Other in a Cure Song," in *Expression in Pop-Rock Music*, Walter Everett, ed.

(New York: Garland Publishing, Inc., 59–74). As she reads them, the song lyrics add an element of self-recognition to the narrator's reaction to the killing: "Staring at myself / Reflected / In the eyes of the dead man on the beach." While her reading of "Killing an Arab" explores this shift in the psychology of the narrator as an indication of the Cure's awareness of Orientalist politics at work in the story, she does not question the cultural unremarkableness of the opening and closing Phrygian music as part of the accompaniment to a non-Western locale.

48. A similar instance of this idea of exotic-music-as-prop can be heard in David Bowie's "China Girl" (1983) wherein blatantly exoticizing lyrics are accompanied by moments of obvious "Chinese" music. Again, I would argue that their use as a special effect is about as deep as Bowie goes with these sounds or their parent culture at this moment in his career. Whatever subtle Self/Other conflict might be occurring in the course of this song is also obscured by its location in the mass media of the mid-1980s.

49. For a discussion of these kinds of images in metal, and their role in the reception of metal, see Robert Walser, *Running with the Devil*, 151–165.

50. My use of "harmonic," a word that implies a vertical orientation, together with "scale degrees," which imply a horizontal or linear orientation, should be clarified. In metal, the power chord is the primary building block of riffs, which are, in turn, the primary building blocks of songs. Generally, power chords blur the traditional distinction between harmony and melody, and convey, in many ways, *both* harmony and melody. In most cases the bass guitar doubles the motion of the guitar's power chords, linking the two further. Among other critical accomplishments, MTV's *Beavis and Butthead* provide a good example of this linkage when they "sing" to emphasize how much they like a metal video. One of their favorites is the main riff from Black Sabbath's "Iron Man," comprised entire of power chords. Throughout my discussion I will also use Arabic numerals to identify chords, instead of Roman numerals, because Roman numeral-labeled chords carry with them the added indication of quality (whether major or minor), a tertian context that also implies a very specific kind of functionality rarely found in (or really relevant to) metal.

51. Throughout the following discussion the Arabic numerals are meant to indicate scale degrees derived from the diatonic minor scale. Thus, for a song based around E the pitch D is scale degree 7, not ♭7.

52. This riff was originally the chorus riff to a very early song by Exodus called "Die By His Hand," and is one of several riffs contributed by guitarist Kirk Hammett after leaving Exodus in early 1983 to join Metallica.

53. The verse riff in "Ride the Lightning" (from *Ride the Lightning*) demonstrates this kind of relationship quite clearly. The riff is comprised solely of power chords on E and B♭.

54. The influence of timbre on this idea is important because distortion on unfretted notes such as Low E sounds different than it does on higher fretted notes.

55. Quoted in Gore, ibid.

56. The widespread popularity, since the mid-1990s, of seven-string guitars in metal (with the seventh string tuned to Low B) has only emphasized this idea. While some guitarists did tune their E string down to D for specific songs before that time (including Metallica on "The Thing That Should Not Be"), the possibilities enabled by lower pitches were constrained both by the loss of tone quality in a string not designed to be so loose. In a standard tuning power chord fifths are also physically impossible to play using the sixth and fifth strings once the sixth string goes below D.

57. The importance of the seventh-fret E was discussed in Chapter 2 with respect to "Fade to Black." Affective range is also powerfully demonstrated in the chorus music for "Frayed Ends of Sanity" from ...And Justice for All where the riff "breaks out" of the low, palm-muted and chromatic sludge of the first half into the comparatively brighter sound of a power chord on the higher E for the chorus' hook.

58. The creation of a temporal world around the E and F power chords even seems to allow for the possibility of another half-step climb, to F#. Indeed, exactly that kind of gradual climb happens during the coda to "Outlaw Torn," from Metallica's 1996 album Load. In that song, the chords climb chromatically in one-measure increments from Low E to Low G.

59. Hetfield plays the B♭ power chord at the first fret of the A string and not at the sixth fret of the Low E string in order to continue the arpeggiation pattern begun with the Low E and Low F harmonies. However, playing the B♭ chord up at the sixth fret would have introduced a large physical movement of Hetfield's left arm, one that would have also injected a distinct experiential component into the six half-step leap from E to the B♭ chord.

60. Scott Lash and John Urry, Economies of Signs and Space: Theory, Culture, and Society (Newbury Park: Sage, 1994, 259).

61. Susan Fast, In the Houses of the Holy: Led Zeppelin and the Power of Rock Music (Oxford: Oxford University Press, 2001), 103.

62. Ibid., 104.

63. Andrew Goodwin and Joe Gore, "World Beat and the Cultural Imperialism Debate" in Socialist Review 20/3, 1990: 70.

64. Goodwin and Gore, ibid. p. 73. The example of Paul Simon is also discussed in Charles Hamm, "Graceland Revisited" in Putting Popular Music in its Place (Cambridge: Cambridge University Press, 1995, 336–343). See also Steven Feld's essays "Notes on 'World Beat' " and "From Schizophonia to Schismogenesis: On the Discourses and Commodification Practices of 'World Music' and 'World Beat' " in Charles Keil and Steven Feld, Music Grooves (Chicago: Chicago University Press, 1994, 238–246; 257–289).

Chapter 5

1. David Fricke, "Pretty Hate Machine." Rolling Stone, no. 737 (1996): 33.

2. This dialogue is catalogued in "Rockumentary Intv. w/ James Hetfield," #453768 on Tape B37 of the Behind the Music footage. I give 1996 as the date

of the interview because of Hetfield's short haircut and the discussion of the new album, *Load*.

3. The position of Cliff Burton in the mythology of Metallica's 1980s past remained steadfast throughout the 1990s. I discuss his role in the formation of the band's structural complexity in previous chapters.

4. Also known as "SymphonicA", recorded with the San Francisco Symphony but under the direction of noted arranger Michael Kamen. Though the performance can be heard in the context of previous interpretations of rock music by classical ensembles (the long line of London Symphony Orchestra performances of the music of artists like Yes, Sting, and the Beatles is the best known), *S&M* is not simply the music of Metallica arranged for symphony orchestra. Rather, Kamen composed new orchestral parts to augment the original Metallica songs.

5. The album *Metallica* is currently certified at 14x platinum (14,000,000+ sales) in the U.S. and continues to sell in the top 200 every week on *Billboard's* catalog chart. The sales of that album more than quadrupled the sales of any of the band's previous releases, as well as dramatically out-selling *Load* and *Reload*, which followed in 1996 and 1997. I discuss the notion of "thinking-man's metal" in Chapter 3.

6. Martha Woodmansee, *The Author, Art, and the Marketplace: Rereading the History of Aesthetics* (New York: Columbia University Press, 1994, 41).

7. One of the most historically important manifestations of musical autonomy lies in the equally complex notion of "absolute music," theorized during the same period and centering on Beethoven's *Eroica* symphony from 1803. Daniel Chua explains that the assertion of the absolute made in the service of musical authenticity is a spiritual claim in the sense that absolute music is "something too ethereal to have a history and too transcendent to be soiled by the muck of contextualization." See Daniel K. Chua, *Absolute Music and the Construction of Meaning* (Cambridge: Cambridge University Press, 1999, 4–6) and Tia DeNora, *Beethoven and the Construction of Genius: Musical Politics in Vienna, 1792–1803* (Berkeley: University of California Press, 1995).

8. For an overview of the history of copyright see Mark Rose, *Authors and Owners: The Invention of Copyright* (Cambridge: Harvard University Press, 1993) and Siva Vaidhyanathan, *Copyrights and Copywrongs: The Rise of Intellectual Property and How It Threatens Creativity* (New York: New York University Press, 2001).

9. Ulrich and Hetfield were more apt to share publicity duties in the first year or so of the band's existence, but soon thereafter Hetfield left most of the in-person publicity duties (interviews, and so on) to Ulrich. Hetfield still did a great deal of interviews, but far fewer than Ulrich in the 1980s and 1990s, and many times for guitar magazines (and often alongside lead guitarist Kirk Hammett). Reflecting in 1999 Hetfield remarked that he felt he had been misquoted too often by the general rock press in previous years to warrant continued interaction. At the same time, he noted that during those years he himself "didn't understand the press game." See Lorraine

Ali, "Metallica: Symphony of Destruction." *VirginMega Magazine* (November 23, 1999). http://www.virginmegamagazine.com/default.asp?aid=19D (accessed December 15, 2004).

10. In this regard, the position of the NWOBHM in Ulrich's later life gains its powerful "authenticity" precisely because it has been removed from its original context. On the notion of the authentic and context, see James Clifford, "On Collecting Art and Culture" in *The Predicament of Culture: Twentieth-Century Ethnography, Literature, and Art* (Cambridge: Harvard University Press, 1988, 215–251).

11. Steve Jones and Kevin Featherly, "Re-Viewing Rock Writing" in *Pop Music and the Press,* edited by Steve Jones. (Philadelphia: Temple University Press, 2002, 22).

12. Sinclair's solidarity with the Black Panther party, and his views on whites' role in American youth culture, operated within a complex network of (often primitivized) racial imaginings about black masculinity. See Steve Waksman, *Instruments of Desire: The Electric Guitar and the Shaping of Musical Experience* (Cambridge: Harvard University Press, 1999, 217–229).

13. Quoted in Charles Hamm, *Yesterdays: Popular Song in America* (New York: W.W. Norton & Co., 1983, 453–454).

14. Ibid.

15. Jones and Featherly, p. 28.

16. Ibid., p. 35.

17. Charles Hamm, "Modernist Narratives and Popular Music," in *Putting Popular Music In Its Place* (Cambridge: Cambridge University Press, 1995): 2. To be sure, Hamm's purpose for discussing the use of the "youth" narrative in rock criticism is ultimately to critique the totalizing representation of "youth" by academic sociologists in the 1970s and 1980s as a foundational impetus for the scholarly study of popular music. Employing the narrative of "youth," writes Hamm, "results in distortion, through omission, of the larger view of popular music," and provides no way to talk about "youth" outside of rock or popular music cultures where age is less important. See Hamm, 23.

18. Lawrence Levine, *Highbrow/Lowbrow: The Emergence of Cultural Hierarchy in America* (Cambridge: Harvard University Press, 1988), 8. See also Motti Regev, "Producing Artistic Value: The Case of Rock Music," *The Sociological Quarterly* 35 no. 1 (1994): 85–102.

19. Ibid.

20. Simon Frith, *Performing Rites: On the Value of Popular Music* (Cambridge: Harvard University Press, 1996, 67).

21. Jon Stratton, "Between two worlds: art and commercialism in the record industry," *Sociological Review* 30 no. 2 (1982): 272.

22. Frith, *Performing Rites*, ibid.

23. David Fricke, "Pretty Hate Machine," 33.

24. After hiring the well-known management company Q-Prime, Metallica left Megaforce Records in 1984 in order to sign with Elektra Records, a much

larger company. The band has described those moves as clear attempts at broadening their audience.

25. M.M. Bahktin, "The Problem of Speech Genres," in *Speech Genres and Other Late Essays*, ed. Caryl Emerson and Michael Holquist (Austin: University of Texas Press, 1986, 91).

26. Ibid., p. 69.

27. I discussed Bahktin's notion of a speech genre in Chapter 2.

28. The label "Organization Man" comes from William H. Whyte's *The Organization Man* (1952), an exposé of the sociological implications for business culture due to the increased economic prosperity of mainstream America in the 1950s. See Thomas Frank, *The Conquest of Cool: Business Culture, Counterculture, and the Rise of Hip Consumerism* (Chicago: University of Chicago Press, 1997, 10–12).

29. Ibid, 69. Emphasis added.

30. Instances of hip consumerist advertising in contemporary culture are almost too many to mention. Some that come to mind are Apple Computer's "Think Different" campaign, Miller's Outpost's "It's a free country, dress accordingly," and Verizon Wireless' "People want to be free." Frank notes that the hip consumerist technique underwent a huge resurgence in the 1990s, partly as the result of the view that the 1980s shared similar approaches to consumerism and culture as the 1950s. See Frank, 233–235.

31. The initial quote is from the chorus of "Escape," a relatively obscure song from *Ride the Lightning*.

32. Newsted's quote comes from an interview in *Metal Edge* from 1997. The full text of the interview is available at http://www.metallicaworld.co.uk/Interviews/1997_metal%20edge.htm.

33. "Sex and Violence," Addicted to Noise (1996). In 1997 the online rock journal Addicted to Noise was incorporated into SonicNet.com, which was then swallowed by VH1, with the result that the original article noted above is no longer available. However, an archived copy is available at // www.4horsemensite.com/multimedia/interviews/text/frameinterview33.html.

34. Thrash metal musicians were far more likely to feature aggressive, teeth-bared facial expressions in their photos designed to convey a sense of powerful menace.

35. It is also a feeling expressed by learned academics disgusted with Metallica's legal proceedings against Napster in 2000. In a post to the metalstudy listserv one scholar included the video topic in positioning the Napster issue as "the end of a long train of abuses, starting with the video ("we will never do a video"), the ballads, the haircuts, Alternica, etc." The post was at: http://groups.yahoo.com/group/metalstudy/message/49 (June 12, 2000, no longer available). That making a music video after allegedly vowing never to do so can be described as an "abuse" in the sense usually reserved for criminal activity seems an extreme condemnation.

36. Many of those statements about early plans for a video are quoted in Putterford, *Metallica in Their Own Words*, 64.

37. Quoted in Steffan Chirazi, "Napster and Beyond: An Interview with Lars Ulrich," *So What!* 7 no. 2 (1998): 30.

38. The RIAA never actually used the word "control" to describe their efforts. Instead, the lawsuit relied on the rhetoric of "protecting" artists' work. Metallica, on the other hand, was explicit in describing their own lawsuit as an issue of control.

39. Reebee Garofalo, *Rockin' Out: Popular Music in the USA*, 2nd ed. (Upper Saddle River, NY: Prentice Hall, 2002, 414). Garofalo's general discussion of the events of the various file-sharing controversies in the late 1990s is a useful and informative starting place on the topic.

40. The U.S. Congress allowed various sectors of the entertainment industry to craft the DMCA as they saw fit in exchange for the online availability of industry-controlled content.

41. Some examples were http://www.killmetallica.com, http://www.paylars.com, http://www.metallicasucks.com (a portal to other backlash reactions, many sarcastically humorous), and the series of animated cartoons produced at http://www.campchaos.com. The cartoons, in particular, foreground greed as the object of their humor, caricaturing Lars Ulrich along the lines of a fast-talking weasel and James Hetfield as a hulking gorilla capable of speaking only in two-word grunts and growls. All sites were accessed June through August, 2001.

42. Ted Drozdowski, "Heavy Mettle," *Musician* 220 (March, 1997), 28.

43. See Garofalo, p. 416.

44. Napster's primary source of income was the millions of dollars it received in venture capital, but the existence of such capital only indicated that the company was being primed for a business model.

45. The discussion aired on May 12, 2000, and the full segment can be accessed at http://www.rapstation.com/promo/lars_vs_chuckd.html (last accessed on June 23, 2005).

46. The moral issue of Metallica's power to effectively halt a major component of Internet usage remained untouched in the interview except for Ulrich's comment that the band's concerns were also shared by other artists who lacked the capital and visibility to confront Napster in the way Metallica could.

47. Quoted in "If I Share My Sandwich: The Future of Digital Music," *So What!* 7 no. 2 (2000): 27.

48. Ulrich's testimony closely following his dramatic hand-delivery of the Napster user names to Napster corporate headquarters. His statement, though significant in the history of the band, is nevertheless fairly straightforward in its presentation of many of the band's concerns with Napster. The statement itself is still available on Metallica's official Web site, http://www.metallica.com.

49. Bassist Jason Newsted even sported a short hair style in the early 1990s, during the *Metallica* tours, but that move was never read as indicative of any form of selling out.

50. The word "Mama" is also featured in the song "Hero of the Day," in a song with much of the same interiority and vulnerability characterizing "Mama Said." In "Hero of the Day" the word is used as an address by a son as he struggles to define his identity in the face of continual pressures to maintain an image long past its usefulness. The phrase "Mama, they try and break me" opens the song and is repeated, mantra-like, throughout the last half of the song over galloping double bass flurries and off-beat distorted power chords. The words "try and break me" gradually rise in pitch and eventually shift the whole phrase up an octave, subjecting this section to a very high vocal presentation. Hovering around F# and A above the staff, Hetfield resists switching to falsetto (literally, to allow his voice to "break") to sing the "try and break me" sections with the result that he can't quite hit the notes using his chest voice. The strained sound thus comes from the uneven tone and cracks in that range.

51. Arpeggiating open-faced chords does not have the same direct affective connotation as strumming them does. With arpeggiation, affect is also determined by timbre and other performative gestures, such as palm-muting.

52. Quoted in Ted Drozdowski, "Heavy Mettle," 30.

53. See "Heavy Mettle" 29; and B.M., review of *Load* in *Stereo Review 61* (September 1996): 108.

54. James Rotondi, "Write the Lightning." *Guitar Player* 30 (October 1996): 51.

55. In 1996 Jennings participated in the *Lollapalooza* tour (apparently at the urging of Hetfield), and in 2003 Hetfield contributed a performance of "Don't You Think This Outlaw Bit's Done Got Out of Hand" for a Jennings tribute album.

56. Metallica wrote 27 songs after returning to the studio in 1995, an unparalleled level of productivity for the band. Initially the plan was to release one double album, but according to Hetfield and Ulrich time ran out and the fourteen songs that became *Load* were the group of songs most complete by the recording deadline. Hetfield provides a further explanation and says that "complete" referred to whether or not the song simply had useable lyrics. All of the remaining thirteen songs were released on *Reload*.

57. Press Kit, *Reload*. Elektra Records, October 1997.

58. Press Kit, 2.

59. In terms of songwriting credit, Hetfield and Ulrich still received most of the credit for the 27 songs. Hammett received third-line credit on thirteen songs while Newsted only received third-line credit once (for "Where the Wild Things Are"). Of the band members, producer credit for both *Load* and *Reload* go only to Hetfield and Ulrich.

60. Newsted's constant extracurricular jamming had been tolerated by the rest of Metallica, but the leakage of recordings of some jam sessions to a radio station in San Francisco caused Hetfield significant concern as Hetfield's desire to maintain and project a sense of unity conflicted with Newsted's desire to play music outside the role proscribed for him in Metallica. In 2001 Newsted quit Metallica, in part because of this conflict.

61. David Sprague, review of *Load* in *Rolling Stone* 738–739 (July 11–29, 1996).

62. Two songs on *Reload* also tune that Low E♭ down to a Low D♭.
63. Quoted in David Fricke, "Married to Metal: The Rolling Stone Interview with Metallica's Lars Ulrich" *Rolling Stone* 708 (May 18, 1995): 98. Original emphasis.
64. See for example David Ake, *Being Jazz: Identities and Images* (Ph.D. Dissertation, University of California, Los Angeles, 1997); and Robert Walser, *Keeping Time: Readings in Jazz History* (London: Oxford University Press, 1999).
65. Ake, 5.
66. The vocal style in large parts of "Poor Twisted Me" departs from the rough timbral characteristics of Hetfield's usual style. Not only does he dispense with a distorted tone on high notes, but he also allows his voice to break slightly. This breaking of the voice, commonly understood as a sign of an "untrained" voice, only adds to the appearance of a more direct and "real" vocal sound. Much more could be said about Hetfield's vocal style on *Load* and *Reload* and its relationship to an overall "blues" aesthetic.
67. Berry's close working relationship with Johnson not only shows up in Berry's guitar techniques, but in the key areas Berry chose for his songs. In particular, Berry favored keys such as B♭ and E♭, both very unusual and more difficult on guitar because the open strings of the guitar generally lie outside these keys. In contrast, B♭ and E♭ areas are widely used on the piano because of the ease of playing with the quality of the third scale degree. However, it must not be overlooked how pianists, as typically subordinate performers in jazz bands, were themselves adapting to the primary key areas of wind and brass instruments.
68. Steve Waksman, *Instruments of Desire*, 196–203.
69. See for instance the lengthy expose on Hammett in *So What!*, wherein Hammett describes in detail his view of Hendrix as his "hero."
70. Erik Davis, "...*And Justice for All*," *The Village Voice* 36 no. 37 (September 10, 1991): 77.
71. Jonathan Gold, "Metallica: *Load*," *Spin* 12 no. 5 (August 1996): 98.
72. This visual image might also be described as borrowing from a version of rockabilly, or more precisely the "outlaw rockabilly" image adopted by rock musicians such as Mike Ness and Scott Weiland. These particular adaptations remain quite different from the more Mod-style rockabilly image cultivated by Brian Setzer and the Stray Cats in the early 1980s.
73. In looking to Southern Rock for answers, it must be noted up front that there seems to be little in the sonic details of Metallica's music that directly descends from Southern Rock bands such as Lynyrd Skynyrd or the Allman Brothers Band. Yet, examining how blues-based guitar music influences Southern Rock makes more sense than an examination of other hard rock groups such as Led Zeppelin, AC/DC, or even 1980s bands like Mötley Crüe, Badlands, or Guns n' Roses. Excluding one set of blues-based rock bands from another may seem like splitting hairs, but Metallica's 1990s aesthetic clearly avoids the swaggering braggadocio that was so important for the reception of all of those groups.

74. Ted Ownby, "Freedom, Manhood, and White Male Tradition in 1970s Southern Rock Music" in *Haunted Bodies: Gender and Southern Texts*, Anne Goodwyn Jones and Susan V. Donaldson, eds. (Charlottesville: University Press of Virginia, 1997).

75. Paul Wells, "The Last Rebel: Southern Rock and Nostalgic Communities" in *Dixie Debates: Perspectives on Southern Cultures*, Richard H. King and Helen Taylor, eds. (New York: New York University Press, 1996, 123).

76. Mike Butler, "'Luther King Was A Good Ole Boy': The Southern Rock Movement and White Male Identity in the Post-Civil Rights South." *Popular Music and Society* 23 no. 2 (Summer 1999): 41–63.

77. Of course, the very artists who received much of the mythologizing treatment, such as Muddy Waters in the 1960s and Leadbelly in the 1930s, were oftentimes glad to participate in the process to some extent in order to pursue their own careers. See Benjamin Filene, *Romancing the Folk: Public Memory & American Roots Music* (Chapel Hill: University of North Carolina Press, 2000). The difference, then, between the kinds of myth used by Southern Rock musicians and those used in previous eras is that Southern Rock's mythology of the blues did not center around any single individual to any significant extent. Instead, Southern Rock seems to have globbed together in one fluid bunch of authenticity a much more conceptual understanding of the blues.

78. Country has always been such a repository, but in the 1980s and 1990s the character of that existence needs to be understood in the historical context of the changed media world in the 1990s, a world which specifically enabled the kind of pop-country-nostalgia of that decade.

Epilogue

1. James Hetfield, quoted in *So What!* 9 no. 4 (2002): 44–45.

2. The name "Jump in the Studio" was a pun on the title of Metallica's song "Jump in the Fire" from *Kill 'Em All*. The Web address is http://www.metallica.com/its/logon/logon.asp. Free registration is required to access the archived photos and video clips.

3. According to Berlinger, Elektra's response to the drama of Hetfield's departure and the intra-band turmoil documented by him and Sinovsky was to demand the footage be shaped into a weekly "reality" series along the lines of MTV's *The Osbournes*, then one of the most watched shows on television. The episodes of the show were to lead up to the release of *St. Anger* in June 2003. The details of how this situation led to Metallica's buying out Elektra's interest in the project is discussed in Joe Berlinger, *Metallica: This Monster Lives*. (New York: St. Martin's Press, 2004, 236–243; 249–251).

4. Once Hetfield returned from rehab, the band members, at the initiative of Towle, did not allow themselves to bring in finished (or nearly finished) songs written by just one or two members. Instead the three members of Metallica and Bob Rock met every day to write and arrange music (Rock played bass on the album). Additionally, in one of the most significant

changes from prior albums, all involved were expected to contribute to the group lyric sessions (including Rock). Songwriting credit (both music and lyrics) is listed on *St. Anger* as attributed simply to "Hetfield/Ulrich/Hammett/Rock," while the producer credit is listed as "Bob Rock & Metallica."

5. Q-Prime hired Towle after he'd come to their attention through his successful work with the St. Louis Rams football team, who won a Super Bowl championship after working with him, as well as his work with Rage Against the Machine, another Q-Prime band. However, Newsted was adamantly opposed to Towle's presence and seems to have finalized his decision to leave on the fact that Towle was not going to be dismissed. In addition, the publication of a *Playboy* "interview" with Metallica in April 2001 was the most public revealing of intraband problems at the time. The fact that the statements by the band members in the interview were pieced together from separate and unrelated conversations with the author before Newsted quit (thus enabling a more dramatically dysfunctional atmosphere than might have otherwise existed to be scripted) could not conceal the tabloid-like sniping that marked the relatively poor relations within the band.

6. Andrew Dansby, "Slayer: Steady Metal." *The Houston Chronicle*, December 2, 2004: Preview 4. In *Some Kind of Monster* Newsted himself describes Metallica's desire to use Towle to mediate his disagreements with the others (particularly Hetfield) as "weak."

7. During this scene (Chapter 33), Towle tries to hang on by telling the band members that he's still needed because he's prepared personalized performance notes for each of them. In the context of his new representation as a feminine meddler the concept of personalized performance notes is made to seem as superficial as the personalized astrological charts Pettibone prepares for each member of Spinal Tap once she takes over management of the band.

8. The "Madly in Anger with the World" tour lasted from June 2003 through November 2004.

9. The beginnings of such an examination were presented by the author as "Scream For Me Tarzana!: Subcultural Dynamics and Performance Practices in the Southern California Metal Tribute Scene," paper presented at the Society for American Music annual meeting, Cleveland, Ohio, March 13, 2004.

10. Susan McClary, *Feminine Endings*, 21.

Selected Discography

Metallica

Metal Massacre, Vol. 1. Metal Blade, 1982.
Kill 'Em All. Megaforce/Elektra, 1983.
Ride the Lightning. Megaforce/Elektra, 1984.
Master of Puppets. Elektra, 1986.
Garage Days Re-Revisited. Elektra, 1987.
...And Justice for All. Elektra, 1988.
Metallica. Elektra, 1991.
Load. Elektra, 1996.
Reload. Elektra, 1997.
Garage, Inc. Elektra, 1999.
S&M. Elektra, 2000.
St. Anger. Elektra, 2003.

Megadeth

Killing Is My Business ... And Business Is Good. Combat, 1985.
Peace Sells ... But Who's Buying?. Capitol, 1986.
So Far So Good ... So What!. Capitol, 1988.
Rust in Peace. Capitol, 1990.

Anthrax

Fistful of Metal. Megaforce, 1983.
Among the Living. Island, 1987.

Slayer

Show No Mercy. Metal Blade, 1983.
Reign in Blood. Def Jam, 1986.
South of Heaven. Def Jam, 1988.
Seasons in the Abyss. Def American, 1990.

Testament

The Legacy. Atlantic, 1987.
Practice What You Preach. Atlantic, 1989.

Exodus

Bonded By Blood. Combat, 1985.
Fabulous Disaster. Combat, 1989.

Venom

Black Metal. Neat, 1981.

Motörhead

Ace of Spades. Roadrunner, 1980.

NWOBHM

New Wave of British Heavy Metal: '79 Revisited. Caroline/Metal Blade, 1990.

Selected Bibliography

Adams, Rachel, and David Savran, eds., *The Masculinity Studies Reader*. New York: Blackwell Publishers, 2001.

Ake, David. "Being Jazz: Identities and Images." Ph.D. dissertation, University of California, Los Angeles, 1997.

_____. *Jazz Cultures*. Berkeley: University of California Press, 2002.

Ali, Lorraine. "Metallica: Symphony of Destruction." *VirginMega Magazine*, November 23, 1999.

Allen, Theodore V. *The Invention of the White Race*. 2 vols. London: Verso, 1994, 1997.

Azerrad, Michael. "Metallica: ...And Justice for All." *Rolling Stone*, no. 538 (1988): 143–145.

B.M. "Metallica, *Load*." *Stereo Review* 61, no. 11 (1996): 108.

Bahktin, M.M. "Discourse in the Novel." In *The Dialogic Imagination: Four Essays by M.M. Bahktin*, Ed. Micheal Holquist, 259–422. Austin: University of Texas Press, 1981.

_____. *Speech Genres and Other Late Essays*. Ed. Caryl Emerson and Michael Holquist. Austin: University of Texas Press, 1986.

Baudrillard, Jean. *Simulations*. Trans. Paul Foss. New York: Semiotext(e), 1983.

Baum, Dan. *Smoke and Mirrors: The War on Drugs and the Politics of Failure*. Boston: Back Bay Books, 1997.

Bellman, Jonathan. "Indian Resonances in the British Invasion." In *The Exotic in Western Music*, Ed. Jonathan Bellman, 292–306. Boston: Northeastern University Press, 1998.

Bennum, David. "Good Day for a Battle." *Melody Maker* 69, no. 23 (1993): 8–9.

Berger, Harris M. *Metal, Rock, and Jazz: Perception and the Phenomenology of Musical Experience*. Hanover: Wesleyan University Press, 1999.

Berlinger, Joe. *Metallica: This Monster Lives*. New York: St. Martin's Press, 2004.

Blacking, John. *How Musical Is Man?* London: Faber and Faber, 1976.

Bowman, Durrell. "Permanent Change: Ambiguities of Ideology and Genre in the Music of Rush." Ph.D. dissertation, University of California, Los Angeles, 2003.

Brackett, David. *Interpreting Popular Music.* Cambridge: Cambridge University Press, 1995.

Brothers, The Stud. "Garageland." *Melody Maker* 63, no. 35 (1987): 33.

————. "Metallica: The Men in Black." *Melody Maker* 67, no. 30 (1991): 34–35.

Bruce, Steve. *The Rise and Fall of the New Christian Right: Conservative Protestant Politics in America 1978–1988.* Oxford: Clarendon Press, 1988.

Bush, Steven. *American Hardcore: A Tribal History.* Los Angeles: Feral House, 2001.

Butler, Mike. "'Luther King Was a Good Ole Boy': The Southern Rock Movement and White Male Identity in the Post-Civil Rights South." *Popular Music and Society* 23, no. 2 (1999): 41.

Carby, Hazel V. "'It Jus Be's Dat Way Sometime': The Sexual Politics of Women's Blues." *Radical America* 20, no. 4 (1986): 238–249.

Cateforis, Theo. "How Alternative Turned Progressive: The Strange Case of Math Rock." In *Progressive Rock Reconsidered*, Ed. Kevin Holm-Hudson, 243–260. New York: Routledge, 2002.

Chambers, Ian. *Urban Rhythms: Pop Music and Popular Culture.* New York: St. Martin's Press, 1985.

Chester, Andrew. "Second Thoughts on a Rock Criticism." *New Left Review* 62 (July/August 1970): 75–82.

Chirazi, Steffan. "Napster and Beyond: An Interview with Lars Ulrich." *So What!* 7, no. 2 (1998): 24–28.

Christgau, Robert. "Consumer Guide Turkey Shoot." *Village Voice* 41, no. 49 (1996): 84.

Chua, Daniel K. *Absolute Music and the Construction of Meaning.* Cambridge: Cambridge University Press, 1999.

Clifford, James. *The Predicament of Culture: Twentieth-Century Ethnography, Literature, and Art.* Cambridge: Harvard University Press, 1988.

Corbett, John. "Experimental Oriental: New Music and Other Others." In *Western Music and Its Others: Difference, Representation, and Appropriation in Music*, Ed. Georgina Born and David Hesmondhalgh, 163–186. Berkeley: University of California Press, 2000.

Covach, John. "We Won't Get Fooled Again: Rock Music and Musical Analysis." *In Theory Only* (1997): 119–141.

Covach, John, and Graeme M. Boone, eds., *Understanding Rock: Essays in Musical Analysis.* New York: Oxford University Press, 1997.

Crawford, Richard. *America's Musical Life: A History.* New York: W.W. Norton & Co., 2001.

Crocker, Chris. *Metallica: The Frayed Ends of Metal.* New York: St. Martin's Press, 1993.

Davis, Erik. "*...And Justice for All.*" *The Village Voice* 36, no. 37 (10 September 1991): 77.

————. "Freedom of Screech: Metallica." *Village Voice* 36, no. 37 (1991): 77, 80.

DeNora, Tia. *Beethoven and the Construction of Genius: Musical Politics in Vienna, 1792–1803*. Berkeley: University of California Press, 1995.

Dome, Malcolm, and Mick Wall. *The Complete Guide to the Music of Metallica*. London: Omnibus Press, 1995.

Doughton, K.J. *Metallica Unbound: The Unofficial Biography*. New York: Warner Books, Inc., 1993.

Drozdowski, Ted. "Heavy Mettle." *Musician*, no. 220 (1997): 28.

Dyer, Richard. *White*. New York: Routledge, 1997.

Eddy, Chuck. "Metallica: Against the Wall." *Village Voice* 33, no. 39 (1988): 85.

Fast, Susan. *In the Houses of the Holy: Led Zeppelin and the Power of Rock Music*. Oxford: Oxford University Press, 2001.

Filene, Benjamin. *Romancing the Folk: Public Memory & American Roots Music*. Chapel Hill: University of North Carolina Press, 2000.

Fink, Robert. "Orchestral Corporate." *ECHO*: a musical centered journal, 2, no. 1 (Spring 2000)

Fiske, John. "The Jeaning of America." In *Understanding Popular Culture*. New York: Routledge, 1989.

Foege, Alec. "*Metallica*." *Spin* 7, no. 6 (1991): 75–76.

Forte, Allen. *The American Popular Ballad of the Golden Era 1924–1950*. Princeton: Princeton University Press, 1995.

————. *Listening to Classic American Popular Song*. New Haven: Yale University Press, 2001.

Frank, Thomas. *The Conquest of Cool: Business Culture, Counterculture, and the Rise of Hip Consumerism*. Chicago: University of Chicago Press, 1997.

Fricke, David. "Married to Metal: The Rolling Stone Interview with Metallica's Lars Ulrich." *Rolling Stone*, no. 708 (18 May 1995): 95–102.

Fricke, David. "Pretty Hate Machine." *Rolling Stone*, no. 737 (1996): 33, 64.

————. *Garage Inc.*: Elektra Entertainment Group 62299–2, 1998. Liner notes.

Frith, Simon. *Performing Rites: On the Value of Popular Music*. Cambridge: Harvard University Press, 1996.

Frost, Deborah. "Metallica: Not Confused." *Village Voice*, 15 September 1987, 83.

Gaines, Donna. *Teenage Wasteland: Suburbia's Dead End Kids*. New York: Harper Perennial, 1992.

Garofalo, Reebee. *Rockin' Out: Popular Music in the USA*. 2nd ed. Boston: Allyn and Bacon, 2002.

Goff, Jacques Le. *The Medieval Imagination*. Trans. Arthur Goldhammer. Chicago: University of Chicago Press, 1988.

Gold, Jonathan. "Metallica and the Poetry of the Power Chord: The New Metal is Soul Music for Suburban White Boys." *The Los Angeles Times* 1988, Calendar section, 69.

————. "Metallica, *Load*." *Spin* 12, no. 5 (1996): 97.

Goldstein, Patrick. "Pop Eye: The PMRC Is Back on the Attack." *Los Angeles Times*, 7 December 1986, Calendar section, 88.

Goodwin, Andrew, and Joe Gore. "World Beat and the Cultural Imperialism Debate." *Socialist Review* 20, no. 3 (1990): 63–80.

Gore, Joe. "Metallica: Hell of Energy, No Posing." *Guitar Player*, April 1989, 24–28.

_____. "Metallica: Escape from Blues-Box City." *Guitar Player,* April 1989, 24–29.

Gracyk, Theodore. *I Wanna Be Me: Rock Music and the Politics of Identity.* Philadelphia: Temple University Press, 2001.

Hamm, Charles. *Music in the New World.* New York: W.W. Norton & Co., 1983.

_____. *Yesterdays: Popular Song in America.* New York: W.W. Norton & Co., 1983.

_____. *Putting Popular Music in Its Place.* Cambridge: Cambridge University Press, 1995.

Harrington, Richard. "Metallica's Platinum Overdrive: The Band and Its High-Decibel Departure from the Heavy Metal Mind-Set." *The Washington Post*, March 9, 1989, C1.

Hayward, Philip. "The Cocktail Shift: Aligning Musical Exotica." In *Widening the Horizon: Exoticism in Post-War Popular Music*, Ed. Philip Hayward, 2–19. London: Perfect Beat Publications, 1999.

Hill, Mike. "Introduction: Vipers in Shangri-La: Whiteness, Writing, and Other Ordinary Terrors." In *Whiteness: A Critical Reader*, Ed. Mike Hill. New York: New York University Press, 1997.

Hinds, Daniel. "Stormtroopers of Death." Cited 2002. Available from http://www.the-plague.com/sod.html (no longer available).

Hisama, Ellie. "From *L'étranger* to 'Killing an Arab': Representing the Other in a Cure Song." In *Expression in Pop-Rock Music*, Ed. Walter Everett, 59–74. New York: Garland Publishing, Inc., 2000.

Hochman, Steve. "Metallica Does Itself Justice with 'New Metal'." *The Los Angeles Times*, December 9, 1988, Calendar section, 1.

Holmes, Tim. "Metallica: *Master of Puppets*." *Rolling Stone*, no. 475 (1987): 51–52.

hooks, bell. "Representations of Whiteness in the Black Imagination." In *Killing Rage: Ending Racism*, 31–50. New York: Holt, 1995.

Jameson, Fredric. "Reification and Utopia in Mass Culture." *Social Text* 1, no. 1 (1979): 120–157.

Jhally, Sut, and Justin Lewis. *Enlightened Racism: "The Cosby Show," Audiences and the Myth of the American Dream.* Boulder: Westview Press, 1992.

Johnson, Marc. *The Body in the Mind: The Bodily Basis of Meaning, Imagination, and Reason.* Chicago: University of Chicago Press, 1987.

Jones, Steve, and Kevin Featherly. "Re-Viewing Rock Writing." In *Pop Music and the Press*, Ed. Steve Jones, 3–29. Philadelphia: Temple University Press, 2002.

Kahn-Harris, Keith. "The 'failure' of youth culture: Reflexivity, music and politics in the black metal scene." *European Journal of Cultural Studies* 7, no. 1 (2004): 95–111.

Keil, Charles, and Steven Feld. *Music Grooves.* Chicago: Chicago University Press, 1994.

Keil, Charles C. "Motion and Feeling through Music." *Journal of Aesthetics and Art Criticism* 24 no. 3 (1966): 337–349.

Kennedy, J. Gerald. *Imaging Paris: Exile, Writing, and American Identity.* New Haven: Yale University Press, 1993.

Kimmel, Michael. *Manhood in America: A Cultural History.* New York: Free Press, 1996.

Kirkendale, Warren. "Circulatio-Tradition, Maria Lactans, and Josquin as Musical Orator." *Acta Musicologica* 56 (1984): 69–92.

Kitts, Jeff. "Metal Reflectors: Kirk Hammett and James Hetfield Look Back on Some of Metallica's Brightest Moments." *Guitar World*, October 1991. Reprinted in *Guitar World Presents Metallica*, 11–20. Wayne, New Jersey: Music Content Developers, Inc., 1997.

_____. "Metallica Plays the Heavy Hits & Kills 'Em All." *Guitar World*, December 1998, 54, 98.

Kotarba, Joseph A. "Baby Boomer Rock 'n' Roll Fans and the Becoming of Self." In *Postmodern Existential Sociology*, Ed. Joseph A. Kotarba and John M. Johnson, 103–126. New York: AltaMira Press, 2002.

Krantz, Steven. "Rhetorical and Structural Functions of Mode in Selected Motets of Josquin Des Prez." Ph.D dissertation, University of Minnesota, 1989.

Laderman, David. "What a Trip: The Road Film and American Culture." *Journal of Film and Video* 48, no. 1–2 (1996): 41–57.

Lash, Scott, and John Urry. *Economies of Signs and Space: Theory, Culture, and Society.* Newbury Park: Sage, 1994.

Lauretis, Teresa de. *Technologies of Gender.* Bloomington: Indiana University Press, 1987.

Le Guin, Elisabeth. " 'One Says That One Weeps, but One Does Not Weep': Sensible, Grotesque, and Mechanical Embodiments in Boccherini's Chamber Music." *Journal of the American Musicological Society* 55, no. 2 (Summer 2002): 207–254.

Levine, Lawrence. *Highbrow/Lowbrow: The Emergence of Cultural Hierarchy in America.* Cambridge: Harvard University Press, 1988.

Lidov, David. "Mind and Body in Music." *Semiotica* 66, no. 1 (1987): 69–97.

Lienesch, Michael. *Redeeming America: Piety and Politics in the New Christian Right.* Chapel Hill: University of North Carolina Press, 1993.

Lipsitz, George. *Dangerous Crossroads: Popular Music, Postmodernism, and Poetics of Place.* London: Verso, 1994.

_____. *The Possessive Investment in Whiteness: How White People Benefit from Identity Politics.* Philadelphia: Temple University Press, 1998.

Lott, Eric. *Love and Theft: Blackface Minstrelsy and the American Working Class.* Oxford: Oxford University Press, 1993.

Macan, Edward. *Rocking the Classics: English Progressive Rock and the Counterculture.* New York: Oxford University Press, 1997.

Mainer, Greg. "Smashing through the Boundaries: The Late Cliff Burton." *So What!* 5, no. 1 (1998): 33–35.

Males, Mike A. *The Scapegoat Generation: America's War on Adolescents.* Monroe, Maine: Common Courage Press, 1996.

Manuel, Peter. "From Scarlatti to 'Guantanamera': Dual Tonicity in Spanish and Latin American Musics." *Journal of the American Musicological Society* 55, no. 2 (2002): 311–336.

Marcus, Greil. *Lipstick Traces: A Secret History of the Twentieth Century.* Cambridge: Harvard University Press, 1989.

————. *Mystery Train: Images of America in Rock 'n' Roll Music.* New York: Obelisk/Dutton, 1990.

Marshall, Wolf. "Introduction." In *Ride the Lightning*, 2–3: Cherry Lane Music Co., Inc., 1990.

McClary, Susan. *Feminine Endings: Music, Gender, and Sexuality.* Minneapolis: Minnesota University Press, 1991.

————. *Georges Bizet: Carmen.* Cambridge: Cambridge University Press, 1992.

————. "Music, the Pythagoreans, and the Body." In *Choreographing History*, Ed. Susan Leigh Foster, 82–104. Bloomington: Indiana University Press, 1995.

————. *Conventional Wisdom: The Content of Musical Form.* Los Angeles: University of California Press, 2000.

McIver, Joel. *Justice for All: The Truth About Metallica.* London: Omnibus Press, 2004.

Middleton, Richard. *Studying Popular Music.* Milton Keynes: Open University Press, 1990.

————. "Form." In *Key Terms in Popular Music and Culture*, Ed. Bruce Horner and Thomas Swiss, 141–155. Malden, Massachusetts: Blackwell Publishers, 1999.

Mitchell, Tony. "World Music and the Popular Music Industry." *Ethnomusicology* 37, no. 3 (Summer 1993): 309–338.

Moore, Allan. *Rock: The Primary Text.* Buckingham: Open University Press, 1993.

————. *The Beatles: Sgt. Pepper's Lonely Hearts Club Band.* Cambridge: Cambridge University Press, 1997.

————. "Authenticity as Authentication." *Popular Music* 21 (2002): 209–223.

Morris, Mitchell. "Kansas and the Prophetic Tone." *American Music* 18, no. 1 (2000): 1–38.

Morrison, Toni. *Playing in the Dark: Literature and the White Imagination.* New York: Vintage Books, 1992.

Mowitt, John. *Percussion: Drumming, Beating, Striking.* Durham: Duke University Press, 2002.

Negus, Keith. *Popular Music in Theory: An Introduction.* Hanover: Wesleyan University Press, 1996.

Nicholls, Phil. "The Terminator Race." *Melody Maker* 64, no. 35 (1988): 36–37.

Ownby, Ted. "Freedom, Manhood, and White Male Tradition in 1970s Southern Rock Music." In *Haunted Bodies: Gender and Southern Texts*, Ed. Anne Goodwyn Jones and Susan V. Donaldson, 369–388. Charlottesville: University Press of Virginia, 1997.

Palmer, Gareth. "Bruce Springsteen and Masculinity." In *Sexing the Groove: Popular Music and Gender*, Ed. Sheila Whiteley. New York: Routledge, 1997.

Palmer, Robert. "Metallica Ko." *Rolling Stone,* no. 612 (1991): 89–90.

Pareles, Jon. "Heavy Metal, Weighty Words." *The New York Times,* July 10, 1988, Section 6, 26.

Perry, Neil. "Metallica: Fan-Tastic Voyage." *Melody Maker* 67, no. 33 (1991): 7.

Pfeil, Fred. *White Guys: Studies in Postmodern Domination and Difference.* New York: Verso, 1995.

Powers, Ann. "Ice Princes: Metallica, *Load.*" *Village Voice* 41, no. 26 (1996): 53.

Putterford, Mark. *Metallica In Their Own Words.* London: Omnibus Press, 1994.

Randall, Mac. "Monsters of Pop: Metallica, *Load.*" *Musician,* no. 213 (1996): 85.

Regev, Motti. "Producing Artistic Value: The Case of Rock Music." *The Sociological Quarterly* 35, no. 1 (1994): 85–102.

Reynolds, Simon. "The Killing Machine: Metallica, *...And Justice for All.*" *Melody Maker* 64, no. 37 (1988): 36.

Roediger, David. *The Wages of Whiteness.* London: Verso, 1991.

Rose, Mark. *Authors and Owners: The Invention of Copyright.* Cambridge: Harvard University Press, 1993.

Rose, Tricia. *Black Noise: Rap Music and Black Culture in Contemporary America.* Hanover: Wesleyan University Press, 1993.

Rotondi, James. "Write the Lightning." *Guitar Player* 30, no. 10 (October 1996): 48–55.

Said, Edward. *Orientalism.* New York: Vintage Books, 1979.

Sedgwick, Eve Kosofsky. *Between Men: English Literature and Male Homosocial Desire.* New York: Columbia University Press, 1985.

Shepherd, John. *Music as Social Text.* Cambridge: Polity Press, 1991.

Simmons, Sylvie. "I Confronted Metallica on Their Own Terms!" *Creem* 18, no. 2 (1986): 32–35.

Small, Christopher. *Musicking.* Hanover: Wesleyan University Press, 1998.

Sommer, Tim. "Metallica: Suck Off No One." *Village Voice* 31, no. 18 (1986): 73, 80.

Sprague, David. "Metallica, *Load.*" *Rolling Stone,* no. 738 (1996).

Stoute, Lenny. "Metallica Ponders the Inevitability of Death, Taxes." *The Toronto Star,* April 7, 1989, Entertainment section, D10.

Tagg, Philip. "Kojak—50 Seconds of Television Music." Musikvetenskapliga Institutionen, 1979.

——————. "Analyzing Popular Music: Theory, Method, and Practice." *Popular Music* 2, no. 1 (1982): 37–67.

Taylor, Timothy. *Global Pop: World Music, World Markets.* New York: Routledge, 1997.

Taylor, Timothy. "World Music in Television Ads." *American Music* 18, no. 2 (2000): 163–192.

Théberge, Paul. *Any Sound You Can Imagine: Making Music/Consuming Technology.* Hanover: Wesleyan University Press, 1997.

Thornton, Sarah. *Club Cultures: Music, Media, and Subcultural Capital.* Hanover: Wesleyan University Press, 1996.

Tichi, Cecilia. *High Lonesome: The American Culture of Country Music.* Chapel Hill: The University of North Carolina Press, 1994.

Tolinski, Brad. "Speed Kills: A Thinking Man's Guide to Thrash." *Guitar World*, October 1989, 66–77, 128–129, 38.

Toombs, Mikel. "Nothing Plastic about Metallica; in Fact, Honesty is the Key Element." *The San Diego Union-Tribune*, December 4, 1988, Entertainment section, E–2.

True, Everett. "Viva Metallica!" *Melody Maker*, no. 41 (1996): 32–34.

Ulrich, Lars, and Geoff Barton. *New Wave of British Heavy Metal '79 Revisited*: PolyGram LTD, 1990. Liner notes.

Unsworth, Cathi. "Metallica: Lords of Loud." *Melody Maker* 68, no. 18 (1992): 28.

Vaidhyanathan, Siva. *Copyrights and Copywrongs: The Rise of Intellectual Property and How It Threatens Creativity*. New York: New York University Press, 2001.

Waksman, Steve. *Instruments of Desire: The Electric Guitar and the Shaping of Musical Experience*. Cambridge: Harvard University Press, 1999.

Walser, Robert. *Running with the Devil: Power, Gender, and Madness*. Hanover: Wesleyan University Press, 1993.

_____. "Highbrow, Lowbrow, Voodoo Aesthetics." In *Microphone Fiends: Youth Music, Youth Culture*, Ed. Andrew Ross and Tricia Rose, 235–249. New York: Routledge, 1994.

_____. *Keeping Time: Readings in Jazz History*. London: Oxford University Press, 1999.

Weinstein, Deena. *Heavy Metal: The Music and Its Culture*. New York: Da Capo Press, 2000.

Wells, Paul. "The Last Rebel: Southern Rock and Nostalgic Communities." In *Dixie Debates: Perspectives on Southern Culture*, Ed. Richard H. King and Helen Taylor, 115–129. New York: New York University Press, 1996.

Wieder, Judy. "Metallica: Back to the Garage." *Creem* 19, no. 5 (1988): 38–40.

Woodmansee, Martha. *The Author, Art, and the Marketplace: Rereading the History of Aesthetics*. New York: Columbia University Press, 1994.

Zak, Albin. *The Poetics of Rock: Cutting Tracks, Making Albums*. Berkeley: University of California Press, 2001.

Zasky, Jason. "Taking Care of Business: Metallica's Lars Ulrich Shares a Wealth of Music Business Experience." *Musician*, no. 243 (1999): 50–59.

Song Lyric Permissions

Index

Dickenson, Bruce, 9, 203n45
"Die By the Sword" (Slayer), 193n33
　see also Mosh part
Digital Millennium Copyright Act
　　　(DMCA), 155–156, 215n40
Dio, 33
Do It Yourself (DIY), 190n11
　and thrash metal, 6, 140
Dokken, 3, 54, 189n5
Dome, Malcolm, 101
Dream Theater, 98, 194n40, 199n6
Dyer, Richard, 96

E

Egypt, ancient, 121
Electronic dance music, 23
Elektra Records, 2, 155, 185, 189n2
European culture
　cultural prestige of, 26
"Exciter" (Judas Priest), 8
Exodus, 28
Explorer (guitar), 15
Expressive register, 45, 127–128, 197n23,
　210n54, 211n57

F

Fade-out, rhetoric of, 52
Fade to Black Paradigm
　characteristics, 34–35, 42, 53–55,
　　198n35
　songs, 34, 55
Fair Use, 155–156
Falling Down (film), 195n58
Falwell, Jerry, 74
Fast, Susan, xi, 49, 130, 197n27
Filene, Benjamin, 218n77
Fink, Robert, 208n28
Fiske, John, 29, 204n56
Fistful of Metal (Anthrax), 190n9,
　193n33
Flying V (guitar), 16
Form, musical
　analytical prestige of, 20–21
　open versus closed, 22–23
　relationship to content, 21
　relationship to texture over time, 23
　thrash metal's approach to, 20

　see also Modular structure
Forme fixes, 193n36
Forte, Allen, 193n37
Fortuna desperata, 49
Foucault, Michel, 89
Frank, Thomas, 145–146
Franklin, Benjamin, 86
Fricke, David, 143–144
Friedman, Marty, 82
Frith, Simon, 143

G

Gaines, Donna, 51–53
Garage Inc. (Metallica), 99, 194n47
Garofalo, Reebee, 154, 215n39
Gender, as representation, 60, 89–90
　see also Masculinity
Genre
　and musical identity, 36
　as conversation, 3–5, 170–176, 180
　versus style, 39–41
　see also Speech genre; Selling out, fan
　　discourse about
Genre song, 27–28, 193n33
Gesualdo, Carlo, 195n55
Glarean, Heinrich, 118
Gleason, Ralph, 141
Gold, Jonathan, 94–95, 176–178, 179
Goodwin, Andrew, 130–131
Gore, Joe, 130–131
Grant, Lloyd, 191n17
"Greenhouse Effect" (Testament), 83

H

Haggard, Merle, 162
Hair, 91–92
Halford, Rob, 8, 191n15, 191n16
Hamm, Charles, 142, 213n17
Hammett, Kirk, 2, 54, 100, 143, 164,
　210n52
　and *Load* cover, 148
　closing solo in "Fade to Black," 49–51
　drug use, 61
　importance of Hendrix to, 175,
　　217n69
　opening solo in "Fade to Black," 42